CONTENTS

David Dabydeen is Lecturer in Caribbean Studies
at Warwick University
and Junior Research Fellow at Wolfson College,
Oxford University.
He was winner of the 1984 Commonwealth
Poetry Prize.

For Robin and Ravi Dabydeen
and
Joseph Harte, tireless campaigner and spokesman
for values.

A HANDBOOK FOR TEACHING CARIBBEAN LITERATURE

EDITED BY DAVID DABYDEEN

HEINEMANN

Heinemann Educational Books Ltd
22 Bedford Square, London WC1B 3HH

Heinemann Educational Books (Caribbean) Ltd
175 Mountain View Avenue, Kingston 6, Jamaica

Heinemann Educational Books Inc.
70 Court Street, Portsmouth, New Hampshire 039001, USA

IBADAN   NAIROBI   GABORONE
EDINBURGH   MELBOURNE   AUCKLAND
SINGAPORE   HONG KONG   KUALA LUMPUR   NEW DELHI

A Handbook for teaching Caribbean literature.
1. Caribbean literature (English) —
Examinations, questions, etc.
1. Dabydeen, David
810.9′91821   PR9205

ISBN 0–435–91185–6

Set in 10/12 Garamond Book
Printed in Great Britain by Thomson Litho Ltd,
East Kilbride, Scotland.

Cover illustration: oil painting by
Aubrey Williams, part one of the
series 'The Olmec, Maya and Now'.
From the exhibition organised by the
Commonwealth Institute, London, 1985.

INTRODUCTION

George Lamming, in his book *The Pleasures of Exile*, declared that there were three major moments in British Caribbean history. The first, he said, was the European descent into the region; the second, the abolition of slavery and the arrival of peoples from the East; the third, 'the discovery of the novel by West Indians as a way of investigating and projecting the inner experience of the West Indian community'. Lamming's bold claim has been borne out by the extraordinary richness of writing that has emerged from the region. It is generally acknowledged that some of the finest writers in English are from the Caribbean. Their books have international reputations, have been translated into dozens of languages and have won many of the world's leading literary prizes. It is a remarkable achievement, given the historic forces ranged against the production of such great literature. Peoples newly emerged from slavery, indenture-ship and colonial rule have not only mastered an alien tongue but have asserted a major presence, through sheer talent, in the world of 'English' literature.

The force and vitality of this new literature from the Caribbean are beginning to make an impact on the British educational curriculum. Today the literature is being taught increasingly in British universities (Stirling, Edinburgh, Warwick, Kent and London, to name but a handful) and in British secondary schools throughout the country. Schools examination boards are responding by setting Caribbean texts, and publishers are ensuring that the literature is readily available.

This handbook aims to assist the process of introducing Caribbean texts into the British classroom. It guides teachers to particular texts and provides critical analyses as well as supportive pedagogic information. There are twelve units, each dealing with a particular text or set of poems. Each unit is divided into the following sections (with the exception of the poetry units, which have slight variations):

Section A: Critical Approaches   A critical essay on the text, highlighting its main themes and concerns and providing insights into its literary merit.

Section B: The Setting   This section deals briefly with geographical context and supplies other background information necessary for a fuller appreciation of the text.

Section C: A Closer Look   Two passages are isolated for closer critical scrutiny, to suggest to the teacher ways of reading the text.

Section D: The Author   A short biographical note including reference to the author's other work.

Section E: Classroom Use   This section indicates level of use, isolates points of focus and emphasis, lists several questions for essay writing or classroom discussion and suggests 'creative approaches' to the text. Response to a literary text goes beyond the boundaries of 'textual' analysis into areas of politics, economics, sociology and cultural history. The essay questions and 'creative approaches' seek to stimulate appreciation of the wider significance of the texts and to invite the personal and imaginative involvement of both teacher and pupil.

Section F: Teaching Aids   Audio-visual materials and bibliographical data are given, as well as suggestions for further reading.

I am grateful to Elizabeth Gunner's *A Handbook for Teaching African Literature* (Heinemann Educational Books, 1984) for ideas about the format for this book. Although there are significant points of departure, I have retained some of the headings and subheadings employed in her book.

The contributors, all eminent academics and teachers, responded readily to the call for essays. This book was conceived after a conference on Caribbean literature that I organized at London University in 1984, and I am grateful to those who chaired workshops at that event, including Faustin Charles, David Simon, Morgan Dalphinis, Ken Parker, Beryl Gilroy and Susheila Nasta. I owe a special debt to Mr R. A. German and to the Commission for Racial Equality for providing funding for me to organize a teachers' conference on Caribbean literature at Warwick University in 1986, which helped to develop many of the ideas contained in this book. Finally I am grateful to the Department of Continuing Education at Warwick University for financial support between April and September 1986, without which the work on this book would have been impossible.

David Dabydeen
Centre for Caribbean Studies/
Department of Continuing Education,
Warwick University, 1986

Unit 1
V. S. Naipaul: *Miguel Street*

FRANK BIRBALSINGH and DAVID DABYDEEN

Section A: Critical Approaches

V. S. Naipaul's *Miguel Street* is a collection of seventeen fictional sketches describing people who live on Miguel Street, in Trinidad, during the 1930s and 1940s. Each sketch describes activities associated with one or more residents. The narrator is an unnamed boy who in the early part of the book is still at school, but by the end has left school and is preparing to emigrate from Trinidad to England. The street itself, the people and events are all imaginary; but we quickly realize that they are based on actual people, places and events which the author observed during his youth and adolescence in Trinidad. The subject of *Miguel Street*, therefore, is Trinidadian people and society, as observed by Naipaul around the period of the Second World War when the island was still a British colony.

The main theme that emerges from Naipaul's observations is the incongruity of manners and morals which seems to pervade the whole of Trinidadian society, influencing everyone, in domestic or public life, and affecting all institutions, whether they concern law or government, education or sport. When one of the most popular Miguel Street residents, Hat, is charged for adding water to the milk that he sells, this is what he tells his friend Edward:

V. S. Naipaul, *Miguel Street*, first published 1959; page references in this unit are to the Penguin edition, 1971.

'Edward, you talking as if Trinidad is England. You ever hear that people tell the truth in Trinidad and get away? In Trinidad the more you innocent, the more they throw you in jail, and the more bribe you got to hand out. You got to bribe the magistrate. You got to give them fowl, big Leghorn hen, and you got to give them money. You got to bribe the inspectors. By the time you finish bribing it would be better if you did take your jail quiet quiet.' (pp. 158–9)

In Hat's experience of everyday life in Trinidad, things do not work out coherently, logically or as expected. By his own account, Hat inhabits a universe in which moral values and social manners are topsy-turvy or incongruent. Truth is regarded as a vice, and bribery is not simply a virtue, but one that has to be practised carefully, with skill, caution and generosity. Innocence ensures guilt, and justice, far from being associated with honesty and fairness, is a matter of quick-witted trickery or expert cunning and deception. Hat's experience fits that of most other residents of Miguel Street, all of whom encounter incongruity and react with a variety of attitudes including incomprehension, confusion, amorality or cynicism.

These attitudes give rise to a second theme — an appreciation of life's transience — that is closely related to the incongruity that pervades Miguel Street. Because of their confusion, the residents of Miguel Street develop a flexible approach to life which expresses itself in fickle or casual behaviour and unpredictable, improvised actions. Characters in the stories shift with remarkable ease from one occupation to another, or from one course of action to another. Changeability is the norm rather than the exception. If fixed beliefs, customary practices or agreed conventions exist, they are either happily ignored or freely adapted, to suit each individual's convenience or the temporary demands of each passing situation. The experience of Elias, son of George, forms a good illustration of this. Elias's ambition is to become the driver of a scavenging cart. As he grows up, his ideas change. He takes the Cambridge School Certificate exam and seems headed for a different career. But he fails the exam. He passes it at a second attempt, but with a low grade. He takes the exam a third time, but fails. He then changes course and sits for the sanitary inspectors' exam:

> For three years Elias sat the sanitary inspectors' examination, and he failed every time.
>
> Elias began saying, 'But what the hell you expect in Trinidad? You got to bribe everybody if you want to get your toenail cut.'
>
> Hat said, 'I meet a man from a boat the other day, and he tell me that the sanitary inspector exams in British Guiana much easier. You could go to B.G. and take the exams there and come back and work here.'
>
> Elias flew to B.G., wrote the exam, failed it, and flew back.
>
> Hat said, 'I meet a man from Barbados. He tell me that the exams easier in Barbados. It easy, easy, he say.'
>
> Elias flew to Barbados, wrote the exam, failed it, and flew back.
>
> Hat said, 'I meet a man from Grenada the other day —'
>
> Elias said, 'Shut your arse up, before it have trouble between we in this street'. (p. 36)

Elias's actions appear stongly conditioned by his awareness of the transience, insignificance or impermanence of things. He changes intentions, methods and attitudes with ready ease. One thing will do as well as another. When he fails his exams and has to resort to driving a scavenging cart for a living, he claims to enjoy the job and argues that this was the job he wanted anyway from the beginning. Because he is not committed to anything except survival, Elias avoids disappointment or grief, and his repeated failure does not hurt as much. His fluid, flexible approach shields him from the full force of worry, anxiety and frustration which he could have felt if his attitudes were more strongly committed.

The negative quality of his observations and the laughter they provoke suggest that Naipaul's chief aim in *Miguel Street* is to expose those aspects of Trinidad society which he considers undesirable or unhealthy. Satire originates in dissatisfaction, working through ridicule to achieve exposure or, if possible, reform. One way of reading *Miguel Street* is to identify those aspects of Trinidad society which dissatisfy the author, and examine how effectively he is able to expose them through ridicule. In addition to major dissatisfactions such as incongruity and transience, *Miguel Street* reveals other unsatisfactory aspects of life in Trinidad – for example, corruption, violence and physical deprivation. These themes are as common in Naipaul's writing as they are in the work of other Trinidad and West Indian writers such as Samuel Selvon and George Lamming. What differentiates Naipaul from most of these writers is the satirical techniques which he employs.

One of Naipaul's favourite techniques is exaggeration. It is unlikely that Elias would take so many exams so many times, or that, after passing the Cambridge School Certificate exam at least once, he would settle for a career as the driver of a scavenging cart. By exaggerating real aspects of Elias's character and conduct – for example, his flexible attitude and lack of serious commitment to success – Naipaul ridicules and successfully exposes the incongruity and transience which, in his view, have an adverse effect on most people in Trinidad. Another technique is the humorous use of nicknames such as Hat, Popo, Bogart, Big Foot, Razor and Man-man. Humour is produced, too, by unlikely associations or juxtapositions, as when Bogart leaves a game or cards to go to the latrine, and his friends 'didn't see him for four months'. Most of all, humour is abundantly evident in witty remarks and jokes, crudely abusive expressions and swear-words. Eccentricities of behaviour are often amusing – for example, the habit of the poet Wordsworth, who writes at the rate of one line per month and plans, in about twenty years, to compose 'the greatest poem in the world'. Much humour is also produced by sheer absurdity, as when a spectator at a cricket match bets one dollar that any fieldsman will field the first ball, or when Man-man secures exactly three votes in each election for which he runs. One vote is his own, but the other two remain a mystery. One of the most effective satirical techniques employed by Naipaul is irony. Irony is evident when Man-man claims to have seen God after having a bath. Naipaul comments.

> This didn't surprise many of us. Seeing God was quite common in Port of Spain, and, indeed, in Trinidad at that time. Ganesh Pundit, the mystic masseur from Fuente Grove, had started it. He had seen God, too, and had published a little booklet called *What God Told Me*. Many rival mystics and not a few masseurs had announced the same thing, and I suppose it was natural that since God was in the area Man-man should see Him. (p. 41)

Naipaul's irony makes fun of the superstition and ignorance of Trinidadians. It also brings to public attention the gullibility and exploitation which the author observes in Trinidad.

Since *Miguel Street* publicizes so many negative aspects of life in Trinidad without also advancing any apparently positive or redeeming Trinidadian virtues, the book opens itself to the charge that the author's opinions are one-sided or unbalanced, and therefore prejudiced or unfair. Some readers believe that the characters are made to look ridiculous because the standards used to judge their behaviour are unfair. Other readers argue that an author's function as a satirist requires him only to expose inadequate or negative aspects of his subject, regardless of the standards he uses. But a close reading of the sketches in *Miguel Street* shows that they are not entirely negative. While the predominant emphasis is on weak or inadequate aspects of Trinidad behaviour, very often these weaknesses or inadequacies are shown to be the result of factors over which the characters can have no control. We therefore see the characters as victims who deserve sympathy, rather than as villains to be condemned for their mistakes, faults or wrongdoing. B. Wordsworth, for example, is guilty of the most absurd fantasies and certainly cuts a ridiculous figure. But from the love-story he tells the narrator we realize that he is a sensitive individual who has been victimized by personal and local as well as universal factors. It appears that the early death of his sweetheart, as much as the cultural disadvantages in colonial Trinidad,

conspired to ensure the failure of Wordsworth's artistic efforts. Although we laugh at his failure, and through our laughter gain some insight into the socio-cultural inadequacies that help to limit his achievement, we also recognize the pain he endured and the efforts he made. Ridicule is tempered with sympathy. Similarly, in the sketch on Hat, we are given much insight into corruption, violence, incongruity, transience and other inadequacies, and we laugh heartily at the follies of Hat and his associates; but we also observe that, in their inadequacy, the residents of Miguel Street demonstrate basic gestures of human togetherness. Hat's fellow residents show genuine concern for the facts of his case and the outcome of his trial. As the narrator confesses, 'When Hat went to jail, part of me died.' For people so disfigured by the fragmentation of a colonial history, it is something close to triumph to display the flickerings of human community when one of their number is in distress. While we laugh at their disfigurement and fragmentation, we do not reject or dismiss the residents of Miguel Street as irredeemable. They emerge as imperfect human beings like most of us.

Section B: The Setting

Trinidad lies at the south-eastern end of the Caribbean Sea, slightly north-east of the coast of Venezuela. After intervention by Columbus in 1498, Trinidad became a Spanish colony. It was surrendered to the British in 1797 and remained a British colony until 1962, when it gained independence. It is now a member of the British Commonwealth. African slaves were brought to Trinidad, as to most other Caribbean territories, and descendants of these slaves today form the most substantial section of the population of Trinidad. After the abolition of slavery in all British territories in 1834, labourers were brought in large numbers from India to work on the plantations vacated by the slaves. The descendants of these Indians (of whom V. S. Naipaul is one) form the next largest ethnic group in the Trinidadian population. There are also sizeable minority groups of French Creoles, Europeans and Chinese, not to mention people of mixed blood. The result is a population of very mixed racial ancestry.

The variety of people is matched by the variety of cultural forms, of which steel band and calypso are perhaps the best known outside the Caribbean. Naipaul's novel is most obviously Trinidadian in its relation to calypso; there are many snatches of calypso in the narrative, but apart from these the sharp wit and racy satire are reminiscent of calypso expression. Both steel band and calypso have been, in some measure, commercialized and corrupted by outside influences, in line with the general commercialization of the society resulting from oil revenues. *Miguel Street* exposes this process of corruption (e.g. 'They made a calypso about Popo that was all the rage that year. It was the road-march for the Carnival, and the Andrews Sisters sang it for an American recording company': pp.18–19) and constantly reveals how the United States presence in Trinidad ludicrously affects the behaviour and outlook of some of its inhabitants.

circumstances there is no justice in the sense of what is fair or equitable. Bolo's mistake is not in attempting to deceive, but in not practising deception ingeniously enough. Hence his frustration.

Despite the unsavoury events described in the passage, it is noticeable that the reader is not made to feel anger or disgust. We laugh at Bolo's frustration and bitterness partly because his efforts to evade the Venezuelan authorities have backfired on him. He is the victim of his own trickery to some extent. Far from being angry, we are a little relieved that Bolo's attempted deception did not land him in worse trouble; for we are told that he might have been killed and thrown overboard. Thus, as he does in most sketches in *Miguel Street*, Naipaul uses satire to expose personal weaknesses or social failings, yet without inducing the reader to feel disgusted by the characters who exhibit the weaknesses and failings. By provoking the reader to laughter without anger, Naipaul is able to capture our interest and ensure a more balanced or thoughtful reaction to the issues on which he reports.

Section C: A Closer Look

(1) 'Trickery' (p.135, paragraph beginning 'Bolo said, "When I get my hand ..."')

Bolo is one of the most interesting characters in *Miguel Street*. He vividly demonstrates the upturned values by which he and his fellow residents in Miguel Street operate. Nothing is straight, honest, logical or coherent. All is deception, trickery and chance. The passage describes Bolo's reactions after he has paid someone to take him to Venezuela and is left abandoned on some unfamiliar part of the Trinidad coast. Firstly, we notice that Bolo is dissatisfied enough to want to emigrate from Trinidad. Secondly, the most convenient means of emigration is to sail secretly by night and enter Venezuela without going through immigration formalities. These circumstances produce a double deception. By trying to deceive the Venezuelan immigration authorities, Bolo is himself deceived. He has no valid recourse to justice; for in his

(2) 'Hat's trial' (pp.163-4)

The passage describes Hat's trial on a charge of beating his lover, Dolly, after finding her with another man. The incident at once reminds us of the rough-and-ready sexual mores of Miguel Street. People cohabit rather than marry, and sexual jealousy is expressed in brutal physical action. So brutal was the beating that Hat thought that Dolly was dead. He faces a serious charge; yet his first response to the prosecutor is humorous. The humour immediately dilutes any grief or serious emotional reaction which the reader might have. When this is followed by Naipaul's caricature of Hat's lawyer Chittaranjan as 'a short fat man ... who wore a smelly brown suit', the reader loses all the moral assumptions which may have induced us to take sides in the case; we are prepared simply to listen with an open mind. By the time it is clear that Chittaranjan's defence is to be based entirely on lengthy allusions to Shakespearean drama, the exact outcome of Hat's case becomes less important than the general process of administering justice in Trinidad. Hat's fate – his four-year sentence – proves less interesting than the manner in which he was defended.

The passage ridicules the local judiciary. Not only is Chittaranjan caricatured, his defence is shown to be fatuous and irrelevant. His reference to Portia's speech on mercy in *The Merchant of Venice* actually implies that his client is guilty. If the speech has any relevance to Hat's case, it is simply to plead that he should be spared punishment because Portia (or Shakespeare) said so. The second point in Chittaranjan's argument is an attempt to dignify Hat's guilt by his wholly incongruous association with a Roman general from classical history, who also happens to be the hero of one of Shakespeare's great tragedies. The misplaced accuracy of Chittaranjan's third point – that Hat's offence is a *crime passionnel* – is brilliantly demonstrated by means of the ironic comment that it is based on the authority of a personal visit which Chittaranjan once made to Paris. After Chittaranjan's defence is revealed as utterly ridiculous, the reader can appreciate the ironic truth of Eddoes's remark, 'Is this sort of lawyer who does get man hang, you know.' In keeping with the general tone of events in *Miguel Street*, Chittaranjan's defence achieves the opposite of what it is intended to do. Naipaul's satirical revelations about the workings of the Trinidad judiciary confirm his depiction of incongruity and incoherence throughout the society.

Section D: The Author

V. S. Naipaul was born in Trinidad in 1932. After primary school, he attended Queen's Royal College, the government secondary school for boys, in Port of Spain, the capital city of Trinidad. In 1950 Naipaul won a scholarship to Oxford University. After his degree at Oxford, Naipaul began his writing career, which is still in progress. To date he has produced nine novels, two collections of short stories and a work of autobiography. Naipaul has travelled in many parts of the world and written travel narratives about his experiences. He has also published numerous essays, reviews and commentaries on a wide variety

of subjects. Altogether Naipaul's writing constitutes a distinguished contribution to contemporary literature, and has made him one of the more celebrated authors writing in English today.

Naipaul's satires can be scathing, offering a deep and powerful exposure of the fraudulence of Caribbean rhetoric, pomposity and mimicry. He is particularly gifted in his descriptions of the stupidity and irrationality of human behaviour. His persistent criticisms of West Indian society, and his refusal to be nationalistic or to propagate notions of 'black power' in his writing, have earned him rebuke from certain quarters.

Section E: Classroom Use

(i) Level of use

The novel can be read and studied by pupils in the first to sixth forms. The more mature students (sixth-formers) will be able to analyse the text for its serious contexts (the theme of mimicry, for instance, and its relevance to West Indian society), whereas the younger readers will readily enjoy the sheer humour of particular episodes.

(ii) Points of focus and emphasis

1   The value of education, pp. 32–7, 38–9, 73–83.
2   American influences, pp. 9, 14, 22, 26, 55–6, 143–7, 171.
3   Calypso, pp. 19, 65, 72, 87, 98, 99, 105, 128, 143, 152, 162.
4   Violence to women, pp. 23, 26, 86–7, 103–4, 119.
5   Religious beliefs, pp. 41–4.
6   Journalism, pp. 59–60, 72, 75–6, 82, 130–2.
7   The middle classes, pp. 102–13.
8   Emigration to England, pp. 166–72.
9   The absurdity of history, p. 81.
10 The inability to cope with European technology, pp. 119–25.

(iii) Questions for essay writing or classroom discussion

1   Give your own impression of each Miguel Street resident, including the narrator. Which resident do you like most/least? Why?

2   Identify the satirical techniques employed by Naipaul and examine how each one works to achieve ridicule and exposure. Assess the relative success of each technique, citing particular examples in each case. Which techniques are used most often and why? Some techniques you could consider are: sarcasm, burlesque, parody, travesty, irony, innuendo, invective, humour, scorn, farce, understatement and exaggeration.

3   Identify and discuss the precise aspects of Trinidad society which are either ridiculed or considered in *Miguel Street*.

4   What standards does Naipaul use in judging his characters or measuring the soundness of their actions? Are these realistic in the sense of offering the characters real possibilities of improvement? Or does Naipaul employ ideal standards with the intention of revealing imperfections that he knows can never be improved? Cite specific examples where the characters' imperfections may be fully or partially remedied.

5   How does the story of Titus Hoyt illustrate Naipaul's view that European literature, art and learning become ridiculous in Trinidad?

6   Is Bhakcu's inability to repair his car indicative of the impossibility of a transfer of technology from a developed to a Third World country?

7   People come and go in *Miguel Street*. Make a list of their various journeys. Is there any purpose to these movements?

8   Identify the female characters in the novel. In what ways are they victims of male violence? How are they stronger than the men?

9   The novel begins and ends with references to the Americans. How has the United States influenced the society?

10 Although the novel deals mainly with the lives of the common people, there are oblique references to the affluent section of society. Comb through the narrative for such references. Is Naipaul suggesting aspects of social injustice?

11 How does B. Wordsworth affect the boy narrator? Is Wordsworth depicted sympathetically, or is he a figure of fun?

12 Read pp. 58–9 (the discussion about the war) and p. 81 (the visit to the fort). Naipaul here is suggesting that Trinidadians have no sense of history. If this is true, can you explain this absence of history?

13 Why are there so many references to newspapers in the novel? Is Naipaul suggesting that the superficiality of the society is apt material for journalistic prose? Does the novel suggest an alternative form of expression? (Poetry?) Outline the major differences between poetry and journalistic prose.

(iv) Creative approaches/curriculum links

1   There are snatches of calypso throughout the novel. Why does Naipaul quote calypso? Find out about the origin and role of calypso in Trinidadian society.

2   Write a short history of the United States presence in the Caribbean in the twentieth century. How do the Americans influence the politics, economics and culture of the region? Can such influence be termed 'imperialism?'

3   The narrator emigrates to England to pursue his education. Find out more about emigration from the West Indies to Britain in the 1950s and 1960s. Why did the people come?

4   Read Chapter 5 again, which is about religion in the Caribbean. What are the religions of the Caribbean? How many of its Christian sects originated in the United States? Read newspaper accounts of the Jonestown massacre in Guyana and write your own version of events.

5   Some of the characters in the novel are influenced by Hollywood films. What are the main values propagated by such films and what harmful and corruptive effects can they have on a non-European society? Assess how films can be used as weapons of propaganda.

6   B. Wordsworth is influenced by William Wordsworth, the English Romantic poet. Who are the English Romantic poets and what are the dominant themes of their poetry?

7   Write a series of short sketches on the lives of people in your street or neighbourhood. Are any of them similar to Naipaul's characters?

Section F: Teaching Aids

(i) Audio-visual material

Naipaul has appeared on many television programmes discussing aspects of his life and work. Among the more interesting of these are:

Conversation with Robert Lowell, BBC Television, 19 August 1969.
Review, BBC Television, 2 August 1972.
Writers and Places – Beyond the Dragon's Mouth, BBC Television, 1982.
Interview with Bernard Levin, BBC Television, 9 September 1983.
Bookmark, BBC Television, 12 December 1984.
South Bank Show, ITV, interview with Melvyn Bragg, 8 March 1987.

(ii) Background reading

F. W. Knight, *The Caribbean*, Oxford University Press, 1979.
John La Guerre (ed.), *Calcutta to Caroni*, Longman, 1974.
J. H. Parry and P. Sherlock, *A Short History of the West Indies*, Macmillan, 1971.

(iii) Critical bibliography

E. Baugh, *Critics on Caribbean Literature*, Allen & Unwin, 1978.
R. D. Hamner, *Critical Perspectives on V. S. Naipaul*, Heinemann Educational Books, 1979.
M. Hughes, *A Companion to West Indian Literature*, Collins, 1979.
Modern Fiction Journal, vol.20, no.3, Autumn 1984. Devoted to a study of Naipaul and his work.
William Walsh, *V. S. Naipaul*, Oliver & Boyd, 1973.
L. White, *V. S. Naipaul: A Critical Study*, Macmillan, 1975.

(iv) Reading links

Many of Naipaul's novels are concerned with the theme of fraud and mimicry. Comparisons can be made between *Miguel Street* and novels like *The Mystic Masseur,* Deutsch, 1957; Heinemann Educational Books (Caribbean Writers Series), 1971, and *The Suffrage of Elvira,* Deutsch, 1958. The reader can be directed to other short stories by Naipaul in his collection *A Flag on the Island,* Deutsch, 1967.

Miguel Street can be read in conjunction with either Merle Hodge's *Crick Crack, Monkey,* 1970, – see Unit 9 p.71 – or Samuel Selvon's *The Lonely Londoners,* 1956, – see Unit 4 p.25 both of which present comic but poignant descriptions of the various lives of West Indian characters in Trinidad and London.

Unit 2
Wilson Harris: *Palace of the Peacock*

ROBERT FRASER

Section A: Critical Approaches

Since 1960, when *Palace of the Peacock* was published in London to much éclat, critics have been at pains to explore the special appeal of Harris's first novel and to smooth the reader's path through a thicket of so-called difficulties. Its dislocations of time and place have been noted, as have the freedoms it takes with the identities of individual characters and its flushed prose style. The most unusual critical angle has been to explain all of these features as ways of registering the discontinuities of West Indian, and more especially Guyanese, history. Strong evidence for this theory can be found in Harris's own discursive writing, particularly his 1964 lecture 'Tradition and the West Indian Novel' in which he champions an experimental technique as a means of evading the pressures brought to bear on the conventional, sequential novel by twentieth-century capitalist society.

The disadvantages of such an approach for the younger reader is that it begins at a vantage-point at some distance from the text itself, which it then accounts for as the product of certain historical conditions. The more salutary approach for those confronting this remarkable novel for the first time is to start from the immediate reading experience and then expand outwards towards a consideration of firstly, the place of *Palace* in Harris's *oeuvre* and,

Wilson Harris, *Palace of the Peacock*; page references in this unit are to the Faber edition, 1960.

secondly, its contribution to West Indian literature. Initially the alert reader is likely to feel held in the grip of a strong narrative line. Nine *desperadoes* from the coastal strip of Guyana set off up river in an attempt to make contact with a rural community, 'the folk', and, that achieved, possibly to settle and cultivate the land. In this attempt they are defeated, partly by the intransigence of nature and partly by internal dissensions within the crew. Only three – the leader Donne, Jennings and da Silva – reach their destination, where they are arrested by the steep face of a waterfall on which they perish. This central narrative of quest and self-impalement is framed by an opening section in the form of a prologue, and by a concluding epilogue of two sections which recounts the dying vision of Donne himself. These outer buttresses of the text are most likely to impede the student's understanding, and it is thus as well to examine them carefully.

The first chapter shows us the substantive protagonist, Donne, gradually emerging through successive layers of film. Initially we see him toppling from his horse, struck by a bullet that we later learn was fired by his mistress Mariella. Both the event and its mode of realization seem to belong to the world of dream; the dreamer is then immediately identified as the rider's awe-struck younger brother. Donne himself, who enters the room on his brother's waking, is a natural fighter and man of action, one used to commanding and being obeyed, while the dreamer-narrator is crippled by the sort of intense reflective consciousness characteristic of an intellectual. These two personalities remain constant throughout the principal portion of the book, representing two perspectives from which the action may be viewed. In Harris's language they are the 'dead seeing eye' of the practical man and the 'living closed eye' of the solitary thinker. So closely are they associated that it may be helpful to see them as two aspects of the same person.

Some of the difficulty of the story arises from the fact that the meditative eye of the younger brother is capable of extending events through anticipation or memory. Thus this 'living eye' anticipates Donne's death in its opening dream, and then immediately confounds this by showing us the live man berating Mariella, his obstreperous mistress, in a sequence which appears to be a second dream disguising the fact that she has already escaped inland to join 'the folk'. Donne's discovery of her flight is what prompts him to follow her and hence set in train the expedition which occupies the main body of the book.

Though the manner of Donne's introduction may appear fragmented or even revolutionary, he in fact belongs to a long line of fictional heroes who have pitted their high sense of adventure against the indomitable resistance of the physical world. The quest narrative goes back beyond the novel's beginnings, to *The Odyssey* and *The Aeneid* and to *The Pilgrim's Progress*. With the inception of the novel form proper we have Defoe's Robinson Crusoe, Melville's Captain Ahab and finally the gaunt, possessed protagonists of Joseph Conrad. Harris's achievement in this book has been to yoke the adventure tradition to a resourceful technique which springs from the great fictive experimenters of the 1920s, James Joyce and William Faulkner. Like Faulkner, Harris is describing a decadent planter community in the aftermath of slavery. Like him, too, he has a strong tendency to suggest the shifting and unstable social nuances of a multiracial society by constantly challenging the reader's linear sense of time, place and especially character development.

It has often been remarked that Harris's characters are related to one another in scarcely definable ways, 'one spiritual family living and dying together in a common grave' (p. 40). What has seldom been noticed is that, with the important exception of Donne, the 'last landlord', they are also united in a state of dispossession. The taciturn and morose Cameron, part Scot, part African, dreams of a plot of land that he may call his own: 'He wanted space and freedom to use his own hands in order to make his own primitive home and kingdom on earth, hands that would rule everything, magical hands dispensing life and death to their subjects as a witch-doctor would or a tribal god and judge' (p. 41). Like his 'uncle' Schomburgh, however, like the da Silva twins, like the young African Carroll and the pilot Vigilance, he is enslaved by the sovereign will of Donne. Arriving at the up-river mission, the crew realize that the folk have fled and set off in pursuit of them, and their bickering mirrors their state of frustration. Cameron's jealousy is aroused by da Silva because, having already got one of the folk with child, he has a chance of settling down amongst them. Later when a gorgeous parrot flies overhead and da Silva recognizes it as belonging to the mother of his child, Cameron pelts it in a moment of pique and pays for his petulance with his life. Thus, threshing in impatience for the object of their desires, they destroy one another or are destroyed until the foot of the waterfall is reached.

In all this internecine squabbling the one exception is Donne. It is significant that the leader's name is borrowed from the great seventeenth-century English poet, a quotation from whose 'Hymn to God my God in my sickness' heads Book III. Starting adult life as a dashing courtier and philanderer, John Donne subsequently took to the Anglican ministry and towards the end of a varied life withdrew from the world, wrote a remarkable series of devotional poems and even had his portrait painted shrouded in his own coffin in preparation for death. Many of these characteristics are inherited by Harris's protagonist; the swashbuckling extravagance, the mystical insight and the conviction, shared by many of his crew, that death lies everywhere. Part of this conviction is his belief that the members of his expedition have already perished on the rocks in a previous existence. When Donne reaches the bottom of the cascade his mystical sense, his 'living closed eye', takes over, granting him a succession of visions of peculiar poignancy: the Christ-child as carpenter; the Virgin Mary. Then, gaining the crest, he looks up into the night sky and sees the dead members of his crew reflected in the stars, with the young Carroll serenading them. It is the culmination of their mission; for, tormented by dispossession, they are released at last from the burden of history into a state of emancipation and grace. The enslaved are at length set free, and in the very eye of the enslaver.

The seventeenth-century connotations of the narrative are reinforced throughout by the novel's style. Donne is a sort of late Renaissance *conquistador*, and appropriately Harris peppers his prose with devices that remind one of late seventeenth-century verse and the later plays of Shakespeare. The most persistent of these is the conjunction of two disparate nouns as part of a larger descriptive phrase: 'Schomburgh's age and presence' (p. 40); 'the legend and consciousness of the race' (pp. 71–2); 'one muse and one undying soul' (p. 152). Instances of this kind abound in Shakespeare's tragedies and problem plays: 'The dead vast and middle of the night' (*Hamlet*, I. ii. 198); 'The very head and front of my offending' (*Othello*, I. iii. 80). In Harris's usage it will be found that the first of the two nouns tends to suggest a rambling, floating quality, which is then trapped and fixed by the more assertive second noun. The same may be claimed of another of Harris's distinctive devices, his tendency to qualify a noun with a string of incisive adjectives, the tension between which distils his exact meaning. Two early examples, both *à propos* of Donne, must here suffice. The narrator speaks of his 'stamping terrible voice', the first epithet suggesting a quality of suppressed hysteria, the second a countervailing control. Earlier, addressing his younger brother or musing second self, Donne refers to their recollected kinship as 'this dreaming twin responsibility you remember'. Once again, 'dreaming' suggests the younger sibling's contemplative freedom, which is twinned with the elder's taut mastery.

Section B: The Setting

Palace of the Peacock is set in the interior of Guyana (formerly British Guiana), a country geographically on the coast of South America but culturally bound to the English-speaking West Indies. Harris's feeling for landscape is peculiarly Guyanese; Guyana, unlike the West Indian territories, is not a small island but a vast expanse of continental land. Much of the country consists of dense jungle, with the majority of the population living along a thin coastal strip. The jungle, inhabited by Amerindians (the indigenous people whose pre-Columbian culture survives precariously), is scored by rivers and tributaries, many treacherous and unnavigable. 'Guiana' is itself an Amerindian word meaning 'land of many waters'. Waterfalls, among which are the roaring and majestic Kaieteur Falls (with a drop of some 850 feet), charge the interior with a sense of terror and sublimity: the awesome terrain of the interior is a profound inspiration to Harris's imagination.

Europeans have also been provoked by the mystical presence of the jungle from the sixteenth century onwards. Guyana was one of the fancied locations of El Dorado, the fabled City of Gold; the hidden, impenetrable heart of the jungle fed such fantasies. In more recent times, the El Dorado quest has been carried on by the 'pork-knockers', local adventurers who pan for gold in inland regions and rivers. Guyana, again because of its secret interior, has also been the setting of fabulous stories such as Conan Doyle's *The Lost World* and W. H. Hudson's *Green Mansions*.

A rich mixture of peoples characterizes the human landscape. In the eighteenth and nineteenth centuries, African slaves were transported to work in the sugar plantations. Upon emancipation, Indian indentured labourers ('East Indians') were shipped in by the British administrators to replace the African workers. Chinese and Portuguese labour also flowed into the country. Intermarriage and miscegenation over the centuries have created a 'peacock' richness of skin colours. Racial conflict and competition, erupting occasionally into barbaric violence (the legacy of the British colonial policy of 'divide and rule'), have marred the political and social life of the country. In addition, there is a division and tension between city dwellers and the rural peasantry. The Amerindians, because of their location in the interior, have been spared from these conflicts, but with the increasing presence of Guyana Army personnel in their territory, they are increasingly prey to sexual and economic abuses.

Section C: A Closer Look

(1) 'I saw that Donne was ageing ...' (pp. 54–6)

Harris's verbal dexterity is perhaps best observed in the close working of longer passages. One such occurs when, reaching Mariella, the mission named after his fugitive mistress, Donne realizes that it is his own imperiousness that has caused the folk to flee further into the interior. At this point he takes his younger brother into his confidence.

These paragraphs demonstrate that aspect of Harris's art which leads off from Conrad and, behind him, the long tradition of the European novel. Here Donne seems to be not merely moulded but broken by a history of domination which is reflected in the oppressiveness of the sultry, heat-stilled forest. The phrase 'congealed lightning' captures this to perfection: energy locked into itself and festering. In Donne's private nightmare this has become a lash of rope or 'violent belt of youth' which threatens to throttle him, a danger sensed instinctively by his acutely alert younger self. Behind his mask of mastery Donne is captive to his own wilfulness, the 'horror' of his self-recognition barely held in check by his still overweening 'ambition'. Thus, though his moment of inner awakening has shocked him into temporary mental 'subjection', even *in extremis* he retains a presence of mind which holds sway over his emerging terror.

Once more the balance of feelings is poised between pairs of contrasting nouns. Donne's remarks are a 'medium and translation', at once an avenue of confession and diplomatic evasion of the real intensity of his self-doubt. In the pool of light amid the forest glades his head appears as a 'face and brow', a vehicle of disclosure and yet of imposition of conscious purpose. Typically when he finally voices his dismay it is in a mood of detached soliloquy which enables him to ascribe his misgivings to his *alter ego* or brother: '"Why you're looking as haggard as hell," he said to me in solicitude. "Put on ten years overnight, old man."' The second person singular betrays the unease beneath the reserve, the disclaimer of vulnerability, as does the bluff hail-fellow-well-met tone of his words. Here is a man trapped in hell but wishing us to believe him merely out of doors for an evening stroll. When he voices his real doubt it is in the manner of a bureaucrat admitting an administrative blunder. It is an old colonial ploy — callousness masquerading as ineptitude — and Donne has caught the swagger to a tee: '"I do wish," he spoke musingly, "somebody would lift it from my shoulders. Maybe who knows" — he was joking — "you can."' Only a man with his back against the wall and inwardly screaming would treat his own fleeting younger self as if he were an Assistant District Officer invited on to the Residency veranda for tiffin and a chat. Here Harris shows us with benign asperity the spectacle of a man suddenly frightened at the extent of his own power.

(2) From 'This was the palace of the universe . . .' (pp.146–8)

Strengths of a different kind are evinced by the description of Carroll's posthumous song of liberation in *Palace of the Peacock*. It is a passage at once peaceful, sardonic and profound.

The listener in this passage is both Donne and his nudging conscience, at last at peace with one another. He is situated in the crest of the peacock's head from which he is able to observe the faces of his fellows as they appear transmogrified in the markings of the creature's tail. Harris's chosen word is 'free'; Donne is 'free to observe the twinkling stars and eyes and windows on the rest of the body and the wings'. It is a turn of phrase echoed towards the close of the same paragraph where Schomburgh is described as 'free to listen and to hear at last without fearing a hoax'. In this visionary trance, then, Donne and his crew are on one level and at liberty to take disinterested pleasure in the cry which issues through Carroll's pursed lips. What they hear, however, is not the shrill shriek of the strutting bird, crowing with exultation and defiance but the soothing diapason of an organ.

The state evoked in these paragraphs therefore is one in which possession and dispossession miraculously have no meaning. Donne and his crew have beaten their spears into pruning-hooks; their rapture images a world at peace with itself. In Harris's own delicate image, 'Tall trees with black marching boots and feet were clad in the spurs and sharp wings of the butterfly': butterfly because such an insect is at once fragile and irresistible, and because Donne's dying vision is essentially transient, held between the cruel realities of life and the neutrality of death.

A question inevitably arises as to whether the vision is religious in order. The answer is supplied by Book III, 'The Second Death', which describes the last stage of the journey as corresponding to the seven days of Creation, but in reverse. As the story unwinds we notice that the travellers are retracing human history, so that by the time they reach the cascade they are ready for the refracted Christian iconography staring out from the rock-face. By the time Donne reaches the summit he must be supposed to have regained the dawn of Creation itself. The chant of the aptly named Carroll, then, is none other than the song of the spheres which greeted the very first morning of the newly created universe. It is a stage beyond human history and hence beyond oppression. What Donne and his companions have recovered is the original innocence which preceded the first act of bondage. Though mystical, therefore, the concluding vision is not optimistic. For Carroll's 'sad and . . . glorious music' is compounded by 'mixing blind joy and sadness and the sense of being lost with the nearness of being found'. The wording here is scrupulous; the 'sense' of loss is an absolute experience, while repossession, though 'near', is never fulfilled. In Harris's chart of dispossession there are no free zones, merely furtive glimmerings in the margin.

Section D: The Author

Considering the suggestiveness of his prose writing, it is scarcely surprising that Wilson Harris began his literary career as a poet. Born in Guyana in 1921, of mixed Amerindian, Indian, African and European blood, he trained as a land surveyor and worked in that capacity in the interior for three years. His earliest poems were published in the local journal *Kyk-over-al*, the spearhead of the post-war Guyanese literary renaissance, edited by A. J. Seymour in Georgetown from 1946 to 1961.

Eventually Harris's scattered pieces were collected under the title *Eternity to Season*, issued in Guyana in 1954. He then moved to London, where his first novel *Palace of the Peacock* was published by Faber in 1960. It was followed by the remaining three of his so-called Guyana Quartet: *The Far Journey of Oudin* (1961), *The Whole Armour* (1962) and *The Secret Ladder* (1963). Eleven further novels have followed, all published in London, where Harris now lives with his Scottish-born wife.

Though seen by many critics as the archetypal Guyanese artist, Harris is in fact very difficult to classify. The Guyanese literary school embraces writers of a very diverse temper and turn of mind, from the prolific Edgar Mittelholzer (1909–65), of mixed German and African descent, whose 'block-busters' of raw colonial life took the popular market by storm in the 1950s, to the careful poetry of A. J. Seymour and the tales of the direct, yarn-spinning Jan Carew, author of *Black Midas* and *Wild Coast*. Harris's elusiveness springs from the fact that, although by language and antecedent he seems to belong to the world of Anglophone letters, as the many allusions in *Palace of the Peacock* testify, his remorseless and persistent experimentalism would seem to place him closer to the South American novelists Jorge Luis Borges and Gabriel García Márquez, author of *One Hundred Years of Solitude*. When teaching his work in Africa or Britain, the present critic has found it difficult to arouse the immediate enthusiasm of students, but he was greeted with a torrent of euphoric recognition when lecturing on Harris in Brazil. To view Harris in a Latin American context would be a fundamental error, although his energy and dauntless head of intellectual steam connect him with the New World rather than with the English mainstream where the modernist tradition of formal innovation has recently run aground.

In his preoccupation with the open wound of human history and the fluidity of personal identity, Harris is above all a product of the Caribbean. Despite some of his recent work being set outside Guyana, he continues to explore aspects of social perception which have their origin in the cultural confluence of the West Indies.

Section E: Classroom Use

(i) Level of use

Harris offers much to the classroom, yet he also erects hurdles which the athletic teacher will have to surmount. One fairly lofty barrier raised by *Palace of the Peacock* consists in the bifurcated vision of Donne the protagonist, at once pioneer and dreamer. Some help may be offered by a preliminary discussion of the complexities involved in the term 'character', and by recourse to such classic *exempla* of the split body and mind as Robert Louis Stevenson's *The Strange Case of Dr Jekyll and Mr Hyde* (in textual or in cinematic form) or the *doppelgänger* myth. Literature abounds in characters who are different things to different observers: Jane Austen's Emma, so goodly in her own eyes, so vainglorious in the eyes of others, or Charlotte Brontë's Mr Rochester, so sinister on his first wind-blown appearance but in the end so eligible if benighted a husband. The complexity of the novel's themes and its peculiar mode and style of narration make it suitable for sixth-formers.

(ii) Points of focus and emphasis

1 Amerindian life, pp. 48, 71–2.
2 Donne's character, pp. 14–15, 17, 19, 84–5, 127–43.
3 Dream and hallucination, pp. 13–17, 45–8, 102–3, 140–1.
4 Interbreeding of races, p. 40.
5 Landscape, pp. 20–2, 26–7, 102–3.
6 Music, pp. 147–52.
7 Sex, pp. 16, 46, 66–7, 74–5, 78–81.
8 Violence, pp. 13, 66–8, 75–9, 114–16.
9 Mary/Mariella, pp. 15–19, 23, 37–44, 138–40.
10 Technology versus nature, pp. 21–2, 74, 76, 101, 119, 129.

(iii) Questions for essay writing or classroom discussion

1 How many other works – novels, films or stories – can you think of which describe a journey? What does the journey signify in these works and what in Harris's *Palace of the Peacock*? (Comparison can be made with literary texts like *Sir Gawain and the Green Knight*, Conrad's *Heart of Darkness*, Buchan's *Prester John* and Virginia Woolf's *To the Lighthouse*.)
2 The first chapter has much to do with the narrator's way or ways of viewing events. In order to bring these home, Harris plays on the common pun 'I'/'eye'. How many examples of this *double entendre* can you find? Does it occur elsewhere in the text?
3 How many distinctive stylistic devices can you find in this book, and what appears to be their purpose?
4 In the course of the narrative the past and present fortunes of various characters are intertwined and overlaid. It might be useful to extricate them and place each under a separate heading: Schomburgh, Cameron, Carroll, Jennings, etc.
5 The penultimate phase of the story describes an expedition onwards from Mariella itself to the head of a waterfall. The seven days occupied by this further journey are implicitly compared in the text with the seven days of Creation, which Harris runs backwards until on the very last morning Donne seems to have arrived at the point of Genesis. Is there any way of correlating Harris's account with the biblical legend as recounted in the Book of Genesis itself?
6 What factors, apart from his nationality, justify us in calling Harris a Caribbean writer? How much does his writing have in common with that of other authors from the West Indies which you may have read?
7 Is the manner of narration in *Palace of the Peacock* too indirect for its own good? Might one then be tempted to see the book as 'overwritten'?
8 What part does the myth of El Dorado play in *Palace of the Peacock*?

9   The 'dream' mode of writing has been used by a variety of modern novelists, dramatists and poets. What useful comparisons can be made between Strindberg's *Dream Play*, T. S. Eliot's *The Waste Land* and Harris's work?

10 Isolate the references to sexual desire and lust in the novel. How relevant are they to Harris's vision of the brokenness, violence and rape characteristic of West Indian history?

11 What is the relationship between the three women in the novel – Mariella, the Virgin Mary and the nameless Arawak woman?

12 How is the landscape of Guyana perceived and described by Harris? To what effect?

(iv) Creative approaches/curriculum links

1   Find out about the history and culture of Amerindians in Guyana and in the Caribbean as a whole. How does this knowledge help you to understand Harris's concerns with the genocide of cultures in the region?

2   Read about the history of immigration to the Caribbean (East Indians, Chinese, Portuguese, etc.) to appreciate better the complex family relationships of the characters in *Palace of the Peacock*.

3   References to white imperial colonists and African slaves form the background to the story. Read about the history of conquest and slavery in the Caribbean. How are the revelations of greed and violence in *Palace of the Peacock* connected with this imperialist history?

4   Compare the novel with the paintings of Aubrey Williams, the Guyanese artist. Look particularly at Williams's use of pre-Columbian Amerindian myths and patterns and of the fragmentary and dreamlike style of painting called 'abstract expressionism'. What other connections can you make between Harris and Williams in terms of the nature of their art? Both men lived with Amerindians in the jungle interior of Guyana; how do you think this experience shaped and influenced their art? (For posters, catalogues and biographical information on Williams and his work, contact the Library and Resource Centre of the Commonwealth Institute, Kensington High Street, London W8; tel. 01-603 4535.)

5   Look at European landscape-paintings by Claude, Reynolds, Gainsborough, etc. How do the images of orderly beauty, protective warmth and classical clarity differ from the sense of landscape in *Palace of the Peacock*? What do these differences tell us of the differing nature of civilization in the European countries and their colonies? How does landscape affect the opinions and actions of the characters in Harris's novel? Is the novel concerned with 'the conquest of nature', and, if so, in what sense?

6   Find a map of Guyana and trace the course of the Essequibo and its tributaries and waterfalls.

7   Sounds and music play an important part in the novel, especially in the concluding chapter. Can one compare the whole novel to a symphony in view of its multi-layered structure and motifs? Listen to examples of Stravinsky or Shostakovich, modern composers who employ dissonance and dream in their works. Attempt comparisons with Harris's technique of fiction.

8   Every morning, for two weeks, record the details of your dreams the previous night. What are their patterns of consistency or discontinuity? What is the 'language' of dreams?

Section F: Teaching Aids

(i) Audio-visual material

The Caribbean (16 mins.), Gateway Films, 1973. Available from National Audio-Visual Aids Library, Paxton Place, Gipsy Road, London SE27. A film that looks at the economic, cultural and social life of Jamaica, Antigua, Belize and Guyana.

Wilson Harris (tape cassette), British Council Literature Department, n. d. A discussion on the author's work.

Da Silva da Silva (a one-hour drama/documentary broadcast by Channel 4 Television, May 1987).

(ii) Background reading

V. T. Daly, *A Short History of the Guyanese People*, Macmillan, 1975.

M. Noel Menezes, *The Amerindians and the Europeans*, Collins, 1982. A popular book on the life, culture and history of the Amerindians of the Caribbean.

A. J. Seymour, *Cultural Policy in Guyana*, UNESCO, 1977. A very readable and valuable account of the cultural traditions of Guyana.

(iii) Critical bibliography

Flemming Brahms, 'A Reading of Wilson Harris's *Palace of the Peacock*', *Commonwealth Newsletter*, no. 3, January 1973, pp. 30–44.

Anthony Burgess, *The Novel Now*, Faber, 1967, 1971.

John Fletcher, 'The Intimacy of Horror: The Tradition of Harris's *Palace of the Peacock*' in Hena Maes-Jelenik (ed.), *Commonwealth Literature and the Modern World*, Brussels: Didier, 1975.

Michael Gilkes, *Wilson Harris and the Caribbean Novel*, Longman, 1975.

John Hearne, in Louis James (ed.), *The Islands in Between*, Oxford University Press, 1968.

Kirsten Holst Petersen and Anna Rutherford (eds.), *Enigma of Values*, Dangaroo Press, 1975. UK distributor: PO Box 186, Coventry CV4 7HG.

Bruce King (ed.), *West Indian Literature*, Macmillan, 1979.

Hena Maes-Jelenik, *The Naked Design: A Reading of Palace of the Peacock*, Dangaroo Press, 1976. UK distributor as above.

Gerald Moore, *The Chosen Tongue*, Longman, 1969.

(iv) Reading links

Other novels by Wilson Harris

The Far Journey of Oudin, Faber, 1961.
The Whole Armour, Faber, 1962.
The Secret Ladder, Faber, 1963.
Heartland, Faber, 1964.

The Eye of the Scarecrow, Faber, 1965.
The Waiting Room, Faber, 1967.
Tumatumari, Faber, 1968.
Ascent to Omai, Faber, 1970.
Black Marsden: A Tabula Rasa Comedy, Faber, 1972.
Companions of the Day and Night, Faber, 1975.
Da Silva da Silva's Cultivated Wilderness and *Genesis of the Clowns*, Faber, 1977.
The Tree of the Sun, Faber, 1978.
The Angel at the Gate, Faber, 1982.
Carnival, Faber, 1985.

Critical writing by Wilson Harris

Tradition, the Writer and Society: Critical Essays, New Beacon, 1967, new edn 1973.

'The Interior of the Novel: Amerindian/European/African Relations', in *National Identity*, (Proceedings of the Association of Commonwealth Literature and Language Studies Conference, University of Queensland, 1968), Heinemann Educational Books, 1970.

'History, Fable and Myth in the Caribbean and the Guianas', Edgar Mittelholzer Memorial Lecture, Georgetown: National History and Arts Council, 1970.

'The Phenomenal Legacy', *The Literary Half-Yearly*, vol. II, 2 July 1970, pp. 1–6.

'The Native Phenomenon', in Anna Rutherford (ed.), *Commonwealth*, Denmark: University of Aarhus, 1971, pp. 144–5.

'A Talk on the Subjective Imagination', *New Letter* (Kansas: University of Missouri), vol. 40, no. 1, autumn 1973, pp. 141–9.

'Reflection and Vision', in Hena Maes-Jelenik (ed.), *Commonwealth Literature and the Modern World*, Brussels: Didier, 1975.

Hena Maes-Jelenik (ed.), *Explorations: A Selection of Tales and Articles*, Dangaroo Press, 1981. UK distributor: PO Box 186, Coventry CV4 7HG.

Work by other writers

Caribbean writers The theme of psychic disintegration and schizophrenia is central in Caribbean fiction, revolving round questions of individual, racial and national identity. This theme can be fruitfully traced in novels like Jean Rhys's

Wide Sargasso Sea — see Unit 3 — and Edgar Mittelholzer's *Corentyne Thunder*.

European writers   In his work, specifically in the epigraphs to various sections of his novels, Harris quotes from T. S. Eliot, Gerard Manley Hopkins and William Blake. The charged, surrealistic verse and the religious concerns of these writers can yield insights into Harris's own work. Useful comparisons can also be made with Strindberg's *Ghost Sonata* and *Dream Play*, in terms of theme and technique, and with Conrad's *Heart of Darkness*, a novel which in its 'river journey' structure and metaphysical conceptions bears an uncanny resemblance to *Palace of the Peacock*.

East Indian indentured labourers harvesting and breaking cacao (Royal Commonwealth Society)

Unit 3
Jean Rhys: *Wide Sargasso Sea*

LOUIS JAMES

Section A:
Critical Approaches

A summary of the plot of *Wide Sargasso Sea* could make the novel appear simple escapist romance. The Creole Antoinette Cosway, passionate, beautiful and impoverished, is married off to a cold-natured European. After a disastrous honeymoon on a remote and exotic island, in which she attempts to captivate him with native magic, she is taken back to England and locked in a garret as insane. As the book ends she is about to follow a dream and burn down the old house, killing herself in her act of revenge. Part of the problem in approaching the novel is that it is indeed intense, poetic and melodramatic, and any examination of its complexity must not be allowed to lessen the power of its passion. Yet to do the work justice, the reader must explore the quest for truth that undermines the romantic assumptions about the Caribbean and women's experience that the novel at first may appear to follow. Significantly, the novel has its starting-point in the seminal Victorian Romantic novel, Charlotte Brontë's *Jane Eyre* (1847). But it is not to subscribe to Brontë's interpretation of the story; rather, to revalue it from the point of view of Rochester's rejected Caribbean wife, the madwoman locked in the attic.

The male protagonist in Jean Rhys's story we may call Rochester, and indeed, all commentaries I have read do so. Yet Jean Rhys never gives him this name; he remains anonymous throughout the book. Antoinette is from one of the names Charlotte Brontë gives Mrs Rochester, but Rhys makes Mr Mason her stepfather, and much of the story, up to the last section with Grace Poole in the attic, moves into new worlds. These worlds are not fully mapped, however. 'There are blanks in my mind that cannot be filled up', says Rochester (p. 64), and the reader, too, is at times left uncertain. Is Daniel Cosway Antoinette's half-brother? What is the story of the haunted house Rochester strays by, where he finds himself mistaken for a zombie? Was Antoinette the congenitally mad daughter of a congenitally mad mother? Who is Sandi, and what was his relationship with Antoinette? He was Antoinette's childhood friend; there is a strong suggestion they were lovers, even a rumour they were to be married. Yet he never comes directly into the plot. In part, the novel suggests, the 'Sargasso Sea' of the Caribbean, after emancipation, confuses truth and reality; all is lost 'except the lies. Lies are never forgotten, they go and they grow' (p. 108). But Antoinette also says, 'There is always the other side, always' (p. 106). By telling the story alternately through Antoinette and through Rochester's consciousness, Jean Rhys builds an ambiguous understanding of the drama as it unfolds.

Antoinette's character emerges so vividly that it is sometimes easy to forget that there are, even within the world of the novel, alternative and more promising visions. One is Aunt Cora's. Where Antoinette is preternaturally sensitive to the world around her, even as a child sleeping with a stick by her side, her aunt is both aware of the dangers of life

Jean Rhys, *Wide Sargasso Sea*; page references in this unit refer to the Penguin edition, 1966.

and wisely strong in coping with them, as when she faces the rioters. Even more central is her nurse and friend Christophine. Christophine adds to wisdom and courage a knowledge of the psychic and supernatural dimensions of Caribbean life. It is only in refusing to accept her advice that Antoinette plunges herself into disaster. Antoinette herself is a fragile, inherently self-destructive figure. 'I never wished to live before I knew you,' she says to Rochester; 'I always thought it would be better if I died' (p. 76). Both her moments of peace in a convent as a child (p. 47) and her passionate fulfilment in love-making with Rochester (p. 79) are expressed in terms of dying. Even on the island she loves, she is wanting other worlds. Though she instinctively questions the 'reality' of England ('a big city must be like a dream': p. 67), she says, 'I will be a different person when I live in England and different things will happen to me' (p. 92).

Rochester's grasp on reality is even more tenuous. At the time of his marriage he is ill with fever and he moves into the relationship almost sleep-walking. One of the finest achievements of the novel is the way Jean Rhys conveys his weak, detached personality, gathering together a sense of both the island and Antoinette, until for a brief spell (I deliberately use the word) he is caught in a passion so great that his inadequate emotional resources are overwhelmed. When the letter comes from Daniel Cosway impugning his wife, he receives it with a sense of relief and inevitability. Even at the moments of intuition, he has little grasp of 'reality': The 'beautiful island seems to me . . . quite unreal and like a dream' (p. 67); 'What I see is nothing. I want what it *hides* – that is not nothing' (p. 73). The love affair destroys him more radically even than Antoinette: 'She had left me thirsty and all my life would be thirst and longing for what I had lost before I found it' (p. 141).

Yet it is through these two problematic consciousnesses that Jean Rhys chooses to mediate the story to us. What gives them such significance is the way they are a focus for real historical predicaments. Rochester's awareness is focused on money and legalistic views of 'right'. As Christophine says, 'for that man money pretty like pretty self, he can't see nothing else' (p. 94). As a weak person, he also is dominated by personal vanity; his first thought when Antoinette wishes to call off the marriage is that he will go back to England 'in the role of rejected suitor jilted by this Creole girl' (p. 65). This vanity makes him both dangerous and tragic; Antoinette's attempts to give him her love appear threats to his identity and even the beauty of Grandbois is seen as unfair power – 'on her side' (p. 107).

If Rochester brilliantly embodies the hollowness of economic and legal power, uninformed by compassion, Antoinette, in a still more complex way, is in her sensitivity destroyed by the very lack of the power Rochester wields with such coldness. The powerlessness extends in every direction. Historically, as a white Creole, caught in the 1840s between the loss of the old slave-owning structure, dismantled with emancipation in 1838, and the rise of the new moneyed entrepreneurs, she has no status. 'Old time white people nothing but white nigger now, and black nigger better than white nigger,' says Tia (p. 21). Tia, her childhood friend, is separated from her by colour. For if Antoinette as a poor Creole is isolated from the white upper classes, she is kept by colour and race from those towards whom she instinctively reaches, the black islanders.

Further levels of alienation are suggested by Jean Rhys's presentation of *two* islands: Jamaica and Martinique. Antoinette, Christophine and Annette, her mother, are from the French island – small, Catholic and less dependent on the slave structure, at least in Antoinette's experience. They are therefore strangers even in Jamaica, with its legalistic English traditions and hatreds rooted in history. Personal and historical issues merge; the two islands are not only culturally different, they embody Antoinette's rapturous childhood and her traumatic exposure to suffering.

Antoinette becomes through the burning of Coulibri what Kenneth Ramchand has accurately called the 'terrified consciousness' of the dispossessed Caribbean Creole. She has to watch, powerless, while her home is burnt, her brother murdered, her mother driven to insanity, and when she turns to her friend from childhood Tia throws a rock in her face. This is one answer to Daniel Cosway's accusation of her insanity – and indeed, Charlotte Brontë's in *Jane Eyre*. Aunt Cora told Antoinette that the wound on her face 'wouldn't spoil me on my wedding day. But I think it did spoil me for my wedding day and all the other days and nights' (p. 110).

This trauma conditions her entire awareness of her world. As a child she has an instinctive relationship with nature. She becomes conscious of a world of evil in her vision of rats in the moonlight, and her fear 'of everything, of nothing' leads her to sleep with her stick at nights (p. 69). But Christophine is her protection, and she lives at one even with her fears, unharmed by the *fer de lance* snakes, bathing with an intuitive knowledge of where the dangerous crabs hide. The moment of alienation comes when Mason, as stepfather, is introducing a new, English order to the plantation. Suddenly she becomes aware of the magical forces of evil, knowing, although she does not see it, that the room hides 'a dead man's dried hand, white chicken feathers, a cock with its throat cut dying slowly, slowly. . . . No one had ever spoken to me about obeah – but I knew what I would find if I dared to look' (pp. 26–7). When she seeks help from the magical world to secure Rochester's love, it turns against her with terrifying consequences.

We may see the black Caribbean world as a place of 'obeah' (sorcery) and Antoinette's madness, yet objectively the damaging magic is practised by the English Rochester, and the passages of total madness are spoken by him. In his attempt to crush Antoinette he uses his psychic forces to drain the life from her: 'My hate is colder, stronger, and you'll have no hate to warm yourself. You will have nothing' (p. 140). He denies even her name, calling her Bertha. 'Bertha is not my name,' pleads Antoinette; 'You are trying to make me into someone else, calling me by another name. I know, that's obeah too' (p. 121). Towards the end, Rochester is raving in mental disorder: 'It's an English summer now, so cool, so grey. Yet I think of my revenge and hurricanes. Words rush through my head (deeds too). Words. Pity is one of them. It gives me no rest' (p. 135).

Rochester has no voice in the last section of the book. 'His stay in the West Indies has changed him out of all knowledge,' says Grace Poole; 'He has grey in his hair and misery in his eyes' (p. 145). Antoinette is 'trapped in a timeless, cardboard' world in her garret (p. 148). Yet she is aware that even in England there is a 'reality' she cannot see. Her prison is mental and psychic – Rochester's cold hate. She has a hidden life Rochester could never know, and this is raised by a returning web of memories and the tangible link of the red dress she has been allowed to bring from Grandbois. It recalls the possibility of love with Sandi, who left her wearing a red dress. It is redolent of 'the smell of vertivert and frangipani, of cinnamon and dust and lime trees when they are flowering. The smell of the sun and the smell of the rain' (p. 151). Red is the colour of passion, but this uncovers one of the central paradoxes of the book, for it is also the colour of fire and destruction. Dream and reality, the past, the present and the future to come, with the 'hard stones' awaiting her below, and the sky 'red and all my life . . . in it' (p. 155), all come together. As she carries the candle in the darkness it is the symbol of her death and of her emotional and spiritual survival.

Section B: The Setting

Wide Sargasso Sea is a work of the imagination. Neither the characters nor the places are directly historical, and Jean Rhys had no first-hand knowledge of Jamaica, though Grandbois recalls her childhood Dominica. Nevertheless, the Caribbean, immediately following the emancipation of slaves in the British Colonies in 1838, is the bedrock of the book, and this is given particular poignancy by its relationship to Jean Rhys's own family history.

Her maternal great-grandfather, John Potter Lockhart, acquired the Genever plantation on Grand Bay, Dominica, in 1834. Twenty years later it was being managed by his widow, Jane Maxwell. There had been continual unrest since emancipation, and in 1844 a census was taken as a sign of returning slavery. The plantation was attacked and burnt down, Jane barely escaping with her life. As a child Jean Rhys went to Genever, and the ruins – the rooms on three levels, the steps, the mounting stone – provided the exact model for Coulibri, although the name Coulibri refers not to her family lands but to the neighbouring estate. It is still possible to stand before the ruins today and trace the scene against the surrounding mountains as she describes it in the novel.

The class tensions, economic struggle, fears and incipient violence of the early nineteenth-century Caribbean are accurately explored and portrayed, down to the beginnings of importing indentured labourers from India (most relevant to practices in Trinidad and Guyana) which is mentioned by Mr Mason, injudiciously allowing the suspicious servant girl Myra to overhear. Beyond this, Antoinette's mixture of attraction towards and alienation from the metropolitan culture relates to the experience of generations of immigrants from the islands, including that of Jean Rhys herself.

Section C: A Closer Look

(1) The burning of Coulibri (p. 37, bottom paragraph, to p. 38, end of section, '. . . like in a looking glass')

This climactic scene in the book has been carefully prepared for: the poisoning of the family horse, Tia's robbing Antoinette of her new pennies and dress in jealousy, Mason's insensitivity to the dangers of their situation. Mason's attitude is a combination of patronizing condescension and flabby romanticism. 'They are children,' he says, 'they would not hurt a fly.' 'Unhappily,' retorts Aunt Cora, 'children do hurt flies' (p. 30). Mason is uncomprehending, Cora strong, Annette hysterical. The black rioters are also divided, motivated by undefined forces of suspicion and jealousy, no doubt reinforced by the servant Myra's news that Mason is contemplating introducing labour from India. Revenge combines with sadism. 'I knew,' says Antoinette, 'the ones that laughed would be the worst' (p. 36). Threatened murder is also motivated partly by the realities of retaliation if white witnesses escape: 'What you think the police believe, eh? You, or the white nigger?' (p. 37). Yet the focused fury of the mob is turned aside not by resistance or compassion, but by the sight of the family pet parrot, its wings clipped, its feathers aflame, falling from the balcony: 'It was very unlucky to kill a parrot, or even to see a parrot die' (p. 36). It is a scene of nightmare confusion of act and meaning.

The passage here exemplifies the economy and intensity of Jean Rhys's style. Each word has the weight of dream-heightened reality. The second sentence sums up a whole childhood experience. The simple colours – gold, silver, blue – convey the directness of a child's vision. Ferns and orchids, ginger lilies and roses combine both the exotic and the domesticated. The rocking-chair and blue sofa intimate relaxed security (compare this with the effect if the sofa had not been blue, the chair high-backed). Precisely significant, the picture of the Miller's Daughter reminds us of Antoinette's tantalizing vision of a world that was to be embodied in the English Rochester. It is a doomed image; even in the English context it would be unreal, an idealized pastoral rather than a real girl in a real place.

Antoinette turns from the destruction of things to people – to Tia and her mother, 'for she was all that was left of my life as it had been' (p. 38). Again the economy gives the account paradoxical immediacy and dream-like distance. Antoinette runs, but we do not sense her footsteps; she is struck by the jagged stone, but in her inner distress she cannot feel the physical pain. Tia's face 'crumples', both the creasing of grief but also an image of disintegration, like a collapsing mask. The mirror image has been prepared for in the novel. The reflected image is one of acceptance and hope; her mother 'perhaps . . . had to hope every time she passed a looking glass' (p. 16). In the peace of the convent all sense of self is eased away, and there are no mirrors. When she is happy with Rochester, Antoinette *accepts* herself in a mirror: 'all day she'd be like any other girl, smile at herself in the looking glass' (p. 76). But in her final madness she cannot recognize herself in the glass and sees her image as 'the ghost. The woman with the streaming hair. She was surrounded by a gilt frame but I knew her' (p. 154). In the burning of Coulibri she identifies herself, not with the white Antoinette, but with the black Tia. Separating the two images are blood and tears and a history of division and exploitation in the Caribbean.

The complexity of the book is shown in the way the episode stands not only on its own but as a recurring image. The blackened walls, the steps and the mounting stone, shape themselves into the images of her thrice-recurring dream, where they are fused with the intimations of Rochester, the alienated garden of England and the steps up to the prison attic of Thornfield. The reflections of Antoinette in the Miller's Daughter and Tia are still to divide her consciousness. But above all, the burning of the house is to shape a recurrent cycle of history in which the burning of Coulibri is to recur in another time and another place.

(2) 'I began to walk very quickly' pp. 86–7

The scene works through evocative understatement. It is vividly realized, yet its power comes from the way it conveys Rochester's inner experience. The 'green' light describes both the presence of vegetation and a sense of the strange. It is forest, but more than trees: 'you cannot mistake forest, it is alien.' The sight of a log swarming with white ants is followed by the thought, 'How can one discover truth?'. In Rochester's free-floating consciousness the sequence implies his anxieties swarming in his mind – silent, directionless and destructive. Then 'I stubbed my foot on a stone and nearly fell.' The pain returns him to his alert rational mind, and he becomes aware of the road and the location of the ruins. The sense of place induces a sudden peace, a liberation from time: 'A beautiful place. And calm – so calm that it seemed foolish to think or plan.'

Only the subsequent experience of a girl seeing him, screaming and running alerts us to other levels of happening. Is his experience real? Baptiste, who has been clearly worried by his disappearance, asserts stubbornly that there is no road there, though Rochester has stubbed his foot on it. The place is haunted by a zombie, 'a dead person who seems to be alive or a living person who is dead. A zombie can also be the spirit of the place, usually malignant but sometimes to be propitiated with sacrifices or offerings of flowers and fruit' (pp. 88–9). Rochester has been standing by offerings of flowers tied with grass. Why should he feel this sudden and hypnotic sense of peace?

The story is one of the episodes which are not given causal explanation. We never learn about the ghost of the place, Père Lilièvre, or why Baptiste was so anxious about Rochester's disappearance. But there are other zombies in the story. Cold and bloodless in his hate, Daniel Cosway is one; Amélie

says of Rochester after reading Daniel's letter, 'Your husband, he outside the door and he look like he see zombie.' (p. 83). And Rochester himself loses his precarious identity – 'he was gentle, generous and brave', Grace Poole says of him – to become a hollow ghost: 'She has left me thirsty and all my life would be thirst and longing for what I had lost before I found it.' When the girl sees him and thinks he is the zombie, the recognition is prophetic. After the burning of Thornfield he is to become the ghost of his own ruin in Charlotte Brontë's story. But it is characteristic of the book that the associations are implicit, subconscious, reaching below the narrative levels of the story into an underlying web of meanings. Even Rochester does not realize the nature of the seductive peace he experiences by the haunted stones.

Section D: The Author

Jean Rhys was born Ella Gwen Williams in Dominica on 24 August 1894. Her father, Rhys Williams, was a seafaring doctor who came to rest in Dominica and married Minna Lockhart, a third-generation Dominican Creole. Jean was educated in a convent school where she was fortunate to receive an enthusiastic grounding in English literature. A remote, sensitive child, she was drawn to the physical and the black culture of Dominica, while finding much in her middle-class family circle frustrating. In 1910 she went with her Aunt Clarice to England, where, after a brief spell at school in Cambridge, she launched into drama at RADA. With the death of her father she was forced to leave and make her own way in the world in a musical theatre group, touring the English provinces.

This often intensely unhappy period is evoked in *Voyage in the Dark* (1934), which she wrote largely while on tour. Anna Morgan, her heroine, is in many ways different to Antoinette, but there are some direct similarities. Both are trapped, emotionally and imaginatively, between the worlds of Europe and the West Indies; both find themselves vulnerable financially and sexually; and Anna's nightmare experience of an abortion has affinities with Antoinette's experience of alienation. The novel makes a meaningful supplement to *Wide Sargasso Sea*.

London and Paris, her first marriage to Jean Lenglet and travels through Europe in the chaotic years following the First World War (to Vienna, Budapest and Prague) brought excitement but disorientation and often further distress to Jean Rhys. Her subsequent life in a *ménage à trois* with Ford Madox Ford helped her emerge into published writing, but the emotional toll – chronicled in *Quartet* (1929) and *After Leaving Mr Mackenzie* (1931) – was to mark her awareness of sexual relations; there are traces of Ford in the cold, predatory Rochester, and Jean Rhys was to analyse herself in the self-destructive Antoinette. After 1934 Jean Rhys disappeared from public view, until with *Wide Sargasso Sea* in 1966 she emerged as, in Alfred Alvarez's publicized words, 'the best living English novelist' (*New York Times Book Review*, 17 March 1974). Her earlier novels were republished, together with collections of short stories and recollections, both early and new pieces. She became a celebrity. She died on 14 May 1979 in Devon, where she had lived in interrupted seclusion.

Section E: Classroom Use

(i) Level of use

Pupils from the age of 16 upwards.

(ii) Points of focus and emphasis

1   The presentation of Coulibri and Grandbois, pp. 16–17, 66-74.
2   Antoinette and Tia, pp. 20, 21, 38.
3   The convent experience, pp. 41–51.
4   Rochester's sense of the Caribbean, Part 2, *passim*.
5   Antoinette's account of her childhood, Part 1, *passim*.
6   The love potion, pp. 113–16.
7   Rochester's disintegration, pp. 135–42.
8   England as seen by Antoinette, Part 3, *passim*.
9   The recurrence of history, pp. 34–8, 153–6.

(iii) Questions for essay writing or classroom discussion

1   How does the title, *Wide Sargasso Sea*, relate to the story?
2   How does Antoinette's view of her Caribbean world change, and why?
3   Examine the characters of three of the following: Christophine, Aunt Cora, Tia, Mr Mason, Amélie, Daniel Cosway.
4   What are the attitudes to 'obeah' (sorcery) that emerge in the novel?
5   Is Antoinette right to say that 'there is always the other side, always'?
6   Does Antoinette force her tragedy on to herself?
7   Can you argue that Christophine is the real heroine of the book?
8   How is England portrayed in the book, and why is Antoinette so drawn to go there?
9   Is Rochester more a victim than a persecutor?
10 Look at the different places in which the importance of money is raised in the book, and assess its place in the story.
11 What is Jean Rhys's attitude to women in the book?
12 The Caribbean landscape in the novel is lush, intense and nightmarish. How does landscape shape or affect personality? Isolate the images of nature; what moods do they convey?
13 Compare Coulibri and Grandbois, both as places and for what they mean in the novel.
14 Can the ending of the novel be seen as either hopeful or despairing? Give arguments for your reasoning.

(iv) Creative approaches/curriculum links

1   Read *Jane Eyre* by Charlotte Brontë and assess how Jean Rhys revalues the story under the following headings: attitudes to the Caribbean; attitudes to Rochester; the presentation of the 'madwoman in the attic'.
2   The novel has never been filmed, although a film has been planned on several occasions. Write the film script for a selected section of the novel. From your experience, discuss the difficulties of writing a scenario of the book.

3   Read historical accounts of the Caribbean around the time of slave emancipation (the 1830s and 1840s). Write your own fictionalized account, based on the historical facts, of a riot in which an estate house was burnt down. How does your account differ from that given by Jean Rhys?

4   Read one or more accounts of immigrants from the West Indies to Britain. Can you relate the contrast that Jean Rhys sets up between the Caribbean and Britain to other experiences of immigration? (You may include in your study Jean Rhys's own fictionalized account of her experience in *Voyage in the Dark*.)

5   The 'obeah' (sorcery) of Afro-Caribbean culture adds to the sinister mood of the novel. Read about African religions and their survival in the Caribbean. Can you find equivalents of 'obeah' in Western Christianity?

6   There is reference in the novel to the importing of indentured labourers from India into the Caribbean. Find out in detail the history of this process of migration. What is the present situation of people of Indian origin in the region?

7   The novel refers to the wildlife and fauna of the country – its dangerous snakes, spiders and wild flowers. Find out precisely what the life-forms referred to look like so as to gain a sense of the colour and strangeness of the land.

8   You have discovered that the novel is in fact incomplete. Add your version of the final chapter.

Section F: Teaching Aids

(i) Audio-visual material

Banana split, Christian Aid film-strip with cassette tape and notes, London, 1983. A film about contemporary British exploitation of one of the main export products of the Caribbean, yielding a sense of the historical continuity of exploitation and abuse from the era of slavery to the present.

(ii) Background reading

Lennox Honeychurch, *The Dominica Story*, Dominica, 1975. The best history of Dominica, written in lively style and with a detailed bibliography.

(iii) Critical bibliography

D Athill, Foreword to Rhys's *Smile Please*, Deutsch, 1979, pp. 5–15. Important biographical notes.

Wayne Brown, 'Wide Sargasso Sea', in *On the Coast*, Deutsch, 1972, pp. 46–7. While a poem, it is a vivid personal view of the book by a Trinidadian.

Edward Brathwaite, 'Contradictory Omens', *Savacou*, Monograph no.1, 1974. A West Indian attack on what Brathwaite sees as the Euro-centric attitudes of *Wide Sargasso Sea*.

Louis James, *Jean Rhys*, Longman, 1980. A critical study, based on research in Dominica, specifically relating *Wide Sargasso Sea* to the Caribbean background, though including notice of her other fiction; bibliography.

W. Look Lai, 'The Road to Thornfield Hall', *New Beacon Reviews*, 1968, pp. 38-52. A counter-view to Brathwaite's essay.

Elgin W. Mellown, bibliography of articles and reviews on Rhys's work up to 1977, *World Literature Written in English*, 16, 1977, pp. 79–122.

H. Nielson and F. Brahms, 'Retrieval of the Monster: Jean Rhys's *Wide Sargasso Sea*', in Kirsten Holst Peterson and Anna Rutherford (eds.) *Enigma of Values*, Dangaroo Press, 1975, UK distributor: PO Box 186, Coventry CV4 7HG. Relates Jean Rhys to the vision of Caribbean novelist Wilson Harris.

K. Ramchand, 'Terrified Conciousness', in *The West Indian Novel and its Background*, Faber, 1970, pp. 223–36. With Frantz Fanon in mind, Ramchand relates the quality of the book to the psycho-social situation of the white West Indians.

K. Ramchand, 'Wide Sargasso Sea', in *An Introduction to the Study of West Indian Literature*, Nelson, 1976, pp. 91–107. Excellent introductory essay; bibliography.

T.A. Staley, *Jean Rhys*, University of Texas Press,

1979. A sound survey, with a chapter on her background, of her works published up to her death, taking a straight literary-critical approach.

(iv) Reading links

Other books by Jean Rhys

Quartet (also known as *Postures*), Chatto & Windus 1928. Lightly concealed autobiographical account of Marya Zelli, who is taken up by a middle-aged literary editor with mixed intentions. The sexual betrayal Zelli experiences was to be a recurrent theme in Jean Rhys's fiction. Evocative account of life in Paris in the 1920s skating a thin line between self-exposure and self-pity.

After Leaving Mr Mackenzie, Jonathan Cape 1931. Limbo for the deserted girl. For all her sensitivity, does she have an identity to live for?

Voyage in the Dark, Constable 1934. Written to ease the tedium of touring as a chorus girl in a seedy troupe, this vivid account of a girl's research for identity, caught between memories of a Caribbean childhood and the sordid life and sexual harassment of England around 1914, has a poignancy unequalled in her later work.

Good Morning Midnight, Constable 1939. Those who find her poignant exploration of the isolated woman meaningful will find this final descent into the hell of self the most harrowing of all her novels. Sasha Jensen attempts a bold recovery in London, new clothes, new appearance, only to be picked up by a gigolo down on his luck, who takes her for a rich woman.

Tigers Are Better Looking, Deutsch 1968. Including her first published short stories, this is the best of her collections of short pieces; some show interesting facets on the world of *Wide Sargasso Sea*.

Sleep It Off Lady, Deutsch, 1976. A mixed bag of short pieces, some only fragments, and glimpses of the old misery.

Smile Please, Deutsch, 1979. Subtitled 'An Unfinished Autobiography', it contains some sharp evocative passages but little that has not been transmuted into her earlier fiction.

Work by other writers

The dislocation experienced by white West Indians has been explored by novelists like P. Shand Allfrey (*The Orchid House*, 1953), Geoffrey Drayton (*Christopher*, 1959) and Ian MacDonald (*The Humming-Bird Tree*, 1969).

African slaves working on a plantation, cutting sugar cane (Royal Commonwealth Society).

Unit 4
Samuel Selvon: *The Lonely Londoners*

SUSHEILA NASTA

Section A:
Critical Approaches

The Lonely Londoners is the first in a trilogy of exile novels concerned with the central figure of Moses Aloetta, a 'veteran' black Londoner, and his experiences with a group of ordinary and unlettered immigrants. *Moses Ascending* followed in 1975, and *Moses Migrating* in 1983. The novel examines the old relationship between West Indian and British culture within a new setting and is a seminal work in terms of its exploratory evocation of the development of a black colony in London in the 1950s, when the first major wave of Caribbean islanders migrated to the metropolis. This journey has been a frequent theme in Caribbean literature, and the process, as Louise Bennett once put it, of 'colonizin' Englan' in reverse' is one of the fundamental concerns of Selvon's novel.

With the use of a modified form of 'dialect', or what we should describe as a consciously chosen Caribbean literary English, for both the language of the narrator and that of the characters, *The Lonely Londoners* represented an important landmark in the development of the Caribbean novel; for it moved towards bridging the difficult gap of perspective between the teller of the tale and the tale itself. As one of the first full-length novels to be written in this language form, it also reflected an innovative departure away from the more standard modes of portraying largely illiterate characters in traditional fiction. In style and content therefore it

was illustrative of the process of decolonization. The explicit portrayal of the vitalizing growth and recognition of a specifically West Indian consciousness and identity is one of the novel's definitive features. Paradoxically this occurs after departure from the various islands and after arrival in the city. The sense of celebration that Selvon's black Londoners experience in the discovery of a corporate West Indian identity distinguishes the novel's subject-matter from many other Caribbean novels of exile. (Compare Andrew Salkey's *Escape to an Autumn Pavement*, 1960, or V. S. Naipaul's *The Mimic Men*, 1968.)

With its apparently unstructured, episodic style and the comic dexterity of the dialect form, *The Lonely Londoners* is often regarded as being simply an amusing social documentary of West Indian manners. As such its prime intention is to reveal with pathos and compassionate irony the humorous *faux pas* of the black innocent abroad. The surface textures of the loosely knit sketches or 'ballads' recounted through the ambivalent voice of the third-person narrator seem to support this view. As readers we are swiftly drawn into the pace of the narrative and the rites of initiation experienced by the 'desperate hustlers' as they 'land up' on Moses's doorstep in London 'with one set of luggage, no place to sleep, no place to go' (p. 8). Similarly, the idiosyncrasies and eccentricities of Selvon's various characters ('the boys') are clearly delineated and become easily identifiable to the reader. We witness with the narrator the first shocks of arrival at Waterloo, the disorientating effects of the English weather, the endless and usually abortive search for employment and the constant hunt for the forbidden fruits of 'white pussy'. The 'boys' (this term in itself suggests the almost primeval innocence of the immigrants)

Samuel Selvon, *The Lonely Londoners*, first published 1956; page references in this unit are to the Longman Drumbeat edition, 1979.

come from a variety of the islands, and Selvon is careful both to preserve their individual traits and to develop the sense of a group consciousness. This group of picturesque rogues circle like vultures around the generous figure of Moses Aloetta. Moses has already been in the city for ten years, knows the rules of survival in 'old Brit'n' and acts as a kind of 'liaison officer' for newly arrived migrants seeking their fortune.

From a very early stage in the novel, however, the romance and excitement of being in the metropolis are counterpointed with a frightening sense of dislocation. Sir Galahad's initial buoyancy, for instance, is fractured when he ventures out alone for the first time: 'Is one of those winter mornings when a kind of fog hovering around. The sun shining, but Galahad never see the sun look like how it looking now. No heat from it, it just there in the sky like a force-ripe orange. When he look up, the colour of the sky so desolate it make him frighten' (p. 26). Selvon's description of Galahad's reactions to a different climate, particularly to the difference in appearance of the sun, is fresh and enlightening as he uses terms of reference from a tropical world to describe the incongruities. The psychologically disorientating effect of the new physical surroundings on the newcomer is created implicitly in the way the language is used. Most strikingly perhaps, the collision of the two worlds – of Trinidad and London – in Galahad's mind, with the depiction of the sun as a 'force-ripe orange', introduces an almost surrealistic possibility into the scene, allowing the reader to experience the extremity of Galahad's fear. Similarly, by imposing the language of his subjects on the city, Selvon remakes it in their own image. At times, as Gordon Rohlehr has pointed out, they shrink it by the use of reductive analogies. The walls of Paddington slums, for example, crack like 'the last days of Pompeii' (p. 57).

Moses's developing scepticism about the resources of this community and his need to discover a private identity provide one of the major tensions in the novel. After a visit from Big City, who has ambitions to be a world-wide traveller, the narrator describes Moses's growing awareness of the futility of his existence: 'after Big City leave him Moses used to think bout . . . money, how it would solve all the problems in the world. He used to see

all his years in London pile up one on top of the other, and he getting no place in a hurry' (p. 82). Moses's sense of a pointless repetition here is significantly reflective of a voice that becomes more articulate as the novel proceeds. Set apart from the others as a wise man or sage, with the knowledge of years of 'ballads' behind him, Moses also has to come to terms with a sense of loss. This is illustrated most clearly in his relationship with Sir Galahad; from the opening pages where he attempts to persuade the newcomers to return 'back home' immediately, Moses's words reveal the pain of a superior irony. Whilst Galahad's dreams of the city may by fulfilled by the phrase 'Charing Cross' (p. 66) or by the magnetism of Piccadilly Circus, Moses's consciousness becomes increasingly disturbed. Although he attempts to relive his own past in London through Galahad's experiences, Moses has already reached a point of stasis:

'What you think?' [Galahad] ask Moses.
'Ah, in you I see myself how I was when I was new to London. All them places is like nothing to me now. Is like when you back home and you hear fellars talk about Times Square and Fifth Avenue, and Charing Cross . . . You say to yourself, "Lord, them places must be sharp." Then you get a chance and you see them for yourself, and is like nothing.' (p. 69)

As Galahad begins to feel more and more 'like a king living in London', Moses is drawn further into his introspective reflections and desire to define his own identity. This sense of 'something missing' is also illustrated in the characterization of the 'boys'; their protective self-caricatures and nicknames become recognizable as only a transparent form of camouflage within the black colony. And the nature of the language itself, with its reliance on repetition, drama and anecdote, can also become a regressive force – a form of restricted code with disturbing implications for the possibility of growth either within or outside the community. (These points are illustrated in depth in the analysis of specific passages in Section C.)

Selvon's 'ballad' (folk-tale) style in *The Lonely Londoners* shifts easily between an oral and a literary tone and bears many correspondences with the native tradition of Trinidadian calypso. The oral calypsonian ballad is well known for its use of a subversive irony, the melodramatic exaggeration of farcical anecdotes, racial stereotyping, repetition for dramatic effect and the inclusion of topical political material. Sexual themes are almost always present from a male viewpoint, and Selvon's 'boys' conform in many respects to the urban trickster figures of calypso; their attitudes to women are male chauvinist. However, rather like the ultimately reductive and self-denigratory effects of their nicknames, their view of women as 'pretty pieces of skin' reflects ultimately the boys' uncertainty and insecure sense of self. It is partly because the conflicting values of white society reduce their own stature that they must adopt these postures. This technique of 'naming' or 'labelling' as a means of self-defence is apparent in the episode when Sir Galahad, 'cool as a lord', sets off one day to meet his white date and confronts the colour problem. Never easily deflated, Galahad is left talking to the colour black as if it is a person, telling it that 'is not *he* who causing botheration in the place but Black, who is a worthless thing' (p. 72).

Whilst the calypsonian ballad form was appropriate in many ways to the directionless quality of the early experiences of the 'boys' in the metropolis, it would be a romantic oversimplification of Selvon's concerns if we were to view the novel solely in these terms. Selvon was clearly conscious of the difficulties of using 'dialect' as the principal literary medium in *The Lonely Londoners*. Whereas in *A Brighter Sun* (1952) – his first novel, set amongst the rural East Indian community in Trinidad – he had modified language to demark different racial characteristics, in *The Lonely Londoners* the problem he faced was of dealing with a tension between Standard English and a fabricated Caribbean literary English. The characters in *The Lonely Londoners* speak a language which contrasts markedly with the language of the few English characters, and Selvon also had to make the worlds of Moses and the 'boys' accessible to an international audience, thereby both maintaining the enclosed West Indian world and drawing the non-West Indian reader into it. The language used by Selvon in the novel is a self-consciously created and modified form of 'dialect' which he varies to suit different situations. It is not 'the language of the people or of any one stratum of

the [Caribbean] society'; it 'expresses the sensibility of a whole society' (Kenneth Ramchand, 'Song of Innocence, Song of Experience', in *World Literature Written in English*, 21, 1982, p. 650).

Referring to the composition of the novel, Selvon has himself said that his use of this language form 'was really an experiment ... there are certain physical and emotional scenes where personally I find that the dialect just doesn't ... carry over as efficiently as Standard English exactly what I want to say' (*The English Novel Abroad*, BBC Radio, 1 January 1974). For instance, whilst the oral and dramatic facets of 'the boys'' experience are appropriately depicted by the narrator in dialect, which in tense focuses on the present, and in tone, on the comic, Selvon needed to stretch the boundaries of his linguistic style in revealing Moses's attempts to express an individual consciousness. While still maintaining an essentially West Indian perception of London, at certain points Selvon incorporates the use of Standard English, or, in Moses's lyrical 'epiphany' to summer, turns the dramatic nature of dialect inwards in order to reflect the poetic growth of Moses's private thoughts (see pp. 85–95). Alternatively, in the passage at the close of the novel – 'The changing of the seasons, the cold slicing winds, the falling leaves, sunlight on green grass..' (p. 121) – Selvon uses literary atmospherics and Standard English to convey Moses's nostalgic vision of the English seasons.

There is no beginning or end to the experiences of the 'boys' in *The Lonely Londoners*. Although details about Moses accumulate (pp. 31–50, 77–82), they are unobtrusive and are fitting to his development as a character as the novel proceeds. The surface fragmentation or conscious disorganization of the novel's form therefore becomes part of its main purpose, that 'behind the ballad and the episode' is a 'great aimlessness, a great restless, swaying movement that leaving you standing in the same spot' (p. 125). Similarly, Selvon's experimentation with the language form used by the 'boys' serves only to heighten this illusory sense of movement. Episodes recounted may take on mythological proportions but they later become a small part of the restricted repartee which sustains the community. Only Moses (who by the close of the novel has almost merged in consciousness with the public narrating voice) seems to be moving forward and can perceive the need to discover a new language for existence. The black London of Selvon's 'boys' has become by the close only a city of words; there are no firm foundations, and the surface security provided by this shared code, which reduces the vast metropolis to a manageable West Indian colony within the city, will only perpetuate their isolation, since there is little desire for integration.

The final pages of the novel show us Moses looking down into the river Thames and beneath the surface of 'the boys'' experiences: 'when you go down a little, you bounce up a kind of misery and pathos and a frightening – what? He don't know the *right word* but he have the right feeling in his heart' (p. 126). This search for the 'right word' or an appropriate idiom to express and define a new reality, the experience of exile, is central to an understanding of Selvon's purpose in *The Lonely Londoners* and becomes the preoccupation of a new Moses in Selvon's sequel, *Moses Ascending*.

Section B: The Setting

Perhaps the most useful introduction to the background of Selvon's black London in the 1950s can be found in George Lamming's collection of essays, *The Pleasures of Exile* (1960). It was a period when not only 40,000 West Indians emigrated to Britain to find employment but a number of talented young black writers migrated to the 'metropolis' of London in search of publishers. Of the works that record this movement – the journey from island to city and in many cases from expectation to disillusionment – *The Lonely Londoners* and *The Pleasures of Exile* are central. Whilst Selvon's novel focuses on a fictional rendition of the experiences of a group of ordinary immigrants in the city, 'black immigrants . . . among whom I [Selvon] lived for a few years when I first arrived in London', *The Pleasures of Exile* provides an analysis of the problems from the perspective of the writer or intellectual. For both groups, however, it was an important period in the development and recognition of a communal Caribbean consciousness and identity:

No Barbadian, no Trinidadian, no St Lucian, no islander from the West Indies sees himself as a West Indian until he encounters another islander in foreign territory. . . . In this sense most West Indians of my generation were *born* in England. The West Indian, formerly understood as a geographical term, now assumes cultural significance.

(*The Pleasures of Exile* p. 214)

Whilst this was an early statement by Lamming, its significance is critical to an understanding of Selvon's creation of a West Indian London. Since it was the first time that people from all the different islands were meeting, common codes of reference were established, and these links also provided the resources for a protective shield and a means of survival in the 'grey world city' (p. 11).

At the beginning of *The Lonely Londoners* the atmosphere of Selvon's city is described: 'as if is not London at all but some strange place on another planet' (p. 7). This sense of the 'unrealness' of the metropolis predominates throughout. For the black immigrants it is essentially a hostile world. We meet few British characters, enter few homes, and topographical description in the novel is scarce. The boundaries of Selvon's immigrant enclave are carefully defined and made accessible to new arrivals, who always require initiation into games of survival in a land whose streets are not 'paved with gold' (p. 8). Black London is bounded in the west by 'the Gate' (Notting Hill), in the east by 'the Arch' (Marble) and in the north by 'the Water' (Bayswater); it seems at times as if Selvon has created an island in the city. When the 'boys' do venture out into uncharted areas of experience in the city they always return with a supportive story or 'ballad' to strengthen and reinforce the mythology of the group. Selvon himself has pointed out on several occasions that the London these immigrants inhabited lacked any of the normal pillars of security or cohesion. His characters may see the sights or taste the bitter-sweet attractions of the metropolis but they ultimately live in a restrictive, two-dimensional world.

Section C: A Closer Look

(1) 'Ballad' of Sir Galahad and the pigeon (pp. 106–9)

In Selvon's London, where 'the boys' repeatedly tell Moses sensational stories, where they fail to form deep relationships even amongst their own group, there is no explicit structure to life. It is a world where 'men know what it is to hustle a pound to pay the rent when Friday come' (p. 50), and their 'ballads' stem from their banal and tedious existence. It is essentially a present-orientated world. The 'boys' are trapped, despite the vibrant pulse of the language they speak, in a form of stasis. This stasis is counterbalanced in the novel by the illusion of movement created by Selvon's narrative method and the comic potential of the dialect form.

This tension characteristically informs the movement of Galahad's story. Like many other 'ballads' in the novel, it opens with the unselfconscious voice of the narrator, who swiftly sets the scene in a mode resembling that of an oral storyteller. In fact, Selvon's style embodies many qualities which are characteristic of an oral rather than a literary tradition. This is evident in the condensed and essentially visual presentation of the scene, the frequent use of personification, concrete images, rhetoric and the dramatic portrayal of episodes by the use of a narrator who speaks directly to the reader. The sophistication and economy of Selvon's method and his eye for humorous detail are evident here.

We view the world outside, the world of 'they' people in 'this' country, from Galahad's perspective. An implicit juxtaposition of the two Londons is thus set up. The incident takes place in a familiar park, Kensington Gardens; yet at a time when things are 'brown' for the 'boys', the park is not simply a leisure area. For Galahad it becomes a hunting-ground, a source of cheap food.

The 'ballad' is narrated with an exaggerated sense of drama as Galahad plans his strategy. His logic seems perfectly reasonable considering his predicament, and his father's experience in San Fernando only adds weight to this. The language used supports Galahad's venture, and there is no sense of his actions being morally criticized or ridiculed. Yet the whole episode becomes

increasingly absurd as we realize this is Kensington and not the high street in San Fernando. Sir Galahad's fear of 'the gallows' emphasizes the persecution he must feel, whilst the insular and secure life-style of the British, who have time even to feed the fat birds, contrasts with Galahad's desperation. The pathetic comedy is heightened by the melodramatic manner in which the 'ballad' is narrated. The anarchic antics of the West Indian trickster figure, with his lack of sense of any ethical directives, are beginning to conflict dangerously with the standards of order in the 'mother country'. But Selvon's irony does not condemn; it points to the confusions that result between both societies, and exploits their comic potential. The subtle blend of raw humour and pathos, compassion without sentimentality, a naturalism rendered absurd by the implicit clash of cultural values, is representative of Selvon's method. And the 'heroic' Sir Galahad must, as always, return to Moses for reassurance.

(2) Moses's room as community centre (pp. 122–5)

Towards the end of the novel we are shown a Moses who is becoming aware of a meaningless repetition and circularity beneath the surface preoccupations and activities of the group. The phrase 'what happening?', which echoes throughout the novel and is the fundamental rationale of its numerous episodes, comes to imply less a resilience in the face of complicated experience than a painful sense of futility and incoherence.

In this passage Moses's developing awareness of a position of stalemate is apparent. He gradually recognizes that the 'boys coming together for a old talk to find out the latest gen' is a form of disguise for an appalling sense of chaos, fragmentation and emptiness. The language used by Galahad, Harris, Big City and the rest, as they exaggerate their escapades by dramatic representation in Moses's room every Sunday morning, initially suggests that everyone knows what is happening; but significantly the stories are never finished, and the breathless narration emphasizes this direction-lessness (note the lack of punctuation and the length of the first sentence, for instance). The repartee of the community has become a self-undermining rhetoric, and the feverish questioning undercuts even any modest appearance of control or stability. As the 'boys' attempt to swap well-worn anecdotes, we experience Moses's detachment as he becomes almost a Tiresias figure who can never escape the constant 'moaning and groaning and sighing and crying'. The oral and rhythmic nature of the prose adds weight to this, as the synchronization of voices degenerates into a deflationary climax which then subsides to the original theme: 'So, what happening these days?'. Significantly, the questions do not seem to be addressed to any particular subject; they ring out like voices in the wilderness. The predicament of the 'boys' is exposed by the expectations aroused but not fulfilled by the formal structure.

The pathos of this moment is further highlighted by the fact that their surrogate religious gathering, an occasion which we suspect prepares them for the realities of the coming week's work, of which we hear little in the novel, operates solely in terms of a group identity. Only Moses perceives that beneath the 'kiff-kaff laughter, behind the ballad and the episode, the what-happening, the summer-is-hearts... is a great aimlessness, a great restless, swaying movement that leaving you standing in the same spot' (p. 125). Moses has become both participant in and spectator of the action and begins to see laughter as part of a tragic process. At this stage, he is trapped between the incongruities of several worlds: the world of his private conscience and that of the black community; the sustaining romance of the idea of 'London and life on the outside' and a nostalgia for Trinidad. The self-enclosing and enclosed nature of the experience in his room on Sunday mornings acts as a metaphorical correlative of this tension for the reader.

Interestingly, this extract emphasizes our uncertainty as to who the narrator actually is in the novel. In knowledge, experience and viewpoint he often seems to be indistinct from the reflecting consciousness of Moses. We wonder how the third-person narrator, in a narrative that is largely dependent for its contents upon the passing of the spoken word, knows all that he does. The confusion is not, however, a hindrance to the success of the narrative. Since no particular focus of interest in terms of character is intended (apart from Moses),

Selvon's use of an intimate but public narrative voice is fitting to the 'ballad' style. Nevertheless, the growth of consciousness that Moses articulates here (and in the final pages of the novel) is significant. With his increasing estrangement from the group must come the development of an individual voice; it is a voice that looks forward to the first-person narration by Moses himself in the sequel to this novel, *Moses Ascending*.

Section D: The Author

Born in Trinidad in 1923 of East Indian parents, Samuel Dickson Selvon commenced his writing career whilst working as a wireless operator for the Royal Naval Reserve. In 1945 he became a journalist with the *Trinidad Guardian* and fiction editor of the *Guardian Weekly*, a literary magazine devoted principally to the publication of creative writing. Selvon describes himself as largely self-educated and has observed that from childhood he found literature an important medium of imaginative exploration and discovery. It was during his early adult years in Trinidad that Selvon began publishing short stories, poems and articles in Caribbean literary magazines. Like many other writers of his generation, Selvon emigrated to Britain in 1950, where his first novel, *A Brighter Sun*, was published two years later. Today he is one of the most popular and internationally distinguished of contemporary writers. He has published to date ten novels and a collection of short stories; he has also contributed numerous reviews, essays and poems to a variety of journals. Although critical attention has focused primarily on his fiction, Selvon has written several plays for radio and television (broadcast by the BBC between 1955 and 1978). In recent years Selvon has lived in Canada with his wife and children; he hopes eventually to create a Caribbean vision of Canada.

It is against the background of Trinidad and London that we must place Selvon's major works so far. On the whole Selvon deals with three kinds of people in his fiction. The East Indian peasantry figure in *A Brighter Sun* (1952), its sequel *Turn*

Again Tiger (1958) and *The Plains of Caroni* (1970). Secondly, there are the novels and short stories which focus on urban tricksters or 'calypsonian' figures. Stories included in the collection *Ways of Sunlight* (1958), and the exile novels set in London – *The Lonely Londoners*, *The Housing Lark* (1965), *Moses Ascending* and *Moses Migrating* – fall into this category. And finally, a more introspective and reflective aspect of Selvon's writing can be seen in the less well-known *An Island Is a World* (1955) and *I Hear Thunder* (1963). Selvon has described these as his 'straight' as opposed to his 'dialect' novels and focuses on the metaphysical crises of an educated and professional group of middle-class Trinidadians in the post-war years.

Selvon has been awarded several fellowships and other academic honours throughout his writing career. He has taught creative writing at universities in Britain, the USA, Canada and Trinidad.

Section E: Classroom Use

(i) Level of use

The novel could be studied at a variety of levels, ranging from fourth- or fifth-year GCSE to advanced sixth-form work on language and form. Age: 14–18.

The younger age group might benefit by focusing on particular episodes as an introduction to Selvon's technique: 'ballad' of the pigeon (pp. 106–10); contrast with Cap and the seagull (pp. 118–21); Harris and the fête in St Pancras Hall (pp. 95–106). These episodes would also be suitable for group work and dramatic improvisations.

(ii) Points of focus and emphasis

1 The opening sequence, Moses at Waterloo, pp. 7–19:
- atmosphere of arrivals and departures;
- expectations of new arrivals; Moses's state of mind;
- the portrayal of Henry Oliver (Sir Galahad);
- attitude of English to different islanders; use of neologisms.

2 Sir Galahad and the big city, pp. 19–30:
- London from a Caribbean perspective;
- innocent abroad? calypsonian hustler?
- use of mock-heroic tone;
- unemployment; harsh realities.

3 'The boys'; methods of characterization:
- two-dimensional identities; self-caricatures; why?
- Cap, pp. 33–45; Nigerian in Caribbean community?
- Bart, pp. 47–51;
- Big City, pp. 77-85;
- Five Past Twelve, pp. 94-105.

4 Colour/race consciousness:
- accomodation and limited areas for existence, pp. 11–17;
- Galahad and the child, pp. 69-73;
- attitudes to white women, pp. 48-51;
- Harris's fête, pp. 95-106.

5 Black celebration of the city despite nostalgia for 'back home':
- domestication of specific parts of London, pp. 55–67;
- Moses's 'epiphany', pp. 85-94; style?
- ending of novel, pp. 124-6.

6 The importance of language; banter, anecdotes, etc:
- language as a protective barrier against the city, pp. 121–6;
- Moses's room as surrogate religious centre, p. 122;
- 'what happening?' Questions – no answers, p. 124;
- individual consciousness/social conscience; Moses draws apart; why? pp. 125-6;
- 'dialect' as language of narration, pp. 85-94.

(iii) Questions for essay writing or classroom discussion

1 In what senses are Selvon's black Londoners lonely? From a first reading of the novel one might assume the presence of a vibrant community. Discuss.

2 Is the name Moses appropriate for the central figure in the novel? Why does Selvon use an old biblical name for this character?

3   Consider the names of some of the other characters in the novel. Are they well chosen? What do you think of?

4   Many critics have seen the novel as being simply a humorous social documentary on immigrant life in Britain in the 1950s. Is this an adequate assessment of the book?

5   Very few black women are mentioned in *The Lonely Londoners* apart from Tolroy's relations. Why do you think Selvon has not concentrated more fully on the characterization of women?

6   It is difficult to decide who is telling the story/ stories in the novel. At times the voices of the narrator and Moses seem indistinguishable. Read again the final section of the novel (pp. 121–6). Can you think of any reasons why this should be?

7   Moses's comment at the end of the novel, 'As if the boys laughing, but they only laughing because they afraid to cry', is an important one. Discuss the nature of the humour in the novel.

8   The 'ballads' in *The Lonely Londoners* may describe the quality of West Indian immigrant life in the 1950s but they do not bear much relevance to the black experience today. Do you agree? Is Selvon's novel outdated?

9   Selvon focuses particularly on Moses and Sir Galahad (Henry Oliver). Compare and contrast these two characters and suggest reasons for their differences in attitude. Is it simply a gap between innocence and experience?

10   Selvon's London could be described as a city created by words. Consider the different kinds of language used by Selvon in the novel (compare pp. 7–11, 85-94, 121-2), and discuss the effects of his literary form in relation to the following extract from Louise Bennett's poem 'Colonization in Reverse':

Wat a joyful news, Miss Mattie,
I feel like me heart gwine burs'
Jamaica people colonizin'
Englan' in reverse.
(Louise Bennett, 'Colonization in Reverse',
        ll. 2-4, in *Jamaica Labrish*, 1966)

11   The 'boys' spend much of their time in the novel 'coasting lime'. What do you think this means and what are its implications?

12   'Nobody in London does really accept you. They tolerate you, yes, but you can't go in their house and eat or sit down and talk. It ain't have no sort of family life for us here' (p. 114). How does this comment by Moses add to your understanding of the lives of the 'boys'? Can you find any examples of secure family existence in the novel?

13   'It have people living in London who don't know what happening in the room next to them. . . . London is a place like that, it divide up into little worlds, and you stay in the world you belong to' (p. 58). Discuss how you might feel as a new arrival in London. Are Selvon's characters optimistic about their future in the city?

14   'The old Moses, standing on the banks of the Thames. Sometimes he think he see some sort of profound realization in his life' (p. 125). Read this paragraph and consider whether or not Moses has changed his perceptions by the close of the novel.

15   Selvon once made the following comment on his writing: 'No plot or idea. There never was any beginning.' Is there a 'beginning' as such to Selvon's narrative in *The Lonely Londoners*? Consider why the novel is episodic in form.

(iv) Creative approaches/curriculum links

1   Make a list of all the areas of London mentioned in *The Lonely Londoners*. See if you can draw a map indicating the favourite spots of Selvon's 'boys'. Do they inhabit a large area?

2   Have you ever experienced any form of victimization or prejudice? Write an essay or short story describing your experiences and feelings.

3   '. . . as if not London at all but some strange place on another planet' (p. 7). Read Selvon's description of an arrival and then read the following extract from Jean Rhys's *Voyage in the Dark*, another Caribbean novel of exile:

It was as if a curtain had fallen, hiding everything I had ever known. It was almost like being born again. The colours were different, the smells different, the feelings things gave you right down inside yourself was different. Not just the difference between heat; cold; light; darkness; purple; grey. But a difference in the way I was frightened and the way I was happy.
(Jean Rhys, *Voyage in the Dark*, Penguin, 1975, p. 7)

Are there any comparable features in Selvon's description of the atmosphere of Waterloo and the extract from Jean Rhys? Write your own poem or prose piece on an arrival in a strange or alien place.

4 Find out what you can about why so many West Indians came to London after the Second World War. Which islands did they come from and how were their backgrounds different?

5 Listen to some Trinidadian calypsos (Mighty Sparrow or Lord Kitchener). Is there any comparison between the ironic style of these and Selvon's humour in *The Lonely Londoners*?

6 Find out as much as you can about housing conditions experienced by the black community in inner-city areas today. Do you think things have changed significantly for the children of the West Indians who arrived in Britain in the 1950s? If so, how?

Section F: Teaching Aids

(i) Audio-visual material

Pressure, film, 1978. Selvon was co-author of script with Horace Ové (director). Good background and material for discussion; immigrants in the 1970s. London: British Film Institute.

Interviews and readings

'A Multiracial Society', *The Changing Caribbean*, BBC Radio, 12 October 1960. Selvon contributes to programme.

'Samuel Selvon Talks to Gerald Moore', *The English Novel Abroad* (interview and reading), BBC Radio, 1 January 1974.

'Samuel Selvon Reads and Talks about his Work'. Recording made at annual conference of the Association for the Teaching of Caribbean and African Literature, 24 September 1982. London: British Institute of Recorded Sound.

'Samuel Selvon Talks about his Recent Fiction'. Videotape of Selvon's visit to Warwick University's Centre for Caribbean Studies, 1984.

(ii) Background reading

David Dabydeen, *Slave Song*, Dangaroo Press, 1984, UK distributor: PO Box 186, Coventry CV4 7HG. For insight into male treatment of West Indian women.

Donald Hinds, *Journey to an Illusion: A Study of West Indian Migration*, Heinemann Educational Books, 1966.

George Lamming, *The Pleasures of Exile*, Michael Joseph, 1960, pp. 38–46, 211-25. Important and early presentation of Selvon as a 'folk' or 'peasant' writer.

Kenneth Ramchand, *The West Indian Novel and its Background,* Faber, 1970.

Henri Tajfel and J. L. Dawson (eds.), *Disappointed Guests*, Oxford University Press, 1965.

Keith Warner, *The Trinidad Calypso*, Heinemann Educational Books, 1982, pp. 123–38.

(iii) Critical bibliography

E. Baugh (ed.), *Critics on Caribbean Literature*, Allen & Unwin, 1978.

D. Dabydeen and N. Wilson-Tagoe, *A Reader's Guide to West Indian and Black British Literature,* Hansib Publications, 1988.

Michel Fabre, 'From Trinidad to London: Tone and Language in Samuel Selvon's Novels', *Literary Half-Yearly*, vol. 20, no. 1, 1979.

Jane Grant, *Samuel Selvon: Ways of Sunlight*, Longman (Guides to Literature Series), 1979.

Susheila Nasta, 'Samuel Selvon: A Preliminary Bibliography', *Journal of Commonwealth Literature*, vol. 18, no. 1, 1983. A detailed bibliography of primary and secondary works.

Kenneth Ramchand, 'Song of Innocence, Song of Experience: Samuel Selvon's *The Lonely Londoners* as a Literary Work', in *World Literature Written in English, 21,* 1982.

(iv) Reading links

Other novels by Samuel Selvon

An Island Is a World, Alan Wingate, 1955. Set in Trinidad, London and the USA; interesting contrast to the style and concerns of the 'Moses' novels.

Ways of Sunlight, MacGibbon & Kee, 1957; Longman, 1973. Published only a year after *The Lonely Londoners* and containing many stories written earlier, this collection brings together the two main settings for Selvon's writing: Trinidad and London. The London stories are written in a similar style to *The Lonely Londoners*.

Moses Ascending, Davis-Poynter, 1975; Heinemann Educational Books (Caribbean Writers Series), 1984. Sequel to *The Lonely Londoners*; deals with a different black London twenty years later in which Moses, elevated to the status of 'landlord', attempts to write his memoirs.

Moses Migrating, Longman, 1984. Final novel in the trilogy. Moses returns to Trinidad for Carnival. Ambiguous ending worthy of consideration in relation to *The Lonely Londoners*.

Other novels of exile

Austin Clarke, *Among Thistles and Thorns*, Heinemann, 1965.

Austin Clarke, *The Bigger Light*, Boston: Little and Brown, 1975.

George Lamming, *The Emigrants*, Michael Joseph, 1954; Allison & Busby, 1982.

George Lamming, *Water with Berries*, Longman, 1972.

V. S. Naipaul, *The Mimic Men*, Deutsch, 1967; Penguin, 1973.

Jean Rhys, *Voyage in the Dark*, Deutsch, 1934; Penguin, 1975.

Andrew Salkey, *Escape to an Autumn Pavement*, Hutchinson, 1960.

West Indians emigrating to Britain in the 1950s in search of employment (BBC Halton Picture Library).

Unit 5
Earl Lovelace: *The Wine of Astonishment*

KATHY WILLIAMS

Section A:
Critical Approaches

Thou has showed thy people hard things;
Thou has made us drink the wine of
astonishment.

(Psalms 60: 3)

This novel is a vivid account of the stoicism and
dignity with which a small congregation of Spiritual
Baptists survive all the pressures brought to bear
against them. At one level it is the intimate account
of one family and their friends; at a second level it is
a study of how a village community assimilates and
rejects cultural experiences, at a time of great social
change, in order to retain its own integrity; at a
third level the story is a powerful and poignant
indictment of all those who are oppressors, who
misuse their power. It celebrates the courage of
those who have always been victims and the
creative instinct of such people to transform their
lives into something heroic. They do this through
their family life and relationships, through their
style of worship and religious commitment and
through the artistic statements they make in music
and poetry, in steel band and calypso.

Bonasse village in Trinidad is the home of Bee
Dorcas. With his wife Eva, the narrator of the story,
and his children he lives simply, growing crops,
with a cow for milk in the good times. Their oldest
son has migrated to Port of Spain. Bee is the leader
of the congregation of Spiritual Baptists.

Earl Lovelace, *The Wine of Astonishment*; page
references in this unit are to the Heinemann Educational
Books (Caribbean Writers Series) edition, 1986.

Bolo, once celebrated stick-fighter and local
hero, has been a member of the church, but feels
forced to leave it. While Bee believes that the
church will gain its eventual freedom to worship
without being molested, through the efforts of the
Council's first black member, Ivan Morton, a local
man, Bolo is committed to direct action: 'Bolo, a
warrior still, with his big chest up, and his eyes
bright with dreams that fill him' (p. 16). Bolo's way
is as futile and negative as that of the politicians,
policemen and opportunists whom he despises.
Between Bolo and Bee stands Ivan Morton, who is
educated, modern, civilized — so 'civilized they
can't even break a fart'. The betrayal committed by
this schoolteacher who turns to politics and the
disappointment of the trusting expectations of his
community are all the more painful because he *is* an
insider.

The people of Bonasse have been accustomed to
suffering, in the time of the Richardsons in the Big
House. Behind the verse of the psalm that gives the
novel its title is the earlier verse:

O God thou hast cast us off; thou has scattered
us;
Thou has been displeased; o turn thyself to us
again.

(Psalms 60: 1)

The law and the police have been the most obvious
of the old enemies. 'They was police, but they was
human, too,' says Eva (p. 35). Now a more malign
force appears, to collaborate with the other agents
of destruction: 'Corporal Prince was a different
story . . . power walking down the street . . . to
smash up the church and get promotion' (p. 35).
Throughout the narrative, the tension between
Bee's refusal to be brutalized and Bolo's desire to
precipitate events is mediated through their

relationships with Morton, Prince, the Americans who invade and pollute the village during the war and the emerging group of 'educated' bureaucrats who frustrate the villagers' expectations. Only after Bolo's death, when freedom of worship has been gained, can Bonasse regenerate, build up its own institutions and become socially and psychologically whole, no longer the victims of its history and experiences.

The central theme of the novel is that there is redemption through suffering; the problem of that suffering is viewed from the perspective of a firm faith. There is an insistence that in the very living of their lives, in their endurance, wit and vitality, lies the characters' significance. It is through their own resources, and through God, that the Bonasse congregation will survive, not through the obvious route to material betterment – 'through God we shall do valiantly' (Psalms 60: 12).

While biblical language is a powerful reference point for the people, the language of the novel is that of its narrator, Eva, Bee's wife. Eva's voice is authentic and convincing. It is important for the success of the novel that one trusts her account. She is a deeply religious woman, a realist, clear-thinking, courageous and resilient. While strongly individualized she also represents characteristics and values which are archetypal: Caribbean woman/lover/mother. Her perspective focuses Lovelace's main concerns: his trust in the spontaneous, intuitive and customary aspects of life; and his condemnation of falseness, hypocrisy, politicians and racist opportunists, and those with simplistic solutions. Authorial didacticism is avoided.

The community of Bonasse and its church is close. Eva is able to narrate events directly, or from eyewitnesses. She is a born story-teller, garrulous yet pointed, often repeating, reinforcing and reinterpreting. Great art goes into the apparently spontaneous account. The reader is a confidant – persuaded to see, to understand and to respond. Eva's language is a gentle dialect. It is immediate, compacted and powerful, apparently simple images becoming multi-faceted. Images and associations spark off from one another.

The structure of the novel is dictated by the fact that Eva holds the whole story in her head. There is the initial visit of Bee to Ivan Morton, and the nine chapters after that take up events and resonances introduced there. At one level the time scheme is clear, but this sequential ordering is less important than the cross-associations among the characters and themes. Eva's eye acts like a film director's camera, and the montage effect, the piled-up detail and images, repeated and developed, holds the whole together in a tightly constructed visual mesh. The foreground dominates – the people, their action and dialogue, sometimes self-consciously making 'self-images', as when Ivan Morton rides back in his car, or when Taffy plays with the idea of leaving Bonasse to 'see snow . . . wear a winter coat' and gradually grow more beautiful.

The text is bright with sharp dialogue and short explanatory pieces. But there are also sustained, orchestrated events, developed and detailed, like the service that breaks the law (pp. 58–63) leading up to the inevitable climax and reaction. There are set pieces, too: the conscious Christ-like images of Bee at his first appearance, or of Bolo at his death.

Eva rarely describes the setting of the story; she is preoccupied with anxiety about her family. Only towards the end of the story, on the day when she begins to feel that she may be getting old, does she have time to look at the world around her, as she thinks of her children:

> I sit down on the front steps in the sunshine, catching the little breeze that blowing, cross the yard and swinging the ripening mangoes on their stems, and I combing my hair, plaiting it in rows – long time ago, so long, I used to take out the grey hairs when they was few – and watching the chickens scratching in the yard, and the striped butterflies zigzagging like kites that can't fly well over the hibiscus hedge where the flowers unfolding like red parasols and the bees rushing from flower to flower and listening to the hens cackle as the cocks strut and the wind blow . . . and thinking that even if we bear what He send like the earth bear the rain and hot sun . . . even if we bear all the tribulation that rain down on us for generations, is still not enough just to be here to bear . . . but we have to rise like the sun rise, we have to shine in a sky, and I don't know why, I feel so good. (p. 140)

Despite the harshness and the struggle, despite the betrayals and the changes, the novel is optimistic. The old world of Bolo may have vanished, but the Holy Spirit, so central to the Baptist congregation, is emerging in new and vibrant forms:

> I listening to the music; for the music that those boys playing on the steelband have in it that same spirit that we miss in our church: the same Spirit; and listening to them, my heart swell, and it is like resurrection morning. I watch Bee, Bee watch me . . . the both of us bow, nod, as if, yes, God is great, and like if we passing in front of something holy. (p. 146)

Section B: The Setting

Even the name of Trinidad has a religious connotation. Columbus sighted the Three Sisters, the Trinity Hills, near the Southern Range, in 1492 and probably landed in Moruga Bay, which he named La Trinidad in honour of the Holy Trinity. For many centuries before then Amerindian Arawak people had lived there. Many of their beliefs in their spirit world, and much of their knowledge of herbs and medicine, lived on. Columbus's arrival was just the first of many meetings among the people and cultures which make up modern Trinidad and Tobago, which now form one nation.

Until 1780 the Spanish used Arawak Indians for labour. By 1700 several thousands had been converted to Christianity by the Catholic missions. Settlers objected strongly to the influence of these missions, and so their power was abolished. As plantations developed, the Indian villages nearly disappeared, and Trinidad was a poor and neglected island. Consequently after a decree in 1783 a free grant of land was given to every settler who arrived with his slaves. African slaves therefore arrived very late in this Caribbean island. By 1784 there were more French settlers than Spanish; the Africans formed the most numerous group, while the Indian population had dropped dramatically.

Although the Africans came indirectly to Trinidad, nearly all of the original slaves were African born. They brought with them their oral histories, stories, dance and music, together with spiritual leaders, a system of healing and certain attitudes to life, particularly concerning the necessity to maintain links with their original culture.

The British moved into Trinidad in 1797 having vanquished the Spaniards. Their motives were largely economic, and they already largely monopolized the trade in cotton and sugar.

While the British abolished the slave trade in 1807, slaves continued to be held legally or illegally until 1838, when emancipation came. Slavery was initially replaced by an onerous and exploitative apprenticeship system. As the demand for labour increased, new waves of migrants came, those of African origin largely from America and other Caribbean islands, and several thousands from India.

The stage was set for a twentieth-century Trinidad with a population sharply divided along ethnic and racial lines. Power and prestige were very unevenly distributed. Most Blacks found themselves poor and despised by lighter-skinned groups. In a society which denied them dignity and true freedom, these lower groups developed strong religious and social institutions which validated their way of life and were positive and assertive. Many of African origin, denied access to formal education and missionary endeavour, applied their own wisdom to any new information that they could acquire. The old system gave children a very high value in society, emphasizing endurance, dignity and respect for others. Community values transcended the needs of individuals. When these people encountered the fervour of black preachers with the messianic message and apocalyptic language, new mediating institutions were formed as a creative and self-valuing response to the Trinidadian experience.

The Spiritual Baptists

The Spiritual Baptists are a group of Afro-Caribbean Christians who accept the theology of mainstream Christianity. They are fundamentalists, but their style of worship is largely African.

In 1816 many black Americans who had fought as British colonial marines accepted the offer of settling on Crown lands in Trinidad. These American settlers (Merikins) were placed in six company villages, where the tradition of black

Baptist worship which they had brought with them became their most powerful cultural and social institution. After holding meetings in homes and then in tents, groups of enthusiastic evangelists and prophets travelled widely and gained many converts, largely among poor Blacks.

The denomination which rose from this process became the Spiritual Baptist Church. They were known as Shouters because of the enthusiastic volume of noise sustained at their services. Some of their adherents were originally from St Vincent. The Shouters' Prohibition Order of 1917 banned their worship as an 'unmitigated nuisance', not to be tolerated. They gained the freedom to worship only in 1951.

Attitudes to the Spiritual Baptists were prejudiced and negative. There had been considerable fear that their devotion and their charismatic leaders might encourage them to take the biblical message too fervently, and organize against the authorities. Other 'alternative' social institutions in the Caribbean, such as steel bands, found themselves the target of similar repressive legislation.

A Spiritual Baptist congregation may be small or large. The leader acts as 'father' to the congregation, and the various offices parallel all the roles in the community outside (e.g. doctor, warrior, shepherd). The leader is usually a powerful preacher, and there is considerable interaction between him and his congregation; at times it seems that he orchestrates their responses. He must be able to guide the congregation into an ecstatic state, because the central experience of Spiritual Baptists is possession by the Holy Spirit. They speak 'in tongues' when this occurs.

They have a particular devotion to rivers and beaches, because they believe in total immersion at baptism, and in the cleansing and vital power of water. Places of particular significance are decorated with flags; these may be in the open air or in relatively modest buildings. The congregation is generally robed for services. Colours are important, although white predominates. A bell, book (the Bible) and candle are used. Herbs and flowers decorate the altar and wayside shrines.

During possession, members may have visions. The leader will interpret these, as he will dreams. One of the central functions of the church is healing through the Holy Spirit. The Holy Spirit is similarly useful in preventive medicine; it protects Baptists from malign influences such as 'obeah'.

The style of worship has some similarities to that of other charismatic groups. Services include fervent hymn-singing, prayers and exhortations, and highly personalized accounts. There is a central powerful sermon. Although there may be a regular order of service, spontaneity is pre-eminent. There is much clapping, stamping and dancing. The atmosphere is very emotional. Converts must convince the congregation of their *sincerity*; they *feel* the Spirit; they *know* Jesus; they *love* God.

For those who may be otherwise oppressed, the Spiritual Baptists provide a proud, independent route to self-knowledge, self-expression and assertion. The church supports its members in every aspect of their lives. It tells a person that he or she is somebody.

The Spiritual Baptists have been acknowledged by an Act of Parliament in 1982 incorporating the International Spiritual Baptist Ministerial Council of Trinidad and Tobago. They are currently attempting to establish a cathedral in Port of Spain. Their characteristic flags, their gowned figures on river banks at ceremonies, their prophets ringing bells as they proclaim their message, their pavement shrines and evangelists on city streets — all these make them a very visible part of Trinidadian life.

Section C: A Closer Look

(1) Bee goes to see Ivan Morton (pp. 1–3)

The first chapter starts with the most basic statement of the central theme, expressed by Eva as experienced knowledge. The individual tone of voice and perspective are established immediately. The cyclical structure of the book is initiated by the reference to the harsh terrain and history of the village and men's capacity to survive and grow, even in such bitter ground.

Compactly, Eva poses the central problem of the *cause* and *purpose* of all this suffering: 'What sin we commit?' The parallel between Eva, the caring mother, and a God who appears to behave unjustly to His children is presented lucidly. The narrative teases out some of the possible answers to this question. The injustice of life in Bonasse is seen from the mother's immediate pain at watching her children go hungry and ill-housed – but even worse from the perspective of the people as a persecuted group: 'the police in we tail, and the magistrate trembling to send us to jail'.

'But children ain't fools. They have their own eyes.' What the children see is a society divided harshly along lines of colour. The Blacks alone, it seems, have to carry this heavy burden. The children listen. Bee, the father, stands Christ-like, needing to know, too, why he suffers. Eva's explanation is to make sense of the nonsense. 'Things have meaning,' she insists. 'The strong suffer most': it was Christ who was crucified. Those who suffer most, who are most oppressed, are truthfully God's chosen: the Elect.

Bee must suffer as leader of the congregation, and as the man responsible for the congregation. Beneath the general suffering, one sees that there is the particular: Reggie's tears at failing his examination. Reggie's immediate childish pain is set against the anguish of Ivan Morton's expected betrayal. Morton is introduced as one of 'our own people', elected to the Council. Frustration and pain tear out of Bee: 'Six months now Ivan Morton in the council and he ain't do nothing to make the Church free.' The denial of spiritual freedom is the greatest burden, but Eva's sense of continuity and time puts things into proportion. After four hundred years 'six months ain't nutten' '.

The need for patience, not to be brutalized, is expressed by Eva: 'wait'. But Bee sees the predicament of 'growing more away' from 'ourself' by *not* acting. Nevertheless he has not yet had to face the reality of Ivan Morton's Judas behaviour, as he stands between Eva, 'trying to make her voice calm', and the children 'making a racket laughing'. The effort to accept Eva's encouragement is a hard, physical struggle. The Crucifixion image is repeated, one of travail and suffering: 'Bee sigh and Bee groan and Bee shake his head and put up his arms back on the cross like Jesus crucify in front the door.' Eva interprets the struggle as that of a man who wants to capitulate but cannot, for he is trapped in his own optimism and faith.

The technique Lovelace uses is immensely economic. The characters act out their drama. Their home and family are at once immediate and yet representative of the larger group. Bee's pain is expressed in New Testament terms; the themes of tribulation and endurance are those of the Old Testament.

The pressures of education are seen clearly, both as a highly prized acquisition but also as a possible false goal. Doubt about Ivan Morton's sincerity is introduced immediately, and a tension about his future behaviour is strongly implied. 'The man new, now learning what to do' indicates the unconscious irony of the situation. At the same time beneath the everyday details lie the implications for action and result: 'And Ivan Morton live right there up the street not far from here. You could go and talk to him any time.'

(2) Elections (pp. 78–86)

The first paragraph succinctly presents the effects of United States influence during the Second World War, the years passing and the inevitability of change. The sentences build up – short, sharp statements: 'Things go. And people forget too.' Then the narrative is expanded in longer, reiterative rhythms: 'I guess you could say we was changing over the years, with people dropping out the Church and our children going to their schools and learning their lessons.'

Modifying worship has prevented confrontation, yet has weakened the Baptists' integrity. Anglicanism and Catholicism are the routes to success. Religious worship becomes a matter of instrumental choice. Ironically the parents pressure their children into schools, and are then discountenanced when they discover the lessons that they learn. The better urban life is a 'trick' they play on themselves, for none of the changes, none of the freely made choices, have brought liberty: 'we was still saying that we wanted to be free'.

The anticlimax created by the vote being given to everyone, before Charleau and Buntin can petition the British, diminishes its value. The illusion of political freedom and effective power diminishes all the sacrifices that Buntin has made – for political integrity, and in creating his own mythology of black beauty and power. But it does not lessen the heroic nature of his endeavour and his rejection of false values.

Eva and her family have not been unchanged either. Reggie is now in the competitive school system, and Eva wants that better life for him, not picking coconuts or digging dirt. The gap between the generations, the innocent and the experienced, the scarred and the entire, is concentrated in Eva's recognition that her view of the harsh reality of the world means nothing to Reggie. (He will eventually wish to be a hero figure, a cricketer.) There is such anguish in his mother's acceptance that 'He don't know the world not going to be kind to him because he beautiful'.

The sentences that follow balance out this ambivalence towards education. The conch shell blows, reminding Eva of the beach, of the men fishing, of their catch; the boy is to be pitied, but so is the whole community. There is the pressure for education; there is the hopelessness of life without qualifications, and therefore the inevitability of change, of children 'stuffed' with education. So much pain, faith, determination and knowledge lie behind Eva's assertion, 'You have to learn boy. You have to learn'. Another sound recalls Eva to the world outside; a cow moos, and she sees Bee approaching with that distinctive hurrying walk. There is the accustomed expectation of despair in 'Oh God, something gone wrong again!'

Then Eva cries. Her tears are for Bee – not at pleasure at the news of the vote. Again the reiterative cadences: 'We get it, Eva. We get it. We can vote now'. Bee's concern is for the group, for the principle. He is still optimistic of controlling his own destiny. Eva's concern is for her family and community. It is a protective mantle. Listen to the exasperation – 'no, he can't eat, he can't stay still. He have to go right away' – and then the unexpected gladness of this visit to Ivan Morton. The old oppressions *are* to pass. 'This time we going to release from bondage,' praises Eva. All the biblical references echo and reinforce the knowledge she has that Bee's tribulation has lain in being unable to be true to himself, to Eva, to the children and to Bolo.

Yet there is a sense, since here the novel works retrospectively, that this is false hope. We know that Ivan Morton's election to the Council is going to be a betrayal of Bee's hopes. Bolo, too, is becoming a threatening figure. Nevertheless that night Bee is able to turn to Eva, embracing her, and she 'didn't feel so old any more':

Those days was nice days. For the first time in I can't remember how much years, Bee was smiling and making jokes with the children and giving us a glimpse of how a man does be when he free. (pp. 80–1)

The rest of this chapter provides an extraordinary lull, a peaceful episode, to be shattered by Bolo's return, by Ivan Morton winning the election and moving to the Big House, by Bolo's failure to get a piece of land, by the release of energy at Carnival leading to violence, rather than celebration: the return to reality, the overthrow of false hope.

Section D: The Author

Earl Lovelace is one of the younger Caribbean novelists, whose roots and commitment are West Indian. He was born in Toco, Trinidad, in 1935. He began writing when he was a young man working as a forest ranger, and has produced four novels, plays, short stories and much journalism. He lives in Port of Spain and Matura, where he admits his prestige has been associated more with his prowess as a cricketer than as a novelist! Currently he writes, lectures and is active in a wide variety of cultural events, including Carnival.

All Lovelace's novels show a passionate concern for the oppressed and an insistence that the dignity 'of those who have invented nothing' is the achievement that he celebrates. He is consistent in his belief that the creative artist can heal the wounds of history. His first novel, *While Gods Are Falling* (1965) looks at the experience of a young man struggling to survive in the city, as Winston does in *The Wine of Astonishment*. *The Schoolmaster* (1968/79) is in many respects a harsh book. It describes how a remote rural community is betrayed generally and personally by the education and the schoolteacher it had desired. *The Dragon Can't Dance* (1979) is excitingly complementary to *The Wine of Astonishment*. Set in a slum area of Port of Spain, it centres on the tensions released at Carnival, 'like resurrection morning', with the steel bands and calypsonians. *The Dragon Can't Dance* integrates most of Lovelace's themes and concerns.

Section E: Classroom Use

(i) Level of use

As a whole, fourth- or fifth-year GCSE, age 14-16. As a general text for 'open-ended' sixth-form work, age 16–19; in particular those themes which relate to the students' own experience. Although some of the passages – Christmas; stick-fighting at Carnival; worship in the Spirit; Buntin's shop – might well be used valuably in the 13–15 age group, because so many of them are 'undercut' by subsequent passages, there might be difficulty in using them in isolation.

(ii) Points of focus and emphasis

1 The family:
   - Eva as narrator, p. 1; on Bolo, p. 125f.; on responsibility, pp. 138–40;
   - Bee, p. 2; meeting with Ivan Morton, p. 12;
   - the children, pp. 4, 7; Winston, Taffy, Joyce and Clyde, p. 11; Gem and Reggie, pp. 51–6;
   - Bolo at church, p. 16; the old hero, p. 20; description, p. 27; fight, p. 98; as badjohn, p. 101; dies, pp. 123-8.
2 The Spiritual Baptist Church:
   - history, p. 32;
   - worship, pp. 7, 16, 33 ff., 59–63;
   - Brother Primus, p. 114;
   - law, p. 73;
   - freedom, pp. 143, 146.
3 The 'oppressors' – police, bureaucrats, education:
   - Prince, pp. 34, 36, 65;
   - Ivan Morton, pp. 2, 5, 7 (in England), 38–45, 50, 133–5;
   - civil servants and politicians, pp. 89–91, 137;
   - education, pp. 9, 11, 46.
4 The war and 'outside' influences:
   - the US soldiers, pp. 18, 29–30, 77, 78;
   - film, pp. 5, 23;
   - debasing the village, pp. 29 ff.; migration to town, p. 78.
5 The community:
   - Buntin trying to borrow money, p. 6;
   - Primus, pp. 114–16;
   - Mitchell, pp. 18, 102;
   - Clem, the chantwell, p. 23; calypso, p. 29; Carnival and the stick fight, pp. 92-100;
   - Eulalie, pp. 23, 45;
   - Christmas, music and food, pp. 81-3;
   - Charleau, p. 132.
6 On being significant, refusing to be brutalized; on being truly civilized; redemption through suffering:
   - 'Bee sigh and Bee groan and Bee shakes his head and put up his arms back on the cross like Jesus crucify in front the door', p. 3;
   - Eva: 'and I wondering if the world is a mortar and we is the plantains below the pestle, taking the pounding', p. 4;
   - Bee rejecting: 'we can't be white, but we can act white', p. 13;
   - Bee refusing to let police brutalize the people; Bolo would kill; Oswald: 'We accustom running', pp. 47–9;
   - Eva's description of the church: 'is the root for us to grow out from, the church is Africa in us . . . the instrument to make us legal and legitimate and to free him . . . then he don't have any understanding of himself or of black people', pp. 133–5;
   - 'And a little respect?', p. 135.

(iii) Questions for essay writing or classroom discussion

1 Eva, the mother narrates *The Wine of Astonishment*. Choose one other character and describe from his or her viewpoint two or three major incidents in the novel. How many perspectives on the story of the Bonasse congregation are there? List them.
2 Write a brief biography of Ivan Morton.
3 'Gem, the teacher say, is bright in school, she may be the one to win an exhibition . . . though I did prefer that Reggie win one, seeing that he is a boy and a boy is a man and a man have the burden of the world on his shoulders in a way that a woman don't, can't have it.' (p. 11)

What does Eva hope education will give her children? What effects does education appear to have? Do the men and women in Bonasse appear to live rather separate lives?

4 'And Mr Civilize sit down there in the white man house ... telling me: "We can't change our colour, Dorcas, but we can change our attitude. We can't be white, but we can act white" ' (p. 13). Who are the truly civilized characters in the book? Which categories and individuals are most alienated and/or oppressive?

5 Read pp. 89–100. Write down the various stages in the stick fighting. What do you think is happening amongst the men? Had Innocent continued the fight with Bolo, could the final tragedy have been averted?

6 Compare the behaviour and its result on Bolo (p. 101) and the earlier visit to make a claim for land (pp. 89, 90). By which other individuals and groups of people are the villagers of Bonasse brutalized?

7 'And Bee there too, standing up by the kitchen door, with his two hands stretch out across the door like how Jesus Christ had his hands when they crucify him on the cross.' (p. 1)

   'Bolo pitch forward ... and when he come to rest his head was lying at the foot of the steps and his body was sprawl over the ground, with his two feet close together and his arms stretch out.' (p. 128)

   What is the significance of both these characters being described in Christ-like, Crucifixion images? Compare and contrast the two men, listing their qualities.

8 'We have five children' (p. 51). List the names of the children and, at this point, their achievements and ambitions. Describe what happens to them and how they both wound and reward their parents. How do you think their lives will differ from those of Bee and Eva?

9 Read pp. 32–4. Why is the church so important to Eva? Explain why the size of the congregation fell. Look at the sentence length, repetition and reinforcement that Lovelace uses to create Eva's 'voice'. Choosing a topic of your own about which you feel strongly, try to use these techniques to convey the sincere urgency of your feelings.

10 List characters in the novel with whom you sympathize, and those who make you angry. Then read the following poem. Compare its statement with that of Lovelace. Where would *you* locate yourself in the novel, and in the poem?

Protest Poem for All the Brothers by Pamela Mordecai

(1) An ache is in a man: towns do not ache,
nor ghettoes fester; the ravening gnaws
at bellies, one-one; hurt is personal.
On the corner, again and again, see me
puffin' my spliff, see me splittin' my mind,
see me teenager dead from the blows of
your words that baptize me according to
Lenin and Marx – 'You are no-one, no one.'

(2) Blessed be the proletariat whom
   we must mobilize
   we must motivate
   we must liberate
   we must educate
   to a new political awareness.

(3) Is di ole chatter ting again; di same
slavery bizness, but dis time de boss
looks more like we an im do be smarter.
Not a damn soul goin' mobilize my ass
to rass-dem jokin. Any fool can read
Das Kapital: what is dat to de poor?

(4) We the people propose
the abolition of you
and us: we propose
an acknowledgement
of our persons and
an alliance of poverty;
we propose to share the little
that breeds on these
antilles, one mango
to one mouth:
we propose to speak
your language
but not abandon ours;
we insist that you understand
that you do not
understand us.
You may begin
by not shouting –
we are tired of noise.

(5) On the corner again and again see
me stand with my pride and my children, my

quiverful, lot, my portion of life; see
me labour and wait; see me plan and scratch
dust for a yam root, a corn, bellyful.

(6) See ME
Look!
I am
here
I am
here
I am
here.

11 Almost everything in the novel tells the
character that they are nothing and nobody.
List all the things that *you* think make these
people significant; you may refer to their
families, personal qualities and achievements,
religious and social life, their vigour,
endurance and language.

(iv) Creative approaches/curriculum links

1 'The same two fingers . . . he rest against his
cheek like those screen stars in the magazine I
see Joyce reading' (p. 5). Discuss or describe a
pop or film star whom you admire and show
how he or she creates an image.
2 Describe a 'big house' or stately home that you
have visited in Britain, or describe an
imaginary visit to the Richardsons' house in
Bonasse: 'it was a haunted house, they say;
behind it was a graveyard . . . holding
generations of dead Richardsons' (p. 8).
3 'And talk! Ivan Morton could really talk!' Write
and tape-record the speech you would deliver
if you were a candidate standing in the next
general election.
4 Read pp. 59–63 and 75–6, then listen to the
Reverend Jesse Jackson, *Pushing On: Holy
Day* (Respect Records, TAS-2607). In small
groups construct a voice/chorus (call and
response) on the theme of self-image. You
might start: 'We are . . . We believe . . . '
5 Perhaps also referring to *Mother Poem* by
Edward Brathwaite (Oxford University Press,
1977), consider the special qualities of Eva
and Caribbean mothers. When Eva finally dies,
what would her children, Bee and you, to

whom she told her story, say of her? Write a
poem about your mother.
6 From which other areas of the world do the
current people of Trinidad come? Draw a map
to illustrate their journeys.
7 The novel ends with optimism and reference
to steel bands. Discover and write about the
history and significance of these bands up to
the present day.
8 Clem becomes 'Lord Trafalgar', the
calypsonian. Calypso is a crucial part of the
popular culture of Trinidad and Tobago. Why
are calypsos important? Could you write one?
9 Reggie's ambition is to be a cricketer, a hero.
Find out as much as you can about the game of
cricket in the West Indies, and the public role
which many cricketers have inherited.

Section F: Teaching Aids

(i) Audio-visual material

The following is a small sample of the religious,
steel band and calypso music recordings available.
200 Years of Mas: Fifty Years of Steel, Charlie's
Records, CR 143.
Carnival in St Thomas, Rounder Records, 5002.
Jump up Carnival in Trinidad, Cook 1072.
Catelli All Stars, *Classical Jems III*, Trinstar.
Catelli Trinidad All Stars, *Woman on the Bass*, West
Indian Records.
The Original Trinidad Steel Band, Elektra, PYS
76002.
Steel Drums, *The Native Steel Drum Band*, Everest
Tradition, 2064.
Black Stalin, *The Caribbean Man*, PO Box 910, Port
of Spain, Trinidad (Rastafarian calypsonian).
Blueboy, *Super Blueboy*, Charlie's Records, BCR
313.
The Explainer (W. Henry), *The Bible/Notting Hill*,
Charlie's Records, 328A.
Mighty Sparrow, *The Greatest*, Charlie's Records,
JAF 1007.
Growling Tiger, *Knockdown Calypso*, Rounder
Records, 5S06.

Olive Walke, *La Petite Musicale*, Trinidad Folksongs, Tropico.

George Eaton Simpson, *Cult Music of Trinidad*, Folkways, 1961.

Shepherd Glazier, *Spiritual Baptist Music of Trinidad*, Folkways, 1980.

Paul Keens-Douglas, *Is Town Say So!*, PK-D 005, Trinidad (side one: *Pan Rap, de Christenin'*; side two: *Jumbies, Duppies and Spirits*).

(ii) Background reading

I. B. Beddoe, L. Bernard, B. A. Rohlehr and K. Seepersad, *Social Studies for the Caribbean*, Heinemann Educational Books, 1983.

Brian Gabes (ed.), *Afro-Caribbean Religion*, Ward Lock, 1980.

Margaret Graham and Franklin W. Knight (eds.), *Africa and the Caribbean: The Legacies of a Link*, Johns Hopkins University Press, 1979.

R. Greenwood and S. Hamber, *Arawaks to Africans, Emancipation to Emigration, Development to Decolonization*, Macmillan, 1979.

Errol Hill, *The Trinidad Carnival*, University of Texas Press, 1972.

John Sealey, *Music in the Caribbean*, Hodder & Stoughton, 1982.

Keith Warner, *The Trinidad Calypso*, Heinemann Educational Books, 1982.

(iii) Critical bibliography

Edward Brathwaite, 'Priest and Peasant', *Journal of Commonwealth Literature*, no. 7, July 1969, pp. 117–22.

Helen Payne-Timothy, 'Earl Lovelace: His View of Trinidad Society', *New World Quarterly*, vol. 14, no. 4, 1968, pp. 60–5.

Victor D. Questel, 'Views of Earl Lovelace', *Caribbean Contact*, vol. 5, no. 3, June 1977, pp. 15–16.

(iv) Reading links

Other novels by Earl Lovelace

While Gods are Falling, Regency, Chicago, 1965.
The Schoolmaster, Collins, 1968.
The Dragon Can't Dance, Longman, 1979.
The Wine of Astonishment, Deutsch, 1982.
Jestina's Calypso and Other Plays, Heinemann Educational Books (Caribbean Writers Series), 1984.
A Brief Conversion and Other Stories, Heinemann Educational Books (Caribbean Writers Series), 1988.

Work by other writers

David Dabydeen, *Slave Song*, Dangaroo Press, 1984. UK distributors: PO Box 186, Coventry CV4 7HG. Poetry on peasant life, emphasizing song and survival in the midst of sexual, physical and colonial violence.

Ismith Khan, *The Jumbie Bird*, Longman, Drumbeat, 1961. Set in Port of Spain, the most vivid relationship, that of grandfather and grandson, in many ways parallels themes of *The Wine of Astonishment*: the search for significance and dignity, the centrality of beliefs, the stick fighting, and Hosein.

V. S. Reid, *New Day*, Heinemann Educational Books (Caribbean Writers Series), 1973. Set in Jamaica; eighty years in a family's life; dignity through survival; another 'messianic' figure; the role of the churches; variety of dialect use.

Sylvia Wynter, *The Hills of Hebron*, Longman, 1962/82. The New Believers of Hebron, an independent black church; the struggles of the leader, Obadiah, to re-establish himself; his recognition of Africa; and the birth of his child.

Unit 6
George Lamming: *In the Castle of my Skin*

JEAN POPEAU

Section A:
Critical Approaches

In the Castle of my Skin is the collective story of
the fate of a village in Barbados, and the personal
story of G, the author George Lamming. The village
is in a state of transition and change. The story
begins with a flood: 'Rain, rain, rain'. Flooding is the
symbol of alteration and transfiguration; rain, of
sadness and lamentation. The young boy laments
the flooded day which marks his birthday: 'my ninth
celebration of the consistent lack of an occasion for
celebration' (p. 9).

Like the colonial situation of the island in general,
all seems at first safe and stable in this village world.
The village is owned by Mr Creighton and family,
one of a long line of English owners. They live in a
large house surrounded by trees within a wall,
overlooking the village. Mr Creighton inhabits a
strange, ritualized world up to which the villagers
look with awe. To gain access to this world (as Mrs
Forster does) is to feel an overwhelming sense of
privilege (p. 34). The landowner's house looks
down protectively upon the people; they listen for
its tone and attune their consciousness to it: 'A
custom had been established, and later a value
which through continual application and a
hardened habit of feeling became an absolute
standard of feeling' (p. 29).

The seeds of the forthcoming turbulence which
forms one of the major themes of the novel are,
however, already present in the opening of the
novel. The seedbed for social dislocation is found in
the relationships which operate within the colonial
system. The landlord functions at a seemingly
elevated level, but the people turn their wrath
against his subordinate, the overseer. The overseer
in turn regards them with fear and suspicion as his
'low-down nigger people' (p. 27) and turns his
anger against them when he is upbraided by the
landlord for slacking on the job (p. 26). Thus in the
village the potential revolutionary anger is
temporarily turned towards the landlord's
representative, but it is always likely to be directed
against the colonial authority itself should the right
conditions arise.

The opportunity for channelling this resentment
is seized by the rising bourgeoisie, in the person of
Mr Slime. Mr Slime represents the rising middle
classes who will supplant Creighton. He is an
ambitious and capable schoolteacher, cut short in
his progress through scandal with the
headteacher's wife – although this does not prevent
later collaboration with the headteacher in a
financial scheme. The villagers put their faith in Mr
Slime as the successful organizer of the Penny Bank
and Friendly Society, and Mr Slime betrays them.
Later he sells the shares of the two businesses to
partners, who suddenly appear, to evict the
villagers off their land.

Nevertheless, Mr Slime becomes the agent of
change. The old couple, Ma and Pa, regard him
symbolically as such. Pa says: 'Ever since we get the
news 'bout the schoolmaster Mr Slime [his
dismissal] I feel a sort o' change happen, an' though
I ain't got the words to repeat what's in my mouth I
feel it all the same' (p. 76).

George Lamming, *In the Castle of my Skin*, first
published 1953; page references in this unit are to the
Longman Drumbeat edition, 1979.

Urged on by Mr Slime, the strike in town rages against Creighton's shipping company and spreads to the village. Urban violence threatens the rural scene. Gradually we learn what has happened. A crowd of waterfront workers sent a delegation to the governor. The sentries would not allow the delegation to pass. Fighting broke out, during which the police fired and killed Po, a small boy. Rioting spreads from town and finally arrives at Creighton Village.

Creighton himself seems about to be deposed. He is reduced to ordinary frightened human proportions, reduced to tottering humanity: 'he had reached the track that led through the weed as the men came forward and Mr Slime moved nearer and nearer towards them' (p. 207). But Mr Slime, the harbinger of events, is also fearful. The men look towards him for leadership at their moment of crucial decision. He moves towards them, but is also in dread of their power. He allows Creighton to escape. The men disperse, penitent. Mr Slime, the agent of colonialism, makes a symbolic pact with it; he will assume its mantle.

The novel is both a record of the fate of a Barbadian village and a charting of the narrator G's growing consciousness. At first narrator and author seem one and the same, but later the author records not only the narrator's childhood but events in the village and elsewhere, beyond G's range of consciousness. The opening of the novel sets the inauspicious tone of this record: 'The morning laden with cloud soon passed into noon, and the noon neutral and silent into the sodden grimness of an evening that waded through water' (p. 9). This is not going to be a tale of the joyful opening of a soul to experience. Colonialism permeates every aspect of this childhood; we see its effects in the children's observation of the headteacher's obsequious behaviour before the white inspector, in his brutal beating of a boy whom he considers to have betrayed him before the official: 'No one could say how long he was beaten or how many strokes he received. But when he stood supported by the four boys who had held him down he was weak. The knees tottered and the filth slithered down his legs' (p. 43).

We also see the effects of colonialism in the boys' confused attempts to understand their history, of which they are kept ignorant – for example, their thoughts on slavery: 'slavery was thousands of years before that [the Battle of Hastings]. It was too far back for anyone to worry about teaching it as history. That's really why it wasn't taught' (p. 58). The boys seem to be confusing Greek or Roman slavery with modern slavery here. Slavery, a subject of immense relevance to the study of their own history, is considered too 'ancient' when compared to the distant events of English history.

A Caribbean childhood, however, spent not far from the beach, is relieved by sublime communion with nature. The beach is not just a place to sit and contemplate; rather, it is a place of activity, of swimming, crab catching and conversing in a dreamy sort of way. Dreaming is associated with nature; politics, on the other hand, is associated with the world of adults, like Mr Slime. Through growing awareness the boys learn of the impotence and failure of the adult world, especially the male world. The boys find strength and virtue in their mothers. Many of them are in fact illegitimate children of absent fathers.

The relationship between G and his mother, for example, is emotionally complex and warm. Towards the end of the novel, as he is about to leave home, they draw closer to each other, though the relationship is still troubled. He gazes at her with quiet admiration: 'Bent over the list in the light I had a chance to see her well. Her hair was long and thick, falling in black coils round her face, and in her steady concentration she was like a recluse' (pp. 276–7).

Awareness of failure in the adult world is matched by a growing sense of alienation which will eventually lead to the exile of G himself. It is the youth (Trumper, G) who are most prone to migration. For G the desire to leave the island and not return is mostly for personal reasons stemming from a growing sense of distance from the colonial world of the village. Speaking of the village community he says: 'It was never possible here' to 'strike identity with the other person' (p. 261). Through immigration to the United States, Trumper has discovered the provincialism of the colonial world and that it is necessary to exile yourself from it in order to see it in the right perspective. Speaking of the movement from Barbados as making for a greater solidarity with other blacks, Trumper maintains: 'You're one o' my people all right . . . but you can't understan' it here. Not here. But the day you leave an' perhaps if you go further than Trinidad you'll learn' (p. 296).

After the riots described in Chapter 9, the next chapter begins: 'The years had changed nothing' (p. 209). But the village has clearly undergone an alteration. For G, his gradual alienation and inability to make contact lead to withdrawal and the decision to emigrate. On the eve of departure he has a premonition of the finality of this break with the land: 'The earth where I walked was a marvel of blackness and I knew in a sense more deep than simple departure I had said farewell, farewell to the land' (p. 303).

For the rest of the villagers, the turbulence is followed by dispossession from their land. The strike and the riots make Creighton leave the estate, selling the land to the Penny Bank and the Friendly Society. The people with the most shares are of course members of the bourgeoisie, lawyers, teachers, etc.; it is to them that the title deeds to the land fall, while the peasants are forced to relinquish them. The sense that nothing can be the same again is emphasized by the departure of Pa to the almshouse, having lost his plot of land to the headteacher. The departure of the eldest inhabitant from the village brings home to G the irrevocability of the changes which have occurred:

'You won't see me again, my son,' he said, and felt his way up the steps. The door closed gently behind him.

I stood for a moment waiting to see whether he might put on the light. The feeling had seized me again. You had seen the last of something. (p. 303)

Section B: The Setting

The use of G as a name for the main character indicates the autobiographical nature of Lamming's story, as do the many correspondences between Lamming's own childhood and the events described in the novel. Creighton Village is derived from Carrington's village and St David's village, both of which Lamming knew intimately during his

childhood. He grew up in Carrington's village, previously a sugar estate a few miles from Bridgetown, and spent much time in St David's, where his stepfather worked.

In an interview with Sandra Pouchet Paquet, Lamming has admitted to:

numerous aspects of the novel's experience that derive from his childhood, among them: his elementary and high school experiences at Roebuck Street Boy's School and Combemere; escapades at Gravesend Beach and Shock Hall Beach about fifteen to twenty minutes' walk from Carrington's village; the public baths; the sanitary inspector's visits; the annual floods in Carrington's village and the year of the great flood when Mr Brewster refused to abandon his house; the riots of 1937–8; the purchase of village lands with funds from the Penny Bank and the reselling of the land. In the Carrington's village of Lamming's childhood, there was Papa Grandison who assumed the role of godfather to young Lamming and became the model for Pa; the shoemaker, Dads Harewood, an authority on politics and cricket, and whose shop, complete with clippings on the walls, was a gathering place for adults and children; Brother Lally, the itinerant preacher; Savory and his cart.

(Sandra Pouchet Paquet, *The Novels of George Lamming*, Heinemann Educational Books, 1982, pp. 13–14)

Barbados has long been regarded by the other islands as 'Little England' for the peculiarly English character of its social and class structure. As we are told by F. A. Hoyos: 'The class consciousness among the slaves was adopted from their European masters. . . . By a process of "conferred élitism" the standing of the slave was enhanced by the personal status of his master' (F. A. Hoyos, *Barbados: A History from the Amerindians to Independence*, Macmillan, 1978, p. 74). The enhanced position of Creighton, the solitariness of his house looking 'down' upon the villagers, the villagers' feelings of awe and privilege on coming into contact with his world, all point to the continued influence of this historical social structure on the island.

Although the social scene was relatively quiet in Barbados compared to other islands, as in the novel the seeming tranquillity covered up an oppressive and potentially explosive social structure which resulted in the insurrection of 1816 and the disturbances of 1937, the latter of which is described in the novel. Hoyos notes (*A History,* p. 207), and this is confirmed in the novel, that

> the disturbances were not confined to the city of Bridgetown. It is astonishing how rapidly the spirit of disorder spread from the metropolitan area to the rural districts of the island. Motor cars were stoned, shops were broken into and potato fields raided. . . . But it seems certain that the raiding of the potato fields and the attacks on shops in the country districts were mainly due to 'hunger or the fear of hunger'.

The riots were sparked off by the deportation of a popular union leader, Clement Payne, who had spent his early years in Barbados but was then living in Trinidad. Payne's speeches to the Barbadian working masses on trade unionism were eventually considered to be dangerous and liable to rouse the masses into insurrection. His deportation on 26 July 1937 may have been the immediate reason for the riots, but the underlying causes were eventually exposed in a Royal Commission which found evidence of very low wages throughout the island.

Section C: A Closer Look

(1) A strange catch (pp. 150–2)

One of the major themes of the novel is childhood. Childhood is traditionally associated with 'magic', dreaming and exploration. The boys, Boy Blue, Trumper and G, spend their time by the sea talking, catching crabs and swimming, all of which we associate with the 'magic' of childhood. But a colonial childhood is permeated by the effects of colonialism. One of the effects of colonialism is the failure and compromise of the adult world — typified by the betrayal of Mr Slime. The fisherman who saves Boy Blue is the corrective to Mr Slime, the elemental figure who does not fail the boys. He is outside the world of compromise and degradation associated with adulthood, part rather of the strange world of childhood.

Lamming describes this world with delicacy and exactness. There is, as Boy Blue becomes completely absorbed in crab catching, the casual precision of detail: 'his thumb had found the accustomed spot between the claw and the body of the crab. The crabs were still but buckled tight, so that it was difficult to strengthen the grip.' This precision, coupled with accuracy of figurative language, is exemplified a few lines earlier: 'the crab's claws were free like revolving chairs. They could spin, it seemed, in all directions, and they raised and dropped them to any angle.' The short lapidary sentences are as delicate as the actions they describe.

The fisherman appears before this world like a beacon of light. Earlier the boys watch him disappear behind the lighthouse (p. 148), and he returns from behind it to rescue Boy Blue (p. 151). The purpose of a lighthouse is that of guide and corrective. The fisherman and the lighthouse are associated with the elemental strength of nature: 'there was something powerful and corrective about his big figure', we are told earlier (p. 148). To speak to him is 'like climbing a mountain before anyone else' (p. 149), both thrilling and fearful.

Thus, unlike any other adult male, the fisherman is portrayed in heroic terms. Like Proteus, god of the sea, he suddenly materializes to save Boy Blue, who, absorbed in activity, is almost drowned. The elemental (the fisherman) and the future (Boy Blue), neither of whom the forces of colonialism can completely dominate, meet briefly. There is an exchange; the fisherman loses some of his elemental force but gains in humanity: 'he looked so terribly repentant and at the same time there was an expression which we could not define. Under the marble eyes and the impenetrable stare there must have been something that cried out for life.' He has a double aspect, both human and not human: 'his anger was human. His absolute command and assurance as the waves washed up against his feet and the net spread before him were not' (p. 152).

It is interesting that it is Boy Blue, who we are told has some of the fisherman's assurance and command, who is rescued. The very presence of the fisherman seems to rouse Boy Blue to be equal to it. Standing before this gigantic elemental force which has just rescued him, he gains in confidence and stature. The other boys are astonished by his boldness:

'By Christ, you should have drown,' the fisherman snarled again.

'You mustn't say that,' Boy Blue said. We were stunned by the impertinence of the words. But there couldn't have been impertinence. Boy Blue was shivering like a kitten that had had a bath.

'Why the hell shouldn't I have let you drown?' the fisherman shouted. It was the first thing he had said that made us think he was really human like us. (p. 152)

The fisherman has passed on some of his strength and vitality to Boy Blue and in turn displays his own human vulnerability, for which his anger is really a mask:

'Tell me,' he snapped. 'Tell me to my face why the hell I shouldn't have let you drown?'

''Cause if I'd drown I wouldn't have been able to tell you thanks,' Boy Blue said. He was serious and the fisherman walked back towards the lighthouse. (p. 152)

The fisherman is disarmed by the poignancy and frailty, but also paradoxically the strength, of childhood.

(2) The lost pebble (pp. 215–16)

G, like Trumper, feels most keenly the alienation caused by the colonial world. The loss of the pebble brings home to him the sense of resignation to the loss of things one is going to see for the last time. As with the pebble, the boy once gave his affection to the village. The loss of the pebble presages the waning of attachment to the village, alienation leading to exile.

G has received letters from Trumper and from Trinidad, all connected with loss in some way. From Trumper he is reminded of the loss of friendship, with Trumper himself, Boy Blue and Bob, which accompanied his move to the high school. The Trinidadian letter beckons him to the island, preparing for the departure from the village world he has known all his life.

The lost pebble is a powerful symbol of the hardening and abstraction of soul which accompany the absence of feeling leading to alienation. The boy's emotion, centred on the pebble, is difficult to locate at first: 'and above all I had a vague feeling that there was no reason one should see things for the last time' (p. 215). The loss of the pebble helps to sharpen and focus the feeling: 'It had really started the evening before when I received the letters, and now the pebble had made it permanent' (p. 215). The absent pebble now begins to stand for all the things he will miss in leaving the village: 'You couldn't bear the thought of seeing things for the last time, and things included all that had become a part of your affection or anger, or even the vague feelings which you couldn't corner and define. Things included people, objects and situations' (p. 215).

Lamming was primarily a poet before turning novelist, and this pebble incident is charged with poetic intensity. The pebble is just an ordinary pebble, although 'it stood out from the others' (p. 214). As the boy plays with it, it begins to lose its ordinary 'pebbleness' until it assumes the guise of a material metaphor: 'it was no longer a pebble. It had become one of those things one can't bear to see for the last time' (p. 214). Later it is figuratively connected with the hardness of heart G has to assume in preparation for exile. He had already began to cultivate retreat from others as a means of defending his self's integrity, typified in his reaction to being found reading the letters by his mother: 'It was very embarrassing when my mother came in and saw me re-reading the letters. I threw them aside and walked out of the house. At my age I couldn't risk making a fool of myself, and the safest defence seemed to be a forced indifference' (p. 215).

This growing retreat from others into a self-protective carapace, a stone-like shell, is more fully expanded towards the end of the novel:

When I reach Trinidad where no one knows me I may be able to strike identity with the other person. But it was never possible here. I am always feeling terrified of being known; not because they really know you, but simply because their claim to this knowledge is a concealed attempt to destroy you. (p. 261)

The loss of contact symbolized by the loss of the pebble, and the hardening of feeling, is very subtly captured. This incidence of epiphany in the novel is thus congruent with its major themes of alienation, loss and exile.

Section D: The Author

George Lamming was born in Barbados in 1927. When he was ten years old he was a witness to the Bridgetown riots that followed the deportation of a trade union organizer, Clement Payne, followed by a dramatic rise in union activity. This is clearly reflected in some of the social and political unrest described in *In the Castle of my Skin*. Lamming went to Trinidad in 1946 as a teacher, then left for England in 1950 during the massive wave of emigration of that period. He applied for membership of the Communist Party in London in the early 1950s but was turned down. He returned to the Caribbean in 1956 on an assignment for *Holiday Magazine* and was involved in major political events in the Caribbean.

In Trinidad, Lamming was on the platform introducing the candidates for the first PNM (People's National Movement) election, which was followed by the prime ministership of Eric Williams. He also took part in political activity in Guyana. In 1958 he made a trip to Africa, described in *The Pleasures of Exile* (Michael Joseph, 1960), a book of essays. Though largely staying in England and the USA, Lamming remains in touch with the Caribbean through frequent trips, during which he actively participates in social and political developments.

The issue which dominates Lamming's first novel – that is, the Caribbean people as a product of a colonial past – is also the central subject of his later fiction. His aim has been to chart the history of Caribbean society in its totality, ever since the complete world described in his first novel. Each novel examines an aspect of a developing colonial experience. The novels are unlike certain kinds of European fiction written recently, in that they tend to examine individuals within their complex social and political contexts, rather than focusing almost exclusively upon psychological and personal interrelationships.

Section E: Classroom Use

(i) Level of use

The book would be appreciated by fourth-year pupils onwards. Pupils doing GCSE English would find some of its major themes very useful for thematic work on childhood, colonialism, conflict, etc. Parallels between the situation of the peasants in the novel and the plight of the working class in Britain have been particularly noteworthy in discussions stemming from the novel.

(ii) Points of focus and emphasis

1 The opening of the novel, plangent and sad, pp. 9–10.

2 Establishing the basic physical setting of the village, p. 10 – 'The village was a marvel of small, heaped houses . . .'

3 Some important characters (Ma and Pa) are introduced. The closing of the first chapter ('My birthday drifted outside in a fog of blackness that covered the land', p. 14) recalls the closing of the last chapter ('the earth where I walked was a marvel of blackness . . .', p. 303).

4 The social position of Creighton, the English landowner, p. 25. The relationship between landlord and village ('The landlord was safe. The village was safe'), p. 27.

5 School: pp. 35–7, 53–8, 220-2. The inspector's visit; the beating of the boy whom the head thinks has let him down, pp. 37–43.

6 The significance of the lesson on Queen Victoria, p. 56, and slavery, pp. 57–8.

7 Ma and Pa; their commentary on the relationship between Creighton and Mr Slime, pp. 76–90.

8 (a) The changing relationship between landlord and village, p. 97.
   (b) Mr Slime and the strike; Mr Slime's new role as 'the chief', p. 98.
   (c) The forthcoming strike in Barbados in relation to the disturbances in Trinidad, pp. 100–1.

9 Chapter 6: Blue Boy and Trumper; discussion about life and religion; its demoralizing and disturbing effect upon (a) Jen, Jon and Susie, (b) Botsy, Bambi and Bambina; the names seem to signify the repetitive nature of such stories, probably occurring all over the island.

10 The near-drowning incident, pp. 50–2.

11 The threat to Creighton from the villagers; Mr Slime's part in it, pp. 206–8.

12 The eviction of the shoemaker, pp. 233–6.

13 Final poignant meeting between Pa and G; both going into exile, pp. 302–3.

14 G and his mother, pp. 16–24, 113-15, 262-87.

(iii) Questions for essay writing or classroom discussion

1 Reread Chapter 1. Discuss:
 (a) The mood of this opening chapter.
 (b) What we learn about G.
 (c) What we learn about the village.

2 Discuss the structure of rule in the village (pp. 26–34). Is it similar to the structure of a feudal village in Britain during the Middle Ages, for example?

3 What is it about the school (Chapter 3) which defines it as a typically colonial institution?

4 Have a number of readers prepare and read the section from 'Why you run you fool? . . .' to '"Woolah woolah she put them pon me"' (pp. 43–52). Discuss what we learn about the headteacher and his wife.

5 Have one person read the narration, one play Boy Blue and a third read the fisherman's role in the 'catching a crab' section (pp. 150–3), from 'A master at the art . . .' to '"Yes sir," we said in unison.' Discuss how Lamming makes the incident vivid and exciting.

6 Write a description of the village as if you were writing a letter to a friend, noting in particular (a) the setting and (b) the houses and amenities.

7 What role does the landlord play in the village? How do the villagers regard him?

8 'The landlord was safe. The village was safe' (p. 27). What forces threaten the relationship between landlord and village?

9 Discuss the visit of the school inspector. What does it indicate about the position of the headteacher, in a typical colonial school?

10 'The boy made a brief howl like an animal that had had its throat cut. No one could say how long he was beaten or how many strokes he received. But when he stood supported by the four boys who had held him down he was weak' (p. 43). Describe the incidents leading to the punishment of the boy. What is it that the boy knows about the headteacher?

11 'The idea of ownership. One man owned another. They laughed quietly. Imagine any man in any part of the world owning a man or a woman from Barbados' (p. 58). What do we learn about the history education the boys receive? What does it tell us about a colonial education?

12 What do the stories of Jon, Jen and Susie, and Botsy, Bambi, and Bambina, indicate about the effect of religion on the villagers' lives?

13 What do we learn about the changes that have taken place in the friendship between G and Trumper in Chapters 11 and 14? How does Trumper play his part in G's education?

14 What do we learn about the relationship between G and his mother in the book? (See Chapters 2 and 14 especially.) Why do you think they have this special relationship?

15 George Lamming has said, 'Both Pa and I were exiles.' Discuss how this idea is developed in the novel.

(iv) Creative approaches/curriculum links

1 Fiction and autobiography are closely interwoven in the novel. Creighton Village, as described in the novel, is the kind of place Lamming knew intimately, a composite of Carrington's village and St David's village both of which he knew from childhood. Using a larger map for reference, on your map of Barbados mark Carrington's village, St David's village, Gravesend Beach and Shock Hall Beach (where Lamming went swimming as a young boy), Bridgetown, the capital, and scene of the riots in the novel.

2 The riots of 1937–8 play an important part in

the novel. Find out all you can about the causes and results of those riots.

3   Barbados is often called 'Little England' (p. 39). Find out the various historical reasons for this.

4   A school inspector may have visited your school at one time or other, just as he visits G's school in Chapter 3. Write a story entitled 'The School Inspector's Visit' about an imaginary visit of an inspector to your school.

5   Workhouses were common in Britain right up to the beginning of the twentieth century. Many old couples ended up in such places just as Pa, in the novel, is forced to go to the almshouse. Write a story or a poem about an old couple or an old person who has to go to the workhouse under similar circumstances to those of Pa.

6   There is a reference in the novel to emigration to the United States. Find out more about the history of this process, and account for the reasons for successive waves of West Indian migration. What part did West Indians play in the Harlem Renaissance of the 1920s and 1930s and in the Black Power movement in the 1960s?

7   Find out what you can about the United States presence in West Indian countries? What impact does this presence have on the politics, economics and culture of West Indian societies?

8   Describe a birthday of your own, or of an imagined character. Try to give the piece a dominant atmosphere (as Lamming does with the rain). Make it reflect the state of feelings or life in the family or the main character. You could use snow, drizzle, scorching sun, cloud, and so on, to create different atmospheres.

Section F: Teaching Aids

(i) Audio-visual material

Films

World History Outlines (30 mins.) and *World History Focus* (28 mins./31 mins.), distributed by Central Film Library. Both films describe the social and economic development of the Caribbean area.

Education in Trinidad (30 mins.), Colour Guild Sound and Vision, made for the Open University, 1977. Examines the mismatch between traditional education – a hangover from the colonial era – and Trinidad and Tobago culture, and raises questions about the use of Standard English and local dialect in schools, among other issues. All very relevant to Barbados and to the themes of the novel.

Grenada, Jamaica and *Trinidad* (21 mins. each; black and white), BBC Enterprises, 1971. Three films from *People of Many Lands*, a series of geography programmes for children aged 10–11, which aim to give a sympathetic understanding of other people's ways of life.

Sun, Sand and Bananas (30 mins.; colour), Concord Films, 1972. Shows how reliance on a single crop can distort the economies of the West Indies.

Legacy of Empire (20 mins.; black and white), Concord Films. Designed for school-leavers, a factual retracing of the history of slavery and the reasons for immigration. Tries to cover a lot of ground, not totally with success, and therefore needs a careful introduction.

Filmstrips

The Caribbean (40 frames; colour, with script), Gateway, FGGP 40. Scenes from Guyana, Honduras, Jamaica and Antigua. Indicates similarities and contrasts and shows different racial types. Sugar production and bauxite mining are illustrated.

Maps

Philips Regional Wall Map of the West Indies (1: 2,500,000) Maps of individual islands/countries (Barbados: DOS 955), produced by the Directorate of Overseas Surveys, obtainable only from Edward Stanford Ltd, 12 Long Acre, London WC2 9LP.

(ii) Background reading

History

Julius Lestor, *To Be A Slave*, Longman, 1970. Aspects of slavery are described in detail by former slaves, reconstructed from their memories, written down both before and after the American Civil War. Still relevant to a major theme of the novel – the deliberate obfuscation of the history of slavery in a colonial education.

Philip Sherlock, *West Indian Story*, Longman, 1971. A short but comprehensive history of the Caribbean from 1492 to the present, suitable for third, fourth and fifth years.

Eric Williams, *From Columbus to Castro: The History of the Caribbean, 1492–1969*, Deutsch, 1970. A complete history of the Caribbean, written by the late Prime Minister of Trinidad and Tobago. The book examines the continuing adverse effects of colonialism in relation to the Caribbean.

(iii) Critical bibliography

Edward Baugh (ed.), *Critics on Caribbean Literature*, St Martin's Press, 1978. Contains a very useful essay on Lamming's *In the Castle of my Skin* by Ngugi Wa Thiong'o.

Sandra Pouchet Paquet, *The Novels of George Lamming*, Heinemann Educational Books, 1982. The definitive critical work on Lamming's novels.

(iv) Reading links

Other novels by George Lamming

The Emigrants, Michael Joseph, 1954. Describes the attitudes and motivations of a group of emigrants going to Britain in the wave of immigration which swept the 1950s. Caribbean man is examined as he makes another Atlantic crossing – this time to the 'mother country'.

Of Age and Innocence, Michael Joseph, 1958. Describes the return of the emigrants to the Caribbean and the growth of independence movements in the 1950s.

Season of Adventure, Michael Joseph, 1960. Probably Lamming's most optimistic examination of events in a self-governing Caribbean country. Gort and Fola, masculine and feminine, revolutionary and middle class, team up in a struggle for genuine freedom and independence in the face of the oppressive influences that still exist in a newly independent former colony.

Natives of my Person, Holt, Rinehart & Winston, 1971; Longman, 1972. Describes a sixteenth-century voyage in a ship manned by a white crew on a voyage to the Americas via West Africa. The novel examines the efforts of the crew to come to terms with their personal and social problems at home as well as on board ship.

Water with Berries, Longman, 1972. Title taken from a Caliban speech in *The Tempest* is set in London among a community of West Indian artists. It examines the complex relationship between the artist 'decendants of Caliban' and the indigenous population of London.

Related fiction on childhood

Much of West Indian literature is concerned with descriptions of childhood experiences. It is as if the West Indian writer, in addressing the external world, feels a need to describe his or her personal world from its earliest stages onwards. Excellent examples of fiction on childhood include Merle Hodge's *Crick Crack, Monkey* (1970)—see Unit 9, p. 71 and Zee Edgell's *Beka Lamb* (Heinemann Educational Books, Caribbean Writers Series, 1982). For an African comparison, see Nafissatou Diallo's *A Dakar Childhood* (Longman, 1982).

Unit 7
Michael Anthony: *The Year in San Fernando*

ALASTAIR NIVEN

Section A:
Critical Approaches

The Year in San Fernando is not only Michael Anthony's best-known novel but one of the most familiar titles in Caribbean literature. The reason for this is essentially its accessibility to readers of any age. Though simple in its outlines, this story of a twelve-year-old boy's initiation into an awareness of the adult world has resonances which repay many readings. I have known it to be enjoyed by young teenagers identifying with its descriptions of adolescent feeling and by adults who admire its total lack of condescension. At any age the novel's depiction of a boy's unfolding insecurity, as he finds himself abruptly deprived of his close-knit family environment and exposed instead to the tensions of city life, is certain to strike a chord.

There is an element of the *Bildungsroman* about *The Year in San Fernando* – the form of fiction in which there exists a large measure of self-identification between the protagonist and the author. Michael Anthony has claimed that 'fiction really is not invention in any way', adding that 'I prefer to write about things that I know simply because if I know something when I write, I can believe in it'. These remarks, from the published version of a talk entitled 'Growing up in Writing' which Anthony gave at the University of Kent,

Canterbury, in 1967, are borne out by the best of his fiction. *The Games Were Coming* (1963) and *Green Days by the River* (1967), both drawn from recollected experience, are generally agreed to be more successful novels than *Streets of Conflict* (1976) or *All That Glitters* (1981), which, though they also have moments of acute personal observation, attempt to render a more ambitiously imagined world.

The Year in San Fernando is not, however, primarily autobiographical. It probably has more in common with the mood of James Joyce's stories in *The Dubliners*, where single moments of what Joyce termed 'epiphany' open up for a child vistas of the forthcoming adult world, than it does with the introspective sexual and intellectual self-questioning of the most famous of English-language *Bildungsromans*, D. H. Lawrence's *Sons and Lovers*. Michael Anthony's achievement is to create a novel about childhood experiences unobscured by the overlay of adult perceptions which inevitably distort them. Throughout the book we have a sense of the boy narrator struggling to articulate what he feels to be an apocalyptic change in his life. The West Indian critic Kenneth Ramchand has used the adjective 'Wordsworthian' of parts of Michael Anthony's writing in this novel, and we can indeed recognize that the purpose William Wordsworth claimed to be behind the *Lyrical Ballads*, namely, 'to follow the fluxes and refluxes of the mind when agitated by the great and simple affections of our nature', is Anthony's intention, too.

The central subject-matter of *The Year in San Fernando* will be familiar to readers of Caribbean, African and Indian fiction, or indeed of some English writing after the Industrial Revolution. Societies in a phase of rapid transition and

Michael Anthony, *The Year in San Fernando*, first published 1965; page references in this unit are to the Heinemann Educational Books (Caribbean Writers Series) edition, 1970.

development are likely to mirror this in stories of growing up and moving away from roots. The changes from childhood to being an adult, from the parental wing to self-sufficiency, from the village to the town, from innocence to experience, are indicators, even images, of great social upheaval. In this respect *The Year in San Fernando* is the most socially and politically aware of Anthony's novels, perhaps more than *Streets of Conflict*, though that book has a background of civil unrest. Ramchand argues this point explicitly: 'The image of Francis, deprived, and tethered to the Chandles' house (even to having a lair below the house), in a circumscribed world of which he is trying to make sense, is an image of the condition of the modern West Indian.' This slightly overstates the case, for there is no internal evidence that Anthony intends an allegorical statement about the disorientated West Indian, but the aspiration to belong – to a home or a community or a faith or a nation – which is so frequently a motif of Caribbean writing undoubtedly colours Francis's behaviour and perceptions throughout *The Year in San Fernando*. At the end of his tale, Francis says: 'I had spent a year here and I was standing on the wharf now and I was a stranger in the big place' (p. 135). Here he is expressing a view of his surroundings which has much in common with the overt feelings of displacement allocated to the Caribbean sensibility by V. S. Naipaul in his provocative diagnosis, *The Middle Passage*, (1962), where he talks of being 'lost in a landscape which had never ceased to be unreal because the scene of an enforced and always temporary residence'.

One is tempted to admit, however, that the reader who lets these wider implications pass him or her by is not missing the essence of the book. *The Year in San Fernando* is about the loss of childhood innocence, to be replaced by bewilderment rather than anything as strong as knowingness or corruption. The novel shows the predicament of a child who is uprooted from the calm if poverty-stricken orthodoxy of his home at an especially disquieting stage of his upbringing, and who is obliged to form new attachments not only to strangers but to a different place. He learns in the process that simple values cannot sustain one in every complicated situation of adult life. He changes, too, in his understanding of people,

moving from terror through respect to, finally, a position almost of judgement over his elders. His sharpened moral awareness is touched by pity and compassion. In an utterly unsentimental way *The Year in San Fernando* portrays some of the realities of human sympathy, which must always be based on knowledge of others that one may wish one did not have, since there must be a measure of pain in perceiving the vulnerability of someone who has been held in awe.

Yet there is a positive side to maturing as well, as Francis realizes when he and Mr Chandles are drawn together in friendship while the old lady who has dominated both their recent lives lies dying:

> When people were fooling you knew it and when they were insincere you knew it too, and you knew when they were genuine to you. Mr Chandles wasn't saying much now but he was standing there and I was standing by the window and I was feeling here was a time when he was becoming used to me, here was a time when he felt he could talk to me. I wondered when did all this start up, because it wasn't sudden. I wondered how come he felt he could talk to me like this and be friends with me. I knew he was no tyrant now and I was feeling easy with him. I looked down at the sweetbroom and at the love-birds and inside me I was feeling new. (p. 127)

Anthony delicately intertwines the regeneration and the disenchantment that come together in adolescence.

Such understanding of the process of maturation has to be conveyed with great artistry if the processes are not to seem improbable. Because of its simple vocabulary, the small scale of its events and the fact of a twelve-year-old boy being its protagonist, there has been a tendency to underestimate the quality of Michael Anthony's art. It is hard to imagine, however, in what way the narrator's perceptions could be more acutely imagined. He frequently admits to confusion: 'I looked towards the cane-lands to see how it was over there, but it was no use – the mist was thick in the distance. . . . It was as if everything had moved out to some other part and as if life had stopped for a while' (p. 79). Sometimes, though, there are moments of outburst and clarity typical of unguarded youth; his feelings towards Mrs Chandles are an example of this: 'The truth was, she sickened me' (p. 31).

This clarity is particularly notable in the account of Francis's relationship with his mother, who, for most of the novel, is a touchstone of vanishing childhood bliss, though when she visits him in San Fernando he sees about her a thinness and anxiety he has not detected before. He thinks of her constantly:

> Ma seemed so far away she might have been in some other world. I had written and posted a letter to her but that seemed to have melted in the silence. Ma seemed as lost as she was in the dreams I had dreamed and half-forgot on waking. I was dejected and despaired. (p.48)

The finality of 'silence', 'lost', 'dejected' and 'despaired' blends with the insubstantiality of 'melted', 'dreams' and 'half-forgot' to convey the dual sense of disembodiment and reincorporation – of shedding childhood and taking on the mantle of growth – which is the main theme of the book.

The interplay of town and country helps to assure that *The Year in San Fernando* becomes neither cynical nor too nostalgic. 'How many Pepsi Cola signs were there in the world?' (p. 10) speculates Francis on arriving in San Fernando. But his thoughts are never far from his village, and his face is often turned towards the looming openness of Mount Naparaima behind the city. Anthony infuses much of his novel with a mood of pastoral regret, implying a moral contrast between rural and urban values. In San Fernando 'it seemed that everybody had grown years older. It was as if the sun had sapped all the life from them' (p. 70). When Francis describes to Mrs Chandles the poui poui flowers and immortelles that proliferate around his village at the end of the dry season, she replies excitedly, taking on for a moment a vitality and tenderness she normally lacks. In San Fernando, after all, the vegetation has to struggle for survival as much as the people. The mere description of a fecund life elsewhere is therapeutic. A rainbow appears shortly afterwards, and the distant echo of Wordsworth's poem 'My heart leaps up when I behold' comes back to Mrs Chandles, then dies as she cannot remember the next line (p. 84). It is as if the city has crushed out of her joy which Wordsworth's poem celebrates, to say nothing of the pantheistic links between humanity and nature.

In conclusion it is worth recalling Wordsworth's lines in full. Normally I would advise readers of a West Indian novel to be extremely wary of cross-referring it to a classic text in English literature, since this may be to imply that the right standards of evaluation lie in another island's culture. But in this case the author specifically invites us to recall Wordsworth's poem, secure, perhaps, in his knowledge that his Trinidad topography and his local sources of imagery are too richly rendered to be dispossessed by anything English. The sentiments of Wordsworth's poem correspond with Michael Anthony's in *The Year in San Fernando*, on the same high level of art:

> My heart leaps up when I behold
>   A rainbow in the sky:
> So was it when my life began;
> So is it now I am a Man;
> So be it when I shall grow old,
>   Or let me die!
> The Child is Father of the Man;
> And I could wish my days to be
> Bound each to each by natural piety.

Section B: The Setting

Trinidad, an island 4828 square kilometres in area, lies off the north coast of the South American republic of Venezuela. With the much smaller neighbouring island of Tobago it forms an independent republic which achieved this status on 31 August 1962. Trinidad and Tobago is a member of the Commonwealth. However, when reading *The Year in San Fernando* we must remember that Anthony places his novel in 1943–4, when Trinidad was a British – administered colony. Though officially at war at the time, Trinidad's war effort plays virtually no part in the book. San Fernando, the main setting of the novel, is the second city of Trinidad. Mayaro is a small fishing village on the south-east corner of the island.

The peoples of Trinidad are racially drawn from many origins, including those of African descent, those who are of mixed race and those smaller groups who are Indian, European and Chinese by background. The main crops of the island, as Anthony emphasizes in the novel, are sugar-cane and edible fruits. Today Trinidad produces oil and it also has the largest natural asphalt lake in the world.

Section C: A Closer Look

(1) From 'I felt strange for most of that night . . . ' (pp. 5–6)

Part of the art of writing in a convincing way about the experience of childhood lies in being able to recreate the vocabulary in which the child would be thinking. It is rare in an autobiography, for example, for the writer to recall his or her early years without an interpretative patina of adult awareness. This can lead the author to use a more sophisticated or detached vocabulary than a child would know at the time of the experience being described. The opposite danger is that the writer will self-consciously use an oversimplified language which ends up by being patronizing. Michael Anthony creates in Francis a narrative persona which avoids either pitfall.

We see this at the start of the passage with the repitition of the word 'strange'. A child would think this word to himself as he comes to terms with his situation and would wake up the next day feeling the same. He would not reach for an alternative adjective for the sake of variegating his prose. Yet at the same time the boy is struggling to articulate his feelings. He knows that the change about to happen to him – going to live in San Fernando – is apocalyptic; hence the almost biblical tone of 'It seemed as though I was suddenly changed without and within.' But he does not have a ready-made comprehensive explanation for what he feels: 'Somehow, the knowledge that I was going away made Mayaro look very strange.' The use of 'somehow' reverberates more than a specific word would do.

The passage describes a historic moment in the boy's growth. He needs to be alone while he absorbs it. Significantly within the overall structure of the novel (and in analysing any passage we need to place it in the context of the whole work from which it comes), the narrator has recourse to the surrounding landscape when talking about his feelings. 'The lime trees looked greener, for one thing': a clear image of a new world impinging. This moment may be his last look at his own home, and he sees it with new eyes. Things seem 'rare'; here Anthony selects a word which strikes exactly the right note of credibility and childlike simplicity but which has a hint of Wordsworthian grandeur. Indeed, when at the end of the passage he tells us that 'my heart almost leaped to my mouth' it may not be altogether fanciful to detect a hinted recollection of Wordsworth's 'My heart leaps up when I behold/A rainbow in the sky' – a line of poetry alluded to elsewhere in the novel, as we saw in Section A. Though Anthony is a less overtly visionary writer than Wordsworth, he establishes a correlation between the individual's inner state of being and his sense of the natural surroundings that is similar to the English poet's.

We follow the reflections of Francis's mind and his graduations of mood as he moves from an abstract knowledge of his altered life to the particulars. Seeing the world through new eyes, he does not want to play the normal games of a typical day like stoning the guavas or batting at cricket. His mind moves to the school he will be leaving, what results he will get in a test, then on to his future in San Fernando; finally, like a camera moving into close-up, he sees Mr Chandles. Anthony paces the whole passage with careful dramatic control. The boy's naïveté is suggested in his sense of the 'terrific' size of the Forestry Office, when *we* know how much bigger San Fernando will be. At the end – 'He smiled with me', not 'at me' – we surely have a forewarning of the complicity that will eventually grow up between Francis and Mr Chandles.

(2) From 'I saw the big mango tree rustling . . .' (pp. 113–14)

The Year in San Fernando is not a didactic novel. For much of it we detect the changes in Francis's perception of the world through the author's implicit touch rather than because he has spelt out for us what these changes represent or how they have come about. This passage about the mango tree in Celesta Street illustrates one of the methods whereby Anthony achieves his understated effect. As we read this account of how the boy observes the mango tree through the different seasons, and comes to love it, we may recall that this is the same boy who thoughtlessly stoned the guava tree and earned Mr Chandles's disapproval. A conscious respect for nature seems to have accompanied his maturing.

Michael Anthony successfully creates a poetic mood in many places in this novel but he never permits his prose to be emptily melodic or meaninglessly decorative. He brings off a poetic mood here mainly because the language is straightforward and the observation soundly based on the sights a child would actually see and not on what they might evoke in an adult. The author's choice of words is especially precise: 'The humming-birds had pestered the blossoms as they had pestered all blossoms', for example, where the chosen verb has exactly the right connections, working both as an accurate descriptive term for the natural process it describes and carrying with it a shading of almost moral disapproval as the boy resents the way the humming-birds intrude upon him and his mango tree. The moral tone becomes a little stronger when he talks of the pain he feels at the casual pickers with their bamboo rods. He is like a witness to a private sacred act, the growth of the mango tree. It is left to us to see in its growth a small image of Francis's own development. It may not be over-ingenious to see the unannounced coconut tree – 'very tall . . . far in the distance' – as a reminder of the boy's coming maturity.

The passage demonstrates how risky it is to slide over the moments in Anthony's writing where nothing much appears to be happening. As an 'event' there is no drama in what Anthony writes here; but as an insight into Francis's spiritual development it could hardly be richer.

Section D: The Author

Trinidad has produced many notable writers including Michael Anthony, Ralph de Boissière, C. L. R. James, Shiva Naipaul, V. S. Naipaul and Samuel Selvon. Michael Anthony was born in Mayaro, Trinidad, in 1932 and had his secondary education until the age of fifteen at the Junior Technical School in San Fernando, the second city of Trinidad after the capital Port of Spain. Anthony's first stories were published in the *Trinidad Guardian* and in *BIM*, two publications with a well-established tradition of encouraging new Trinidadian writers. Anthony worked in England for many years in factories and for the General Post Office and British Railways, but he had earlier worked in an iron foundry in San Fernando. He has also lived in Brazil, where his novel *Streets of Conflict* is set. He now lives back in Trinidad, and among his publications is a history of the island.

Anthony's first three novels are about the years of growing up. To read them together enhances one's admiration for his sensitive handling of adolescence, since he never repeats himself but manages to convey in each both the pains and the exhilaration of one's 'green days'. *The Games Were Coming* (1963) centres on a boy's preparations to win a cycle race at the time of the Carnival. In *Green Days by the River* (1967) the main character is older than either of the boys in the first two novels, and there is some emphasis on his sexual awakening. In all three novels the relationship of the child to his parents is stressed, as is the contrast between the values of a rural community and those of the town.

With *Streets of Conflict* (1976), published after what seemed like a long creative silence, Anthony broke new ground. Not only is the novel placed in Brazil but it reflects the political restlessness of the period in the late 1960s when the author lived in Rio de Janeiro. The shifting currents of the various relationships in the novel are gently handled and result in an unfocused but possibly undervalued story in which for the first time Anthony places equal weight upon a female character. In *All that Glitters* (1981) once again he makes a boy his central character, and his setting is Trinidad, but the more complex plotting precludes some of the simple effects that he brings off in the first three novels.

Michael Anthony's other published work includes an anthology of short stories set mainly in Mayaro but including 'Enchanted Alley' and 'The Day of the Fearless', both of which take place in San Fernando. This collection, entitled *Cricket in the Road and Other Stories* (1973), should be read in conjunction with 'Drunkard of the River', a tale appearing in Andrew Salkey's anthology, *West Indian Stories* (1960).

Michael Anthony's work has not been widely praised in the Caribbean, perhaps because it is neither overtly nationalistic in theme nor linguistically experimental. It does not reflect many of the social divisions in Caribbean society — though they are hinted at — and it seldom evokes the folklore, musicality or religions of the islands. Abroad, however, his quiet ironic tone has been much admired. *The Year in San Fernando* is often chosen as a teaching text at all levels of education.

Section E: Classroom Use

(i) Level of use

The Year in San Fernando is about a twelve-year-old boy going through experiences some of which at least will be similar to those that all boys and girls go through at about that age. So it is not unreasonable to presume that the novel will appeal to young people of that age and above. Any younger will probably be to ask for too much understanding of the more perceptual side of the book. Age 14–16 will be ideal and for students around fourth- or fifth-year GCSE. However, there are complexities both of psychology and style within the novel's apparent simplicity that suggests it could be used at a higher level, too; and it is widely read by adults.

(ii) Points of focus and emphasis

1   How Francis reacts to the news that he is to live in San Fernando: Chapters 1 and 2:
   - the presentation of village life;
   - Francis's relations with his family;
   - the journey to San Fernando.

2   San Fernando itself: Chapters 3, 7, 10, 24, 27:
   - the contrast between San Fernando and Mayaro;
   - the quality of people's lives in the city;
   - the use of symbolism to express urban pressures.

3   The presentation of nature in the novel: Chapters 12, 21, 23, 24, 26, 27:
   - the way that descriptions of weather, plants, trees, Mount Naparaima, etc. are used to indicate the stages of Francis's growing up;
   - the chronology of the year in San Fernando and the cycle of its seasons.

4   Francis's key relationships:
   - with his mother (Ma), esp. Chapters 1, 17, 18;
   - with Mrs Chandles, esp. Chapters 3, 14, 19, 22, 23, 29, 30;
   - with Mr Chandles, esp Chapters 2, 4, 5, 8, 25, 32, 33;
   - with Julia, esp. Chapters 11, 20, 27.

5   Education as a goal:

My heart was burning for home. For a moment I felt like crying out, but at the moment of greatest pain my mother's voice came back to me. It was as if she was here and talking. She had said, Stay and take in education, boy. Take it in. That's the main thing. (p. 67)

Education as the main object of Francis being in San Fernando is a constant factor in the background of the novel. There is no single chapter concentrating on this theme, but it needs to be examined as an important motif.

6   Michael Anthony's techniques in portraying the experiences of childhood: again, this is a vital part of understanding the book but since it is the main subject of Michael Anthony's work it is difficult to isolate single chapters as especially representative. As effective a way as any to discuss Francis's growing perception of the world around him is to examine in detail, along the lines used above in Section C, the shifts of emphasis and the imagery within particular passages. Such a passage might be that beginning 'I watched out for my lunch but

it was well into the afternoon before it was ready' down to 'and the darkness fell thickly and heavily that night' (pp. 47–8).

7   Francis's predicament as an image of Caribbean alienation: we need to take seriously the possibility that Michael Anthony intends us to see Francis's developing alienation as a mirror image of what has happened to Caribbean people generally: uprooted from their traditional background, cast adrift in an unsympathetic world, hardened through bewilderment. Chapters 3, 23 (especially the passages 'The rain outside seemed to isolate us from everything . . . the rain had cut us off from everything and had left us together', pp. 82–3, and 'I wished I could just forget about such things for now . . . I went in and made my bed and lay down', pp. 86-7) and 33 will be especially relevant.

(iii) Questions for essay writing or classroom discussion

1   How does Michael Anthony suggest that there are different moral values in the village and the town?

2   Take a particular passage of the novel and examine the means by which Anthony shows how Francis feels within it.

3   Would it be accurate to describe *The Year in San Fernando* as a poetic novel? (Teachers may want to use the word 'Wordsworthian' with a more advanced class.)

4   Write a character study of either Mr Chandles or Mrs Chandles or Julia.

5   Francis's mother sends him to San Fernando for the sake of his education. What kind of education do we see him receiving there? (Teachers might consider with the class the question of whether an education in human understanding and experience is not as valuable as the more formal education of the schoolroom.)

6   Do you see Francis's experiences in San Fernando as mirroring aspects of Caribbean history?

7   Does Michael Anthony make us feel that a child and not an adult is narrating the story?

8   What significance is there in the novel in the emphasis on weather and the changing seasons?

9   Describe Mrs Chandles's house.

10   Take the episodes in Chapters 17 and 18 concerning Ma's visit to San Fernando and show how they help Francis to deepen his understanding of the world.

11   Is Michael Anthony a comic writer? If so, illustrate how he achieves his comic effects.

12   Describe the stages of Mrs Chandles's illness and death and show how these help Francis to understand the adult world.

13   Compare *The Year in San Fernando* with any other novel of childhood (or part of a novel, or opening section of an autobiography, perhaps) that you have read.

14   What have you learned about Trinidad by reading this novel?

15   If you were recommending a friend to read *The Year in San Fernando*, what aspects of the novel would you particularly mention by way of attracting him or her to it? [A very general question like this may encourage the person answering it to think about why the novel is readable for so many age groups and yet clearly a work of considerable quality.]

(iv) Creative approaches/curriculum links

1   In *The Year in San Fernando* Francis narrates what happens to him in the course of one year. Can you describe what has happened to you during either the last year or the last month?

2   Have you ever arrived in a new place where you knew you would be living for a long time and which was very different from the place you had been used to? If so, try to recall what it felt like travelling there and settling in.

3   Think of a very old person you have known and write an account of how you got to know them. If you choose one of your grandparents, write about a typical day you spent with them.

4   What seem to you to be the main differences between growing up in Trinidad during the Second World War and growing up in your own community today?

5   [For someone fourteen years old or over.] Think about what it was like to be twelve years old and write about the highlights of that time.

6   [Fourth years and above only.] Compare Michael Anthony's presentation of Francis with his other boy characters in *Green Days by the River*, *The Games Were Coming* or *All that Glitters*. Or simply read one of these other novels and describe how your own life contrasts with the experiences described in it and in *The Year in San Fernando*.

7   Trace a map of Trinidad and mark on it where Mayaro and San Fernando can be found. Place on it Mount Naparaima and anywhere else that you can locate by reading the novel. Then write underneath it all that you can find out from either the novel or other sources about the climate, vegetation, landscape and main products of Trinidad.

8   Compare the experiences of Francis in *The Year in San Fernando* with the typical year of a West Indian child in an urban community in Britain. You may like to think about how the parents or grandparents of such a child may have arrived in Britain from Trinidad or another part of the Caribbean in the 1950s and why they came to live in Britain.

9   *The Year in San Fernando* is sometimes criticized for making no mention of the contemporary history of Trinidad. Find out what you can about the island in the 1940s, especially in the war years, and see if you can write an account of the political, social and cultural situation that Francis would be aware of – or would be learning about – during his year in San Fernando. If it is difficult to do this specifically for Trinidad, then look into the contemporary situation in the West Indies generally.

Section F: Teaching Aids

(i)   Audio-visual material

Slide sets

Trinidad and Tobago, Chepstow (Gwent): Audio-Visual Productions, 1978.

Trinidad, Bar Hill (Cambridge): Concordia, n.d.

Caribbean in Change (series of five slide sets), by John and Penny Hubley, London: Centre for World Development Education, 1981.

The Caribbean, Bristol: Gateway Educational Films, n.d.

Mixed-media sets

Caribbean Anthology (2 cassettes and booklets), London: ILEA Learning Materials Service.

An Introduction to History and the Caribbean (1 sound cassette, 26 maps, photographs, worksheets, workbook and set of teachers' materials), Sandwell (West Midlands): Afro-Caribbean Support Unit, 1982.

(ii)   Background reading

African, Caribbean and Black American Books for Fourth and Fifth Year Secondary School Pupils: Reading Guide and *Background to African and Caribbean 'A' Level Texts: Reading Guide*, both published by the Association for the Teaching of Caribbean, African, Asian and Associated Literatures, 1983, 1985.

Stella Dunckler, *A Visual History of the West Indies*, Evans, 1972.

F. C. Evans, *A First Geography of Trinidad and Tobago*, Cambridge University Press, 1973.

David Lowenthal, *West Indian Societies*, Oxford University Press, 1972.

(iii)   Critical bibliography

Paul Edwards and Kenneth Ramchand, 'The Art of Memory: Michael Anthony's *The Year in San Fernando*', *Journal of Commonwealth Literature*, no. 7, July 1969. Reprinted in William Walsh (ed.), *Readings in Commonwealth Literature*, Clarendon Press 1973.

A. Luengo, 'Growing up in San Fernando: Change and Growth in Michael Anthony's *The Year in San Fernando*', *Ariel* (Calgary), vol. 6, no. 2, April 1975.

Alastair Niven, 'My Sympathies Enlarged: The Novels of Michael Anthony', *Commonwealth Essays and Studies*, 2, 1976.

(iv) Reading links

Other novels by Michael Anthony

The Games Were Coming, Deutsch, 1963; Heinemann Educational Books (Caribbean Writers Series), 1977.

Green Days by the River, Deutsch 1967; Heinemann Educational Books (Caribbean Writers Series), 1973.

Streets of Conflict, Deutsch, 1976.

All That Glitters, Deutsch, 1981; Heinemann Educational Books (Caribbean Writers Series), 1983.

Michael Anthony's short stories

'Drunkard of the River', in Andrew Salkey (ed.), *West Indian Stories*, Faber, 1960.

Cricket in the Road and Other Stories, Heinemann Educational Books (Caribbean Writers Series), 1973. The stories are introduced by the author.

Critical writings

'Growing up in Writing', *Journal of Commonwealth Literature*, no. 7, July 1969.

'The Return of the West Indian Writer', *BIM*, no. 56, pp. 212–18. Anthony interviewed by I. Munroe and R. Sander.

Work by other writers

The process of growing up is a central concern in Caribbean writing, with many novels having a child narrator or dwelling extensively on the period of childhood. Among such novels are V. S. Naipaul's *A House for Mr Biswas* (1961), Sam Selvon's *A Brighter Sun* (1952) and Merle Hodge's *Crick Crack, Monkey* (1970) – see Unit 9, p. 71. The last is particularly recommended; its racy style, wonderful humour and warmth make it a brilliantly enjoyable book to read, and provide good contrasts and comparisons with Anthony's style.

A small fishing village (Vicky Unwin)

Unit 8
Roger Mais: *The Hills Were Joyful Together*

KARINA WILLIAMSON AND DAVID DABYDEEN

Section A: Critical Approaches

The Hills Were Joyful Together is a tragedy, not of an individual protagonist but of a class. Set in a slum 'yard' (a group of tenements built round a communal courtyard) in Kingston, Jamaica, about the year 1950, the novel provides a microcosm of urban life in Jamaica at the working-class level. It does this by means of a tightly knit structure of interwoven plots, involving a large cast of characters, but the narrative shape is determined principally by the stories of two sets of people: Surjue, his woman Rema and a hanger-on called Flitters; Shag, his woman Euphemia and her lover Bajun Man. These two triangular sets are similar in their psychological pattern, in that each shows a central figure (Surjue, Euphemia), sensuous and morally rudderless, caught between conflicting pulls, good and evil, and succumbing fatally to the worse (this is simplification; the characters are presented both morally and psychologically with subtlety). Both are drawn towards unscrupulous exploiters, against whom the love of their gentler partners proves ineffectual. Surjue, an easy-going idler and gambler, is caught between his love for Rema and desire for money. Aided and encouraged by Flitters, and disregarding Rema's protests, he plans a robbery but is caught while carrying it out, through Flitter's treachery, and is sent to jail. Left on her own, Rema breaks down and goes mad. In a

desperate bid to go to her help, Surjue tries to escape from prison, but even as he does so she sets fire to her room and is burnt to death. Meanwhile, Flitters is hunted down by Surjue's friends and murdered in revenge for his betrayal. In the final scene of the book, Surjue is shot and killed as he climbs the prison wall. The outcome of the other plot is equally brutal. Shag, himself half demented and dying of lung disease, is rejected by Euphemia and hacks her to death after discovering her in the bedroom with her lover.

Interlaced with these main plots are several subsidiary dramas, reinforcing the image of a society in which sexual conflict, violence, treachery and vengefulness are basic elements, but showing other facets as well. The savagery of the adults in this poverty-stricken human jungle is partly reflected but also partly lightened by the portrayal of a group of adolescents in the yard. Between them, Manny, Wilfie, the pathetic young tart Ditty and others play out the same battles and sex-games as their elders, but with a relative innocence that makes them appear pitiable as well as ominous. In Charlotta and Bedosa (the only married couple in the yard), with their children, Manny and Tansy, we are shown the frictions of a loveless family life exacerbated by the grinding struggle for subsistence. Bedosa is another character who meets a violent end, murdered like Flitters in revenge for betraying a mate. Charlotta retreats into narrow religiosity, while Tansy finds refuge and a kind of surrogate father in Ras, one of the first representatives of the Rastafarian cult to appear in Caribbean fiction. Mais is not concerned in this novel with the specific beliefs of the Rastas, but uses the gentle, peace-loving Ras as a counter-image to the aggressive or mean-spirited self-

Roger Mais, *The Hills Were Joyful Together*, first published 1953; page references in this unit are to the Heinemann Educational Books (Caribbean Writers Series) edition, 1981.

assertion characteristic of many of the other male figures. The relationship between Tansy and Ras, though lightly sketched (it was much more prominent in the first version of the novel), hints at the possibility of selfless love as a redemptive force, a theme which Mais was to explore more fully in his second novel, *Brother Man* (1954). It is glanced at again in the self-denying love of Rema for Surjue, and in the prostitute Zephyr's love for Lennie.

Selfless love is not the only positive value demonstrated in the novel. In scenes like that of the great fish-fry (Book 1) and the 'nine-night' for Euphemia (Book 3), we see the strength of a communal feeling that can occasionally override pettier rivalries and conflicts. But both as a symbol and, later, as a presence, the prison overshadows these brave and pathetic attempts to transcend the miseries of the common lot.

In spite of all the violence, *The Hills Were Joyful Together* is neither sensationalist nor melodramatic. Its purpose is twofold. At one level it is a novel of social protest, a ferocious but essentially realistic and compassionate exposure of the conditions under which the deprived classes of Jamaica subsisted. At another level it is a symbolic account of what Mais saw as the tragedy of human existence. To make sense of the cruel and seemingly anarchic world it depicts, the novel offers two kinds of philosophy. On the one hand there is social determinism (usually voiced by the prison chaplain), which explains crime, suffering and moral degradation as the necessary consequences of poverty and social injustice. On the other hand there is a more comprehensive fatalism (expressed in the choric passages which serve as introductions to chapters), according to which human beings are the victims of blind chance in a universe indifferent to their desires or merits. In both, the individual is 'imprisoned' by powers beyond his or her control or, often, understanding. The Christian religion, which influences the attitudes and actions of several of the characters, is shown to be incapable of mitigating either the man-made evils of society or the adversities of fate.

Mais's outlook is not totally negative, however. Beyond both 'philosophies' in the book is a faith in our capacity to take moral responsibility for our own lives. One need not, indeed must not, accept the status of a completely helpless victim. Refusal to succumb and fidelity to positive values (love, courage, loyalty, generosity) are in themselves heroic assertions of the dignity and worth of human existence. Ultimately, the only real defeat is to fail in this responsibility: 'it matters all, that he has turned his back upon life' (p. 184).

The novel should be read in conjunction with *Brother Man* (also in the Heinemann Educational Books Caribbean Writers Series), Mais's subsequent novel. The setting of *Brother Man* is also a Kingston slum in the Jamaica of the 1950s; and although the focus this time is on a street instead of a yard, the second novel again dramatizes the life of a whole community, using once more a structure of interrelated stories. *Brother Man* however has a hero and a central narrative line to which the subplots each contribute. 'Brother Man' (his real name is John Power), a cobbler, is shown primarily in relation to Minette, a young girl he has rescued from the streets where he found her, hungry and homeless and living by prostitution, taking her into his own house. But he is also shown in connection with his neighbours, Girlie and Papacita, Jesmina and her elder sister Cordy, and a range of largely nameless minor figures. The central story is concerned with Brother Man's moral leadership in the local community. He is a Rastafarian, though not altogether a typical representative of the cult. The Ras Tafari movement had not spread and developed by the 1950s to the extent it has since. At that time it was confined to Jamaica, its adherents living mainly in a squalid sector of Kingston, eking out a hand-to-mouth existence and keeping for the most part peacefully to themselves. But because of their poverty, unkempt appearance, devotion to 'ganga' (cannabis) and refusal to conform to social norms, they earned an unjustified reputation for crime and violence, and were readily made into scapegoats, as Brother Man is in the novel.

Mais selects for his hero in *Brother Man* only a few of the specific features of Rastafarianism. Of their doctrines he records only the belief that black men from Ethiopia were the lost children of Israel, and that their hair is left unshaven for religious reasons (p. 74); other Rastafarian facets of Brother Man's character include the use of biblical language and the outlook encapsulated in the Ras Tafari slogan 'Peace and Love'. In other respects his character is fundamentally Christian. He is in fact a Christ figure translated into contemporary Jamaican terms. He is shown praying, preaching, healing the sick and acting out many details of the gospels. At first revered by the people of his locality, he is later betrayed for silver, falsely accused of coining money, abused and beaten up, almost to the point of death, by a hysterical mob. This 'crucifixion' is followed (significantly after three days) by a 'resurrection', and throughout his ordeal he is attended faithfully by Minette and Jesmina, like the two Marys of the gospel.

Subordinate to this main story is the unfolding of Minette's love for Brother Man, his attempts to suppress his own physical desires and the eventual breakdown of his resistance in response to her need. Girlie and Papacita (who contrives the framing of Brother Man) provide a contrasting relationship. For them, sexual passion without tenderness or mutual respect is the only bond, but ultimately it leads to their destruction. Their story ends with Girlie stabbing her lover to death in jealousy over his flirtation with Minette. Cordelia, an unhappy and neurotic woman, is Brother Man's 'Judas'; at Papacita's bidding she plants the counterfeit coins on him. But her degeneration begins when her man is jailed for peddling ganga, and her child falls sick. When Brother Man is unable to cure the child, she turns away from him and falls under the malevolent influence of Bra' Ambo, an 'obeah' practitioner, and ends by killing both her child and herself. As in *The Hills Were Joyful Together*, violence seems to erupt in this world of the deprived and impoverished as if it were an uncontrollable force of nature; but with the difference that the poles of good (epitomized by Brother Man) and evil (Bra' Ambo) seem further apart and less explicable in simple terms of social or economic causes. *Brother Man*, moreover, is more conspicuously patterned than *The Hills*, with fewer and more closely integrated stories and a framework of five episodes (corresponding to the five acts of classical tragedy), punctuated by a chorus. The language, too, exploits more systematically the rhythmic and expressive resources of Creole. The effect of all this is to heighten the dramatic character of the novel and remove it a further stage away from realism, allowing Mais to take liberties with characterization and action that would seem theatrical or sentimental in a more naturalistic mode.

The central theme of both novels is the search for vision. 'Vision' here involves both perception, in the rational and moral sense, and prophetic vision: understanding the meaning of human life within the divine scheme.

Section B: The Setting

Roger Mais announced that his intention in writing *The Hills Were Joyful Together* was 'to give the world a true picture of the real Jamaica and the dreadful conditions of the working class'. The novel is certainly grounded in social realism; we are given detailed insight into the day-to-day existence of the Kingston slum-dwellers. When Mais spoke about 'a true picture' he was certainly correct, for the narrative (especially in the scenes describing the punishment of prisoners) is naked in its revelation of the painfulness of barrack-yard life. The very noises, smells, tastes and sensations of the yard are represented to the reader:

> Ras rolled over on his back, scratched himself all over, broke wind, made a face, getting the first taste of his mouth for the morning, hawked and spat in an earthenware yabba, set beside him for the purpose, and knuckled his eyes coming out of sleep. (pp. 10–11)

> Ditty Johnson, sitting on that top step now, slapped dingie flies on her bare legs, scratched the lumps that they raised with her finger nails to ease the itching, sometimes pulling her dress up her thighs; erased the white scratch marks against the smooth black skin with a spit-wet finger. (p. 10)

At the same time, whilst teeming with such concrete passages, the novel has a symbolic design. The biblical and classical references (for example, the allusion to the myth of Sisyphus and to the Crucifixion in the passage describing Surjue's death) locate the miseries of the Kingston poor within patterns of universal suffering. Mais's purpose is to present the lives of Jamaicans, but in doing so he reveals the life of Everyman. There is a 'political' purpose to Mais's strategy. For him Jamaica is not merely a small island, an insignificant part of the globe (this would have been the view of most British people at the time); the experiences of its people are universal in depth and dimension and are thus deserving of world attention. In 1953, when the novel was first published, Jamaica was still a British colony struggling for independence. Mais's depiction of the lives of its common people (on a realistic and symbolic level) would have educated the novel's British readership to the Jamaican people's claims to freedom.

Section C: A Closer Look

(1) 'The Yard counted' to 'wailing the livelong day' (p. 9)

The immediate purpose of this passage is to set the scene, to provide the verbal equivalent of a stage-set at the moment the curtain rises. This is the purpose of all the directional phrases: 'on the south side', 'to the north', 'at back', 'in the middle', etc. They bring the readers into the theatre, as it were, making them spectators in one sense, but also inviting them to participate as an audience participates in live drama. Mais's description stresses the shabbiness and dereliction of the scene, to indicate the social level of its inmates. Everything is old, worn-out, defective: 'ramshackle', 'termite-ridden', 'dilapidated', 'rotting'. The fence is decaying; the standpipe (no running water supply in these 'shacks') has a leaking tap; the gate is 'wry-hinged'. Moreover this is bleak, not picturesque, shabbiness; the buildings are 'barrack-like' or 'concrete nog' (timber-framed), the only decoration left being 'dirty', 'cracked', 'blistering' paint.

The metaphor of the crustacean shell, as if the building were some sea-creature eaten away by termites until only its shell remains, is subtly but deliberately macabre. For Mais's purpose is not merely to inform and describe. The 'yard' is more than a place where the action is to take place, it is a paradigm of the condition of its occupants. By investing inanimate objects with animate qualities, Mais contrives to tell us something about his human protagonists even before they appear on the scene. The struggle of the trees ('gnarled', 'scraggy', 'scarred') to survive in a hostile environment anticipates the way the lives of the characters are shown to be similarly warped, constricted and worn out in the unequal battle against adverse social conditions. Even the water from the tap is a 'weary' trickle, the sky 'anaemic'. More sinister still is the description of the gate: 'buck-toothed', 'obscenely grinning', hinting at the moral deformity which such conditions induce.

The only human beings introduced are the Sisters of Charity. The irony in Mais's phraseology is significant. Their title, Sisters of Charity, conjures up an image of nun-like gentleness and compassion; but their activities — crooning, gossiping and cooking — contrasted with their lugubrious singing suggest contradictory images of worldliness and hypocrisy. It is an advance warning of the kind of hope Christianity is to offer in the novel.

(2) 'That evening' to 'like children again' (pp. 38–9)

The most notable feature of this passage is the deliberate shift of speech register from simple narrative (para. 1) to quasi-official reportage (para. 2) to dialect (para. 3) and back to narrative (paras. 4–7) but this time mingled with stream-of-consciousness, as Mais reproduces the thoughts of Ras and the other 'scufflers'. The mixture of styles has a strangely unsettling effect. In what sense (the reader is compelled to ask) is this 'true', i.e. real? This suspension of trust is part of Mais's strategy, because what he is about to do is to describe a 'miracle' (as indeed the voices of the crowd testify: 'Is like de quail birds he sen' de children of Israel in de wilderness'). Notice, too, the calculatedly simple, childlike syntax of the narrative paragraphs with their strings of conjunctive clauses ('and . . . and . . . and'), like the language of fairy story or folk tale. It reflects the transformation in the people of the yard: 'they were like children again'.

Later in the evening, to liven things up, Lennie pulls a plank out of the fence and starts to act the song 'Ribber Ben Come Down', inviting everyone to clap hands and join in the chorus (pp. 49-50). Gradually they all get drawn in, not only clapping and singing but, as we see, drumming, dancing and miming. Their happiness is contagious; it spreads to the passers-by in the street beyond the yard. Yet the fence from which the plank is taken, and which marks the limit of their communal patch, is the same paint-blistered, crazy, broken-down fence which helped to identify the poverty and squalor of their existence at the opening of the book. The transformation is like a scene out of *Cinderella*, and as fragile. The malice, anxiety, bickering and fighting, which (we have been shown) are the everyday stuff of their lives, dissolve under the ritualistic, incantatory effect of the song. Mais accentuates its effect on the reader by his own repetition of key words – 'teetering', 'clapping', 'buck-stepping', 'grinning' – giving a powerful sense of joy and movement.

The excitement reaches its climax (pp. 51–2) as Lennie mimetically crosses the river, and in the flush of shared triumph Zephyr's self-imposed restraint is relaxed as she greets the hero of this symbolic *rite de passage*. The final sentence has been criticized as sentimental, and so in fact it would be if Mais had not so carefully placed it in a context which makes it piercingly ironic. The narrative goes straight on to a peculiarly brutal story, related by Shag (partly as a warning to Euphemia, and by hindsight, for the reader, a prefiguration of his own horrible revenge). Even at first reading there should be no doubt that 'miracles' exist only in the wishful imagination of the bystanders in the yard, in the savage world of this novel. Yet what happens at the fish-fry is not thereby devalued; the poignancy of this whole sequence stems from the *reality* and the beauty, as well as the rarity and ephemerality, of the unity achieved. It is a glimpse of what might be in a happier world.

Section D: The Author

Roger Mais was the oldest of the new wave of Caribbean writers who emerged after the Second World War. Born in Jamaica in 1905 and educated privately and at Calabar High School (where he was remembered as a somewhat lawless pupil), he came from a middle-class and deeply religious family. Daily Bible study was a feature of his early life in a rural area of eastern Jamaica. His first job after leaving school was in the lower ranks of the Civil Service, but his rebellious temperament soon made this uncongenial, and he tried a variety of jobs and occupations, settling (in so far as he ever did) for journalism in the 1940s. In 1938, at the time of the labour riots in Jamaica, he underwent what he described as a kind of conversion to socialism and joined Norman Manley's People's National Party. He engaged actively in the nationalist struggles of the 1940s, campaigning at the street level for the PNP. During the war he was sent to prison for publishing an outspoken denunciation of British imperialism, and his experiences in Spanish Town jail provided raw material for the prison sequences in *The Hills*. After the war, while in his forties, he took up painting, and although almost entirely self-taught earned a reputation as an artist of vision and individuality. By this time Mais had come to see that his contribution to the political cause and to the realization of his ideal of a Jamaican national culture should be made through his work as a writer and artist rather than through political activities as such. But it was, he felt, the philistinism of the Jamaican public that was the biggest obstacle in the way of cultural development, and so in 1952 he joined the stream of writers from the Caribbean who were seeking outlets for their work in London. From London he moved for a while to France and renewed his painting, until illness forced him to return to Jamaica, where he died in 1955.

Although Mais had had two volumes of short stories published in Jamaica in the 1940s, *The Hills Were Joyful Together* (1953) was his first full-length novel to be published. The version that appeared in print, and remains the standard text, was the product of drastic cutting and revision; the original manuscript submitted to Jonathan Cape was nearly twice the length of the present text. It was (and is) manifestly the expression of Mais's political concern; never again in his writing was his political commitment to be so explicit, though even here a larger Christian humanist vision is apparent. The religious side of his imagination became increasingly ascendant in his later novels, *Brother Man* (1954) and *Black Lightning* (1955), published in the year of his death. Another novel, *In the Sight of This Sun*, which was left unfinished and remains unpublished, is a dramatization of the Old Testament story of David, Bathsheba and Uriah. All three of his published novels have been reprinted by Heinemann Educational Books in the Caribbean Writers Series.

Section E: Classroom Use

(i) Level of use

The novel is suitable for fifth-year to sixth-form teaching, since its main themes (class division, colonial oppression, universal suffering, etc.) demand a mature understanding. Several passages, however (e.g. the prison scenes), can easily be appreciated by younger readers and can be used to spark off discussion on a variety of issues (e.g. the treatment of prisoners, the work of Amnesty International, the frequency of torture in certain countries) relevant to Britain and the Caribbean.

(ii) Points of focus and emphasis

1   Religion in society, pp. 21, 73, 109, 136, 141, 269–70.
2   Social injustice and class oppression, pp. 225, 226, 228, 237–9, 240.
3   The beating and torture of prisoners, pp. 134–5, 137–40, 184–5, 257–61.
4   The murder of Flitters, pp. 233–4.
5   The murder of Euphemia, pp. 262–4.
6   The death of Bedosa, pp. 130–1, 135–6.

7   The death of Surjue, pp. 287–8.
8   Rema's madness and death, pp. 277, 280–1.
9   The fight between Pattoo and Manny, pp. 114–17.
10 Humour in the environment of suffering, pp. 186–7, 282.
11 Echoes of slavery, pp. 38–9 (reference to the Exodus and to 'Big Massa'), pp. 214 ff. (Flitters as a 'runaway' slave being hunted down).

(iii) Questions for essay writing or classroom discussion

1   What is the significance of the title of the novel? If you had to give it another, what would you choose, and why?
2   To what extent can Surjue be regarded as a tragic hero? How does his character develop in the course of the novel? Compare him with the heroes of other tragedies (plays or novels) you know.
3   There are several adolescent characters in the book. Consider what they show about the experience of growing up, and how Mais differentiates between them.
4   Compare and contrast the relationships between the three couples: Surjue and Rema, Shag and Euphemia, Zephyr and Lennie. Zephyr appears principally in scenes with Lennie or Euphemia (pp. 11–13, 42–4, 73–5, 87–92, 99–102, 143–5, 218–9, 275–6, 282–3). Read those carefully and consider what they tell us about her character.
5   What sort of picture does the novel give of relations between parents and children?
6   In Book 3, the different stories are particularly closely interwoven. What devices does Mais use to link them and to give the impression that they are all going on at the same time?
7   How does Mais build up excitement and suspense in the sequences in which Bedosa and Flitters are pursued? What is the point of having two similar pursuits?
8   Mais said that his purpose in *The Hills* was 'to give the world a true picture of the real Jamaica and the dreadful conditions of the working classes'. How does he make his story appear true? Does he come across as an

impartial witness? Does knowledge of the historical facts about Jamaica up to 1950 help you to appreciate the novel better?

9 The *padre* comments that 'we make criminals out of men and women and children in the kind of society we are satisfied to put up with' (p. 238). Does the novel suggest that the people of the yard are incapable of choosing how to act? To what extent (if at all) does it invite us to pass moral judgement on them?

10 'Twenty centuries of Christ has not assuaged the world of violence' (p. 164). What part does religion play in the novel? Consider particularly the significance of the Sisters of Charity, and the beliefs (or unbelief) of Charlotta, Rema and Surjue.

11 'This is the story of man's life upon earth' (p. 184). How does Mais make his story of a particular time and place appear universal?

12 The cross-cutting between scenes and characters makes the novel at times seem almost like a film script. Consider how a film director might treat it if it were to be made into a film. Which characters would a director focus on? Write a film script based on the episode of the fight between Pattoo and Manny (pp. 114–17).

(iv) Creative approaches/curriculum links

1 The occupants of the yard sing an old slave-song (pp. 48–52). Find out about West Indian slave-songs that survive. What do they tell of the condition of the slaves? Can you compose a slave-song?

2 Look at William Hogarth's engravings of London life in the eighteenth century (*Gin Lane*, *Four Scenes of Cruelty*, *A Harlot's Progress*, etc.). What similarities do you find with Mais's description of yard life in Jamaica?

3 Take any passage in which the characters are speaking in Creole, and translate it into Standard English. What are the differences? Find out more about West Indian language and, in particular, the evolution of Creole. What does the history of the language tell you about the history of the people?

4 What role does religion play in the West Indies? Read a book on the subject e.g. Leonard Barratt's *The Sun and the Drum*, Heinemann Educational Books, 1976, and write short essays on voodoo, the Shouting Baptists (see the Spiritual Baptists in Unit 5, p. 37) and Rastafarianism.

5 Write to Amnesty International for information on political repression and torture in the Caribbean region and in South America. Compose a courteously worded letter to a particular government, expressing your horror at such practices, giving detailed reasons for your attitudes.

6 Zephyr is a prostitute. Imagine that you are Zephyr and write a story about a day in your life. Try to understand and explain the reasons for prostitution and the sordidness of the experience of such prostitution.

7 There are several references in the novel to the use of narcotic drugs. What do you know about such drugs? How and why are they harmful?

8 Are there slum areas in your locality? Investigate and, imagining yourself a journalist, write an article describing the condition of life in such slums.

Section F: Teaching Aids

(i) Audio-visual material

Rastaman (40 mins.), BBC/Time Life Films, 1977. Available from Concord Films, 201 Felixstowe Road, Ipswich, Suffolk. A powerful film on poverty in a Kingston slum, focusing on one family who live in a cardboard shack.

Jamaica (25 mins.), made for British television and available from Concord Films (as above). A film on poverty and unemployment in Jamaica that results in emigration from the country.

The Harder They Come (104 mins.), made in Jamaica in 1972, directed by Perry Henzell. Available from Blue Dolphin Film Distributors, 15–17 Old Compton Street, London W1. A famous film on rural and urban life in Jamaica, dealing with poverty, violence, corruption, commercialism and thwarted ambition.

(ii) Background reading

Horace Campbell, *Rasta and Resistance: Marcus Garvey to Walter Rodney*, Hansib Publications, 1986. A useful account of Rastafarianism in the Caribbean.

Elizabeth Mackie, *The Great Marcus Garvey*, Hansib Publications, 1987. Specially written for use in schools.

Katrin Norris, *Jamaica: The Search for an Identity*, Institute of Race Relations, Oxford University Press, 1962. A brief but lucid account of the social and cultural milieu during the first wave of the literary movements; suitable for sixth forms.

(iii) Critical bibliography

W. I. Carr, 'Roger Mais – Design from a Legend', *Caribbean Quarterly*, no. 13, 1967, pp. 3–28.

Jean D'Costa, *Roger Mais: 'The Hills Were Joyful Together' and 'Brother Man'*, Longman, 1978.

Daphne Morris, Introduction to *The Hills Were Joyful Together*, Heinemann Educational Books (Caribbean Writers Series), 1981.

Kenneth Ramchand, *The West Indian Novel and its Background*, Faber, 1970, pp. 179–88.

Karina Williamson, 'Roger Mais: West Indian Novelist', *Journal of Commonwealth Literature*, no. 1, 1966, pp. 138–47.

(iv) Reading links

Many West Indian novels deal with barrack-yard life and can be fruitfully compared with Mais's *The Hills*. The best of these are C.L.R. James's *Minty Alley* (1936) and Orlando Patterson's *The Children of Sisyphus* (1964). Both novels explore the themes of poverty, violence, class division and social injustice. The latter presents a sympathetic view of Rastafarian culture, showing how the common people struggle, in their daily actions and in their dreams, to escape from 'the worthless, lousy, dirty life' of a Kingston slum.

Slum dwellings in Kingston, Jamaica.

Unit 9
Merle Hodge: *Crick Crack, Monkey*

LIZ GERSCHEL

Section A:
Creative Approaches

Crick Crack, Monkey is a seminal novel. First published in 1970, one of the earliest novels by a Caribbean woman and based on personal experience, it reflects some of the roles and expectations of Caribbean women. It explores the changing sense of self of a girl growing up in rural Trinidad and then in the middle-class world of Port of Spain. Amusing and sometimes painful, capturing mood, event, countryside and character with vividness and vigour, it belongs to that group of powerful novels which explore, often at least partly autobiographically, the theme of childhood in the Caribbean, and is one of the very few to focus on the experiences of women. (For some suggested titles, see 'Reading links', Section F, p. 84.)

Merle Hodge sees the novel as part of a political expression that seeks to affirm Caribbean identity – 'part of a larger movement towards owning ourselves completely' – and her delineation of race and class relationships in Trinidad underpins the story of Tee as an individual. Tee internalizes the conflict between her African origins and the metropolitan values imposed on her through her Eurocentric education, and confirmed by Auntie Beatrice's mimicry of all things European. To resolve these tensions Tee, at first unwillingly and then consciously, rejects her African heritage and thus uproots herself from the life – forces that have

Merle Hodge, *Crick Crack, Monkey*, first published 1970; page references in this unit are to the Heinemann Educational Books (Caribbean Writers Series) edition, 1981.

given her strength. When she leaves the Caribbean for England Tee confirms this cultural dislocation with physical exile; the novel relates in this respect to the novels of exile and dislocation which are discussed in Unit 4, p. 25, in relation to Sam Selvon's *The Lonely Londoners*.

The novel covers about seven years in Tee's life. It starts with the death of her mother and the emigration of her father to England, leaving Tee and her little brother, Toddan, in the care of Tantie, her peasant class, paternal aunt. The first fifteen chapters span six years of Tee's life with Tantie in Santa Clara and her grandmother, Ma, in Pointe d'Espoir. During this time a battle for custody of the children continues between Tantie and their maternal aunt, Auntie Beatrice – The Bitch. Tee wins a scholarship to St Ann's High School and goes to live in Port of Spain with Auntie Beatrice and her family. The last nine chapters of the novel concentrate on the disintegration of her cultural identity and confidence, until Tee (now called Cynthia) and Toddan leave for England to join their father.

The structure invites comparisons and contrasts in the two life-styles, and the dynamic tension of the novel is in Tee's responses: school in the country and school in the town; relationships with neighbours in the country and with those in the town; the holidays at Pointe d'Espoir and at Canapo; going to Carnival; the White Ancestress and Ma's grandmother; Tee's early contempt for Carol and Jessica and her later awe of them; above all, the different approaches of Tantie and Auntie Beatrice to bringing up children, food, clothes, names, friendships, language, colour, morality, education and the proper role of girls.

Merle Hodge has written a number of articles on the role and socialization of girls and women and these form an element of the political background of the novel. One has the sense that part of her concern for the character she has created in Tee is linked to the fact that Tee is an intelligent girl whose scholarship offers her the chance of independence and social mobility. Whereas Tantie recognizes this, Auntie Beatrice's main aims for her daughters are to see them married off to fair-skinned men, no matter how unpleasant. (See Merle Hodge, 'Young Women and the Development of Stable Family Life in the Caribbean', *Savacou*, no. 13, 1977.) It is women who are the planners and the doers in *Crick Crack, Monkey* and whose interactions create the dynamic tension. In 'The Shadow of the Whip' (from *Is Massa Day Dead?*, 1974), Merle Hodge admits that her original intention had been to create a husband for Ma, but that 'even then I had conceived of him as an invalid in a rocking chair, ably looked after by Ma'.

Tantie and Ma both bring up children without male support. Neither of them is a heroic matriarch, but both reflect indomitable spirit, a characteristic born of necessity in Caribbean women and explored by Merle Hodge in 'Shadow of the Whip' and by Lucille Mathurin Mair in 'Reluctant Matriarchs' (*Savacou*, no. 13, 1977). Auntie Beatrice may be scathing about Tantie's morals, but Tantie's relationships with 'the Uncles' appear healthier and more joyous than the loveless marriage of Beatrice and Norman, and no more nor less motivated by economic necessity. Tantie is part of that tradition of Caribbean women whose strength and spirit are directed towards the care and betterment of children. Of the peasant class, she is unpretentious, gregarious, popular and shrewd: 'Tantie's company was loud and hilarious and the intermittent squawk and flurry of mirth made me think of the fowl-run when something fell into the midst of the fat hens' (p. 4). She loves the children with a passion and fights to keep them, but it is her concern for Tee's education which makes her send Tee to live with Auntie Beatrice. Tantie's children love her with the same passion and loyalty she has given them; it is no small part of Tee's unhappiness at the end of the novel that she feels guilty and ashamed of the gulf that has opened between her and Tantie.

Merle Hodge captures, in sharply-drawn scenes the warmth, humour and poignancy of the world of Caribbean childhood that Tee experiences. Her visits to her grandmother root Tee firmly and unquestioningly into what Merle Hodge sees as the real Caribbean culture – that of the working and peasant class. Ma's love of the land, her pride, and her memories of her own grandmother link Tee firmly with the African roots of Caribbean culture and help confirm Tee's values and sense of identity. Tee does not question her role in this world; she is very sure of her place in it and of her relationships with those around her. The worst to fear was one of Tantie's rampages or being caught by Mr Oliver, the irascible and child-hating school watchman. Even when Tee goes to school she accepts the sometimes baffling world of education that adults have devised, conscious that there are things she does not understand (religion; the geography of the West Riding of Yorkshire; the strange behaviour of her teachers) and some injustices (Mr Hinds's explosion at Duncey Joseph for reading 'grapes' as 'chenette'; Sir's whippings). Tee is nevertheless secure and happy within the noisy, protective and exuberant world that Tantie creates. Education is important as a means of social mobility towards a better life but equally important is pride in yourself – 'Jus' you remember you going there to learn *book* do' let them put no blasted shit in yu head' (p. 22–3). Tee has her great-great-grandmother's spirit and stubbornness and, so long as she is rooted into peasant culture, resists all attempts to break that spirit.

Nevertheless, one of Merle Hodge's prime concerns is the destructive influence of colonial education and metropolitan culture on the Caribbean (see Section C). The European influence of books and schooling is subconsciously undermining that confidence in her African heredity and Caribbean cultural background. The conflict within Tee, her personal tragedy, is that when she no longer has Tantie's presence to strengthen her, and under the 'perpetual assault' of Auntie Beatrice's middle-class pretensions, she is vulnerable to increasing self-distrust and shame; the culture she has previously enjoyed comes to seem uncouth and worthless, and she herself inferior. When Tee wins a scholarship to St Ann's and goes to Port of Spain, the change is as abrupt and disconcerting to the reader as to Tee. Through

Tee's eyes we see the sharp contrast between the companionable robustness of Tantie's home and the critical and discordant atmosphere, creating isolation and tension, within Auntie Beatrice's family. Auntie Beatrice devotes her life to aping metropolitan behaviour and distancing herself from her African roots and culture. Maintaining this distance is not always easy, as is shown at Carnival time:

> We went to the Stands on both days, where we sat primly and watched the bands in the company of the tourists and of the nice people who were in two minds about Carnival – saw the unmistakable niggeryness of the affair (real nigger-break-loose, said Bernadette) but were not able either to stay at home and extract themselves from it. (p. 85)

Class and colour prejudice in the Trinidadian society of the novel are interrelated and historically derived. White, Creole, African and Indian form separate cultural groups in a fragmented society, but the power and status are held by Whites and those who are nearest to the European ideal – usually the Creole middle class. African culture and people are seen by these as debased and valueless, a prejudice which Auntie Beatrice reflects within her own family in her attitude to Tee's mother's marriage and in her marked preference for her fairer daughters, Bernadette and Carol, over the dark-skinned Jessica (p. 83). Despite this, Auntie Beatrice is afraid of Mrs Harper, her cleaner, whose strength of character restates the independence and spirit of the black working class and whose moral values prove a sharp and ironic contrast to Auntie Beatrice's. Contemptuously dismissing a light-skinned boyfriend of Bernadette's much encouraged by her mother, Mrs Harper

> muttered about the lil' Pañol prostitute down in the Place-Sainte who had a chile o' every breed God make and couldn' tell yu which Yankee sailorman she make that pissin'-tail runt for – what these people wouldn' scrape-up outa the rubbish-truck to sharpen they gran'-chirren nose, eh! (p. 96)

That Auntie Beatrice also despises Indians – 'coolies' – is shown in her disapproval of Toddan's friend, Doolarie (p. 11) and of Mooney's wedding ('that simmy-dimmy') (p. 78). For further comment on Indians in Trinidadian society, see Section B: 'The Setting', p. 75.

Attitudes to food, closely reflective of culture, exemplify these prejudices; from Tee's horror at Uncle Sylvester's eating 'coolie-food' and saltfish in Auntie Beatrice's living room (p. 107) to the gross affectation of Auntie Beatrice's mimicry of metropolitan culture as she prepares a dinner party at Canapo

> complaining that there was no proper food to be got down here in this bush, barely a bottle of stuffed olives and a bag of potato crisps and as for things like Worcester sauce and French dressing well it was a good thing we'd brought our own supply of food that was all she could say. (p. 90)

A failing aspirant to higher social classes, ignored by her husband and despised by her children, lonely and culturally displaced, Auntie Beatrice attempts to show and gain from Tee the affection she is unable to give her own family, and to remould her in the metropolitan image. Tee is made to feel clumsy and inferior by her cousins – 'some lil relative Mommer found up in the country' (p. 81), and her crisis of identity begins with her isolation. She is sorry for Auntie Beatrice, dependent on her company and no longer able to resist attempts to impose new patterns of behaviour on her: gradually the self-confidence and un-selfconsciousness of her earlier childhood are eroded and replaced by shame and self-loathing.

The holiday at Canapo proves a critical point in this destructive process and in her relationship with Auntie Beatrice whose 'unwearying kindness' radically alters after what she sees as Tee's ingratitude and rejection of her. 'From then on it was a steep slope downhill. Auntie Beatrice announced her firm intention to haul me out of what what she termed alternately my ordinaryness and my niggeryness' (p. 95). When she slaps Auntie Beatrice's hand away, Tee breaks the strange symbiotic relationship between them; her sense of guilt and Auntie Beatrice's withdrawal of affection leave her more isolated then ever. Ironically, her instinctive act of self-preservation becomes inadvertently an act of self-destruction.

At the end of the novel, Tee cannot wait to leave Trinidad. Culturally alienated, out of place equally in Tantie's world and Auntie Beatrice's, England offers her an escape. Psychologically she is in flight from herself. Merle Hodge does not resolve Tee's conflict. Ironically, education for Tee has brought new social, economic and geographical horizons but has simultaneously destroyed her emotional security and cultural locus. Like Auntie Beatrice, she is trapped between a Caribbean peasant past and aspirations towards a metropolitan middle-class society into which she will neither comfortably fit nor willingly be accepted. She is doomed to the same self-distrust, cultural confusion and dislocation experienced by Auntie Beatrice, unless she can find her own identity. The novel has charted a process of destruction; its ending is realistic and unsentimental.

Part of Merle Hodge's success in representing the culture of Trinidad lies in her use of what Kenneth Ramchand calls 'orality'. The use of a first-person narrative voice allows her to move smoothly from standard Trinidadian English, used for much of the narrative, into recorded speech. In this way she integrates the dialect, tone and style of another character:

> Tantie raged all evening. An' she had a mind not to give us anything to eat because allyu belly must be done full wid that bitch ice-cream and sweetie. She raged and rampaged with no indication of subsiding. . . . She reiterated for the hundredth time what could have happened to us: we had jus' nearly get we arse kidnap!(p. 12)

Equally well she captures the affectedly Anglicized tones of Auntie Beatrice: 'Auntie Beatrice was saying on the phone that something *rorther* unexpected had turned up and couldn't Forther please come another day' (p. 106).

Merle Hodge has a sharp ear for the rhythms, range and imagery of Trinidadian speech, from the weighty cadences of Ma's biblical adaptations and maxims, to the graphic vigour of Tantie's rages:

> 'Hear how yu talkin through yu arse again, I ever put yu out? An' go down by yu mother an where she go put yu? On top the roof? Under the house? An' yu ain' shame yu reach a big long youngman an' she still dey ketchin she tail with the lil ol' – house falling – down on she head?' (p. 5)

She captures the rhetorical style of Sir, conveying

the pompousness of his 'discourses' with the passive voice, subordinate clauses piled one upon another and splendidly inverted sentences (Chapter 11). But equally skilfully, in the first chapter of the novel she suggests the simplicity of the young child: 'Then Papa went to sea. I concluded that what he had gone to see was whether he could find Mammy and the baby' (p. 3).

The imagery of the novel is sharp and confident. At the funeral, Auntie Beatrice 'tock-tocked into the room' with 'a voice like high heels and stockings' (p. 2). Later, Tee is conscious that 'the air was a green smell. The night seemed to be blowing like soft wind somewhere out beyond the edges of our patch of light' (p. 3). The images of the countryside symbolize the changes in Tee. Her description of Pointe d'Espoir – 'Ma's land was to us an enchanted country . . .' (p. 14) – where she feels rooted into the beauty and strength of the land, contrasts with her later sense of rootlessness and dislocation at Canapo:

> I was irritated at the sea. I considered it had no right to roll itself to and fro, to and fro, in such a satisfied manner, as though nothing at all was wrong. And the sea-birds and the jumbled footprints in the sand and the dead leaves insulted me, too. (p. 89)

Often startling, always apposite, Merle Hodge's images mark the depth and vigour of her writing.

Much of the humour of the novel is related to Merle Hodge's originality of image, to her ear for dialogue and to her ability to create an atmosphere in a few phrases and then equally quickly change it. Humour is a vehicle for her incisive social comment. All these characteristics, aspects of orality, are used by the calypsonians with powerful effect, to the same end as Merle Hodge, and the description of the use of humour in calypso can aptly be applied to her writing, too: 'The most effective political weapon in Trinidad . . . even when cleverly camouflaged with wit and banter, the sharp tang of social criticism is evident' (Albert Gomes, from Wenzell Brown, *Angry Men, Laughing Men*, 1947, p. 259). We see this at Auntie Beatrice's tea-party, European-style, a gathering of ladies and the priest, for which Tee and Toddan are 'all dressed up and brought forth', a phrase which in itself echoes a biblical tone:

Their talking was clipped-off at the edge, too, and every now and then they fell silent, when all you could hear were the chinking of cups on saucers and Auntie Beatrice's tittery-voice proposing more sponge cake. Then a chinking, tittery silence was devastated by Toddan's voice. 'Ooey!' he suddenly exclaimed, springing down from the lady's lap and pulling at his clothes. 'Take off this damn stupid pants, man! Ah want to ka-ka!' (p. 38)

The humour is not simply of farce. It lies also in the skill with which Merle Hodge has created sound effects at the polite, formal tea, through the use of short vowels, hard 't' and 'k' sounds and words like 'proposing', until Toddan's outburst, with its raucous repeated 'ah' sound, brings the everyday reality of bodily needs, slang and swearing to shatter the genteel atmosphere as effectively as smashing the delicate china might have done.

The title of the novel comes from the folk rhyme 'Crick Crack/Monkey Break 'e back/On a rotten pommerac' (p. 13), – traditionally a question and answer chanted to mark the end of a folk story or used ironically to indicate disbelief (p. 7). As a title it may well have been chosen for its commercial appeal, but its significance is in simultaneously recognizing the peasant culture of the Caribbean and marking the end of Tee's identification with it.

Section B: The Setting

Although Merle Hodge is not specific about time or location, Wayne Brown, reviewing the novel in the *Trinidad Sunday Guardian* (28 June 1970), locates Santa Clara, Tantie's village, as 'somewhere between San Juan and Arima'. The events of the novel take place in the 1950s. After his wife's death, Selwyn, Tee's father, goes to England like so many other West Indians in search of work, leaving Tee and her brother Toddan in the care of his sister, Tantie (Rosa).

Tee grows up with Tantie in Santa Clara, attending first the local Church of England elementary school, run by Mr Hinds (Coriaca RC), and then 'Big School', (Santa Clara RC), run by Mr

Thomas. When Tee goes to live with Auntie Beatrice she moves into Port of Spain itself, to attend St Ann's High School – most probably modelled on St Joseph's Convent.

Trinidad has probably the most ethnically mixed population of all the Caribbean islands. Originally inhabited by Amerindians, it came under European rule from the Spanish and the British. Large numbers of French, both white and free coloured, also came to the island, bringing with them their African slaves, markedly changing the economic and cultural life of Trinidad and having a lasting effect on the language. Tantie's name itself derives from the French *tante* (aunt), 'macommès and compès' (p. 111) are old friends, female and male, and the language of Carnival contains many French contributions; in some rural parts of Trinidad the language spoken is still a French-based Creole.

The emancipation in 1838 of the slaves who worked Trinidad's large sugar estates left plantation owners without a ready supply of cheap labour to work the land, the ex-slaves having overwhelmingly turned away from the plantations. From the middle of the nineteenth century Chinese and Indians were brought as indentured labourers, the Chinese then largely becoming small shopkeepers and traders, the Indians remaining as plantation labourers and peasant farmers, while the African Creoles moved towards the urban areas.

The rural Indians have tended to remain a separate community within Trinidadian society, maintaining their religions, language, food and customs, and are almost as large a percentage of the total population as are those of African origin. Whereas in many rural areas, like Santa Clara in the novel, the communities have begun to integrate, adopting each other's foods and religious festivals and sharing the Creole language (to which the Indians have contributed), in the towns there is still considerable prejudice between Africans and Indians. However, across all ethnic group boundaries cuts what Merle Hodge calls (in 'The Peoples of Trinidad and Tobago', in Anthony and Carr (eds.), *David Frost introduces Trinidad and Tobago*, 1975) the vertical tension of racism – the power structure that locates white and fair-skinned people at the top and black people at the bottom.

In *Crick Crack, Monkey* we find this history reflected in the novel. Tantie (Rosa) and Selwyn

Davis are peasant people of African descent. The village in which Tee grows up has developed around a sugar plantation ('the Estate'), and its population includes the working class, the lower middle class (like Mr and Mrs Hinds, Mr Thomas and the other teachers), and Mr Brathwaite, the owner of the estate. Amongst the peasant class there are also Indians with whom Tantie, Mikey and the children are close friends, Neighb' Ramlaal-Wife being involved in the barricade against 'the Bitch' (p. 10) and Doolarie, their daughter, being Toddan's close companion, much to Auntie Beatrice's disgust – 'You see how she has these coolie children running about with them?' (p. 11). There are also many 'off-stage' characters with Indian names. Tee's ability to imagine exactly what would be happening at Moonie's wedding, and the Indian influence on Tantie's cooking and Ma's sweet-making (bennay-balls, toolum, chilibibi, roti, dalpouri), reflect the closeness of the two communites. It is interesting to read Sam Selvon's novel *A Brighter Sun* (1952) and Michael Anthony's *Green Days by the River* (1967) for their explorations of the interrelationship between Indian and African Creole families.

In town, Auntie Beatrice and Uncle Norman are part of the brown-skinned Creole middle class. They are proud of their white ancestress, Elizabeth Helen Carter, and unquestioningly follow European fashion in clothes, food and behaviour. Living in a street where on one side of the house lives a middle-class man with a white wife, and on the other people from the lower class, probably black, with whom the children are not allowed to play (p. 33), Auntie Beatrice feels a constant pressure to maintain the distinctions of life-style that mark her and her family out as 'nice people', having 'risen above' the mass of the Creoles.

A further influence on Trinidad reflected in the novel comes from the United States bases at Chaguaramas and Wallerfield, set up in 1941. During the Second World War, Trinidad was an important naval and air base; the sudden arrival of thousands of US troops brought many changes. In general, the Americans were thought to be free with their money, and there was much competition among Trinidadians to be employed at the bases, as Mikey is. The Americans also brought their culture – from movies to chewing-gum – and Merle Hodge

pokes fun at the way Trinidadian teenagers imitate their American screen heroes (pp. 7–8). (This is superbly depicted in Michael Thelwell's *The Harder They Come*, Pluto, 1980, and in V. S. Naipaul's story 'Bogart' in *Miguel Street*, 1959 – see Unit 1, p. 1).

Being a 'been-to' (like Manhatt'n, p. 7) has a status in an island where emigration is often the only chance of economic improvement. Thus Mikey goes to the USA and Selwyn himself has remained in England. Eudora comes to Trinidad from a 'small island', Grenada, for the same economic reasons. At a time of widespread unemployment, when there seemed little hope of achieving a comfortable living for the majority of working-class people, most of whom were of African or Indian descent, it is not surprising that so many Trinidadians took to heart what they had had drummed into them at school – that England was the 'mother country' and that life in Europe was better than life in Trinidad – and emigrated. Very often both parents went away, sending back money to their families and intending either to return within a few years or, like Selwyn, to 'send for their children' later. The children were left meanwhile in the care of grandmothers, godmothers or aunts. The situation of women alone bringing up children (often not their own) is not uncommon in the Caribbean and is explored by Merle Hodge, Lucille Mathurin Mair and Edith Clarke (see 'Reading links', Section F, p. 83).

Section C: A Closer Look

(1) Chapter 4, (pp. 16–19)

Ma, Tee's grandmother, appears only once in the novel but is an important part of Tee's emotional security. She is an easily recognizable figure in the Caribbean, foster-mother, market-woman and still young and strong enough to work on the land. Earlier in the chapter Tee describes the peasant culture which frames Ma's daily life: story-telling round the fire at night, authoritative child care, good neighbourliness, cooking African and Indian sweetmeats for sale in the Sunday market, and a closeness to the land she works that makes Tee love it as she loves Ma. When Merle Hodge describes Ma greeting the day with a 'cheups' 'which expressed her essential attitude before the whole of existence' (p. 16), she is conveying not only Ma's fortitude and disdain for life's vagaries but also her African-ness, the 'cheups' being a characteristic of African communication, too, as Merle Hodge has recorded in the broadcast *Some Caribbean Writers*.

The links with Africa emerge through language: 'I was Ma's own-own bold-face Tee' (p. 19), the repetition 'own-own' being characteristic of the influence of West African languages on Creole syntax. They are also there in Ma's belief that Tee is 'her grandmother come back again' (p. 18). Ma's grandmother was an African, 'a tall straight proud woman', but enslaved. 'The People' – the white slave-owners – changed her name to 'Euphemia or Euph-something', by which Merle Hodge intends to suggest 'euphemism': 'a pretty name for something people think is ugly'. Ma's grandmother refuses to accept the 'Euph' name, so 'they had to give up in the end and call her by her true-true name'. Ma cannot remember her grandmother's true-true name, and ironically it is only at the very end of the novel that she remembers and wants it added to Tee's names (p. 110), but by then it is too late; Tee has become Cynthia and rejected her African heritage.

Changing names is a symbolic motif in the novel. In Africa your name is your soul, and using names gives the user power over the named. There are school names and home names. On her first visit to Port of Spain, Tee confronts Auntie Beatrice, who 'always called me "Cynthia", as if I were in school. And she always called Toddan "Codrington" and Toddan never knew she meant him. "It was your Auntie Beatrice who gave you that name, dear . . . " "He name Toddan," I informed her sharply. "Is I who name him"' (p. 36).

Ma's faith in her grandmother's strength from her African past equals her confidence in Tee as the strength and hope for the future: 'They'd never bent down her spirit and she would come back and come back and come back; if only she could live to see Tee grow into her tall proud straight grandmother' (p. 19). Although free and with greater opportunities than her great-great-grandmother ever had, Tee's spirit is not strong enough to resist cultural enslavement. Fittingly, Ma dies before she sees Tee's spirit bent down. Her death is a symbol of Tee's links with her African past being broken.

Merle Hodge varies the pace of her writing with consummate skill. The rush of movement as the children race about the yard 'like mad ants' before the rain 'pounding nearer, racing to catch us', the pandemonium, squeals and commotion, the crowded darkness under the coverlets, rain drumming on the galvanized roof and Ma's own mood of suppressed excitement as she brings special treats for the children (pp. 17 and 18) – all this stops as suddenly as the rain stops. Then, with Ma, they make a ritual visit to the river, and there is a sense of rebirth and renewal, combining worship of an old African god with the biblical story of Noah emerging after the Flood to see the new world and the rainbow: 'the bright air hanging out crisp and taut to dry, and the river ploughing off with the dirt and everything drenched and bowing and satisfied and resting before the world started up again from the beginning' (p. 18).

There is a sharp contrast later at Canapo, which, when they arrive, also promises a storm: 'brooding weather. . . . The sky hung low all around us and the sea was dark and forbidding . . . the cove was filled in with the same dense dark green fury as crowded down the steep slope of The Head, greenness like Ma's land' (p. 86). But it is not like Ma's land; it is neither soothing nor regenerative to Tee's troubled spirit: 'The Head was a monstrous enemy, it was in cahoots with the sea' (p. 94).

Although the narrative is told in the first person, it is not always presented through Tee's eyes as a child. At times Merle Hodge adopts a more adult view, as if Tee is writing with the experience of later years rather than recording events as they seemed at the time. She uses this distancing technique after the visit to the river, changing the focus from the intensity of Tee's involvement with the store and the flooded river to a panorama, so that 'all the holidays at Pointe d'Espoir were one August month', but capturing their mood in a startling and memorable image of the shimmering heat and stillness of noon: 'The cream air in the middle part of the day was like Time staring at itself in a mirror, the two faces locked dreamily in an eternal gaze' (p. 18).

(2) Chapter 13 (pp. 61–2)

'The whole of life was like a piece of cloth, with a rightside and a wrongside', says Tee philosophically, as Merle Hodge ironically examines the effects of literacy on her: 'Books transported you always into Reality and Rightness which were to be found Abroad.' Colonial education reflected only metropolitan culture and life-styles, so that what is real and right is 'the familiar solidity of chimneys and apple trees ... sleighing and snowmen', ludicrous on an island where such things could not be seen. The 'wrongside' of life is the everyday experience and culture of the Caribbean. Denied the validation of print, Caribbean culture is effectively negated. As Merle Hodge said in a radio interview:

> The problem in a country that is colonised ... is that the education system takes you away from your own reality ... turns you away from the Caribbean.... We never saw ourselves in a book, so we didn't exist in a kind of way and our culture and our environment, our climate, the plants around us did not seem real, did not seem to be of any importance – we overlooked them entirely. The real world was what was in books. Merle Hodge, *Some Caribbean Writers* (BBC Schools Radio, 3 April 1987).

Although Tee loves her holidays with Ma at Pointe d'Espoir, enjoys the beauty of the land, sea and river in all its moods and has feasted on the smells as Ma makes African and Indian sweets, she says of 'Helen', her fantasy double, 'the Real Me':

> She spent the summer holidays at the sea-side with her aunt and uncle who had a delightful orchard with apple trees and pear trees in which sang chaffinches and bluetits and where one could wander on terms of closest familiarity with cowslips and honeysuckle. Helen loved to visit her Granny for then they sat by the fireside and had tea with delicious scones and home-made strawberry jam. (p. 61)

'Helen's' life is a romantic pot-pourri of different bits from books, but the whole becomes more real to Tee than her own experience. Merle Hodge's ironic disapproval emerges in the use of capitals for heavy emphasis (reminding us of Sir's discourses), as it does in her choice of high-flown affectations such as 'delightful' and 'wander on terms of closest intimacy' and in the unseasonal combinations of flora and fauna.

The down-to-earth reactions of Tantie and Mikey to Tee's attempts to live out her fantasy emphasize its incongruity, but the long-term effects of de-Africanization and cultural dislocation are not so easily laughed away. Although Tee's first language, and the language of her friends and family, is Trinidadian English Creole, it is not spoken by 'real Girls and Boys' who 'called things by their proper names, never saying "washicong" for plimsoll and "crapaud" when they meant a frog' (p. 61). When working in a children's home in Denmark, Merle Hodge noted the confidence of the children: 'Nobody would say to them "You mustn't speak like that, that is not a good way to speak ... that is wrong, say it this way"' (*Some Caribbean Writers*, BBC *op. cit.*). As Frantz Fanon wrote in *Black Skin, White Mask* (Paladin, 1970, p. 13): 'To speak a language means above all to assume a culture, to support the weight of a civilization.' To replace 'washicong' with 'plimsoll' is to assume the language of the colonizers and to lose the immediacy and power of Caribbean culture.

People, too, are negated; neighbours, guardians and playmates – 'you were all marginal together'. 'Natives and Red Indians and things' are there 'for chuckles and for beating back', thus equating dark-skinned people with objects, ridicule, savagery and defeat. Merle Hodge brings this superbly modulated sixteen-line sentence to a splendidly ironic conclusion, on the prevalence of white faces 'whose exemplary aspect it was that shone forth' (like divine light?) on everything 'from macaroni to the kingdom of Heaven. ... Helen was outgrown and discarded somewhere, in the way that a baby ceases to be taken up with his fingers and toes' (p. 62). The change from parody and bathos in the quiet good sense of the final short sentence, with its implicit sense of 'growing up', marks Tee's return from flights of fancy to reality.

Section D: The Author

Merle Hodge wrote *Crick Crack, Monkey*, as yet her only novel, when she was twenty-five. She started it while she was working in a children's home in Denmark, impressed with the way the Danish children had a grasp of their own world, which she felt she had lacked as a child growing up in the colonial education system of the Caribbean. Talking recently, she said: 'When you have been through a school system like that, you don't really have a normal relationship with your environment, in the sense of the nature around and how the people live, their culture, the food they eat, the way they speak and all of that' (*Some Caribbean Writers, op. cit.*). The novel reflects her own childhood experiences. Her own family epitomizes the rapid upward social mobility that education brings in the Caribbean. Her grandmother, who had a profound influence on her, had been a servant in white households, but her own parents (a nurse and a civil servant) were sent to secondary school; Merle herself and her sisters went to university, so within three generations the 'class' of the family had entirely changed. There was, however, no equivalent to Auntie Beatrice and her family, whom Merle Hodge deliberately invented to illustrate class division.

She was born in Calcutta Settlement in 1944 and was educated in Trinidad, until in 1962 she won the Trinidad and Tobago Girls' Island Scholarship, which enabled her to go to London University. She studied French, got her BA in 1965 and combined her interests in language, Caribbean culture and sociology in her work for her M. Phil., which included translation of the poems of Leon Damas, the French Guyanese writer, and a study of the Négritude Movement. After graduating in 1967, Merle Hodge travelled widely, living in France, Denmark, Spain, Senegal and Gambia. Her interest in travel has since taken her throughout Europe, to the USA and the USSR. Her time away from the Caribbean developed in her a Caribbean consciousness, an experience she discusses in the interview quoted above and which helped her in framing *Crick Crack, Monkey*. Like other Caribbean writers 'in exile' she became aware both of rejection by the people of the 'mother country' and of

the distance between ourselves and these people who we thought we were part of.
. . . Another reason why we began to develop a consciousness of our worth as Caribbean people was that in England we met for the first time Africans. We were able to measure how much of our culture and attitudes had come from Africans. (*Some Caribbean Writers,* op. cit.)

In *Crick Crack, Monkey,* Merle Hodge explores the opposition of a European and a Caribbean culture based on African and also Indian values. Born in an area with a large Indian population, she also questions the mutual prejudice that exists between African Creole and Indian communities in Trinidad, which she sees as socially and politically divisive in the struggle against the remains of colonialism. A linguist and a sociologist, particularly concerned with the roles and relationships of men and women in the Caribbean, she has contributed widely to various journals and continues to be closely involved in education for change.

In 1970 *Crick Crack, Monkey* was published, and Merle Hodge returned to Trinidad, first to teach West Indian literature, French and English at a Port of Spain high school, then to lecture in French Caribbean and French African literature at the University of the West Indies, Mona, Jamaica. Politically active, she taught in Grenada and worked with Chris Searle on a government information paper, *Is Freedom We Makin'*, before the death of Maurice Bishop. She is now lecturing at UWI, St Augustine, Trinidad, and, despite all pressures to bring out 'a sequel' or at least another novel, has written only some (unpublished) stories, as far as fiction is concerned.

Section E: Classroom Use

(i) *Level of use*

Crick Crack, Monkey is suitable for classroom use with fourth years upwards. It could equally well be used for GCSE or at A-level. Although it merits intensive study, the novel is also sufficiently accessible to appeal to less literary readers, and its episodic structure, humour and school-focus will appeal to students aged 14–18. Particular chapters in the novel could be read with pupils in the second or third year, as distinct episodes or as part of wider themes: Chapter 4 (living with Ma); Chapter 5 (starting school); Chapters 8–12 ('Big School', Mr Oliver the watchman, children's games and rivalries, Sir's classroom, raiding the estate).

Various episodes could be used for drama work: pp. 74–7 (joining the dancing class); pp. 41–3 (complaining to Ling about the nails and pebble in the flour); pp. 90–1 (the cancelled dinner party).

(ii) Points of focus and emphasis

1   Education and schools:
- scramble for a place at school, pp. 20–8;
- enthusiasm for learning, pp. 20, 23, 61;
- Sunday school, pp. 6, 30;
- Coriaca church school; Mr and Mrs Hinds, pp. 7, 22–9;
- Santa Clara RC school ('Big School'); Mr Thomas, pp. 55–6, 57, 59; Teacher Iris, p. 44; Teacher Gloria, pp. 45–6; Sir, pp. 46, 54–6, 60–1, 67;
- St Ann's RC High School; Mrs Wattman, pp. 73–4, 83, 97–8, 110;
- dancing class; Miss de Vertueil, pp. 74–7.

2   Growing up in the country:
- with Ma, Chapter 4;
- shopping at Ling's, pp. 40–3;
- going to watch the steel bandsmen and liming, pp. 6–8;
- games: with Mikey, p. 6; at Ma's, pp. 15–16, 17; teasing Mr Oliver, Chapter 9; inter-school rivalries, Chapter 10; raiding the estate, pp. 57–8;
- going to Carnival, pp. 85–6;
- Moonie's wedding, pp. 78–9;
- closeness with neighbours, Chapter 1, pp. 10, 14, 22.

3   Growing up in the town:
- dancing classes, pp. 74–7;
- going to church, pp. 77–8;
- weekends, pp. 80–1;

- going to Carnival, pp. 85–6;
- watching people pass, pp. 99–100;
- relationships with neighbours, pp. 33, 37, 100;
- Eudora and Mrs Harper, Chapters 6, 20, 22.

4   Contrasts and balances:
- names, pp. 19, 34, 36, 52, 70, 110;
- food, pp. 9, 15, 66, 79, 90, 94–5, 103–4, 106–7;
- hair-combing, pp. 18, 84;
- clothes, pp. 18, 34, 62, 72, 77, 85, 88, 108;
- swimming, pp. 6, 14, 88;
- first visit to cousins, pp. 31–4; and later awe of them;
- returning home, pp. 38, 108, 110;
- bringing up children, pp. 12, 15, 32, 34, 38, 71, 77, 83–4, 87–8, 95, 97, 103–4, 107;
- shopping, pp. 40–1, 89–90.

5   Identity:
- early security with Tantie;
- closeness to Ma and to the land, Chapter 4;
- Tee as her great-great-grandmother 'come back again' and true-true name, p. 19;
- confidence of first visit to cousins, pp. 31–4;
- similarity to Tantie (rebelliousness, defiance and swearing), pp. 59-60;
- identification with and rejection of 'Helen', pp. 61–2;
- insecurity at Auntie Beatrice's and sense of inadequacy ('ordinaryness and niggery-ness'), p. 95;
- contempt from cousin, Chapter 16, p. 80;
- shame and guilt related to portrait of Elizabeth Helen Carter and her own mother's marriage, pp. 81–2, 104;
- sense of inferiority at school, pp. 72–4, Chapter 21;
- rejection by Auntie Beatrice, Chapter 19;
- self-negation (desire to be like Dash), p. 97;
- shame and embarrassment at seeing Tantie and Toddan, Chapter 23, p. 111;
- desire to run away; guilt, Chapter 24;
- embarrassment at farewell party; desire for flight, p. 111.

6   Class/race consciousness:
- anti-Indian prejudice, pp. 11, 78, 106;
- anti-African-Creole prejudice, pp. 29, 74, 77, 83, 95, 100;
- prejudice   towards   white/fair-skinned,

pp. 37, 80–2, 87, 98, 105;
- Eurocentricism, pp. 24, 25-6, 30, Chapter 13.

7 Roles of men in the novel:
- Mikey, Chapter 2, pp. 28, 40, 43, Chapter 14, p. 66;
- the 'Uncles', pp. 4–5, 37, 106–7;
- Uncle Norman, pp. 11, 71–2, 82–3, 86;
- Selwyn, pp. 3, 39, 64–5, 109, 110.

8 Roles of women:
- child-carer: Tantie, Ma, Auntie Beatrice;
- market-women/trader: Ma, Mis' Dorothea;
- small farmer: Ma;
- teacher: Mrs Hinds, Teacher Gloria, Teacher Iris, Mrs Wattman, Miss de Vertueil;
- servant: Eudora, Mrs Harper;
- nun: Sister Columba and others.

9 Humour:
- child's understanding of adult world, pp. 1, 23;
- paradox ('Big School' was no place for little children), p. 44;
- bathos, p. 24;
- parody, Chapters 11, 13;
- satire, p. 62;
- irony, p. 48;
- Tantie's language throughout, eg. p. 63;
- comedy of situation, p. 5, 7, 38, 42–3, 60–1;
- comedy through characterization: Mr Oliver, Mrs Harper, Eudora, Manhatt'n.

10 Language:
- standard Trinidadian English narrative;
- Tantie's Creole;
- French and Indian influences on language;
- individual language patterns and accents: Manhatt'n, p. 7; Eudora's Grenadian, pp. 34–6; Ling's Chinese, pp. 41-3; the rhetoric of Sir and Mr Hinds; affected accents of Bernadette and Tante Beatrice, p. 80;
- imagery.

(iii) Questions for essay writing or classroom discussion

1 Tee says at one point: 'At times I resented Tantie bitterly for not having let Auntie Beatrice get us in the first place and bring us up properly.' Do you think it would have been better or worse for Tee if she had been brought up by Auntie Beatrice from the start? Why?

2 'Auntie Beatrice symbolizes the colonized middle class, Tantie the peasant resistance in Trinidadian society.' Discuss this statement using evidence from the novel, and explain Tee's position.

3 Reread Chapter 6, where Tee first goes to stay with Auntie Beatrice, and Chapter 16, where she returns. Compare the two – why are they different?

4 Identify the ways in which Tee's confidence in herself was undermined when she went to live with Auntie Beatrice. Make a list of examples.

5 Tee's memories of her early childhood are largely happy. She describes Tantie's warmth and her rampages as if life with Tantie is dramatic but fun. Choose two scenes which illustrate this and comment on them.

6 In Chapter 16 (p. 72) Auntie Beatrice says: '"You don't hear how these children talk to me, Norman, you don't hear anything at all in this house." Uncle Norman eyed her curiously and sat down to finish his food.' Describe Auntie Beatrice's family and their relationships with her and with each other.

7 Explore and explain, as far as you can, the changes in Auntie Beatrice's attitude to Tee during the novel.

8 Tee loved her holidays with Ma at Pointe d'Espoir. What did she learn from Ma? Compare her relationship with Ma to her feelings about 'the white ancestress', Elizabeth Helen Carter. Why is Ma's death especially significant for Tee?

9 This novel has been criticized for presenting a very negative picture of men. Write about the men in the novel and the roles they play.

10 Although there is a first-person narrative, sometimes Merle Hodge seems to be writing as an adult author and sometimes through the eyes of a child. Choose two examples of each narrative style and say why you think they are effective in their context.

11   One of the reasons for the novel's success is its humour, which ranges from satire, irony and parody to farce and Tantie's vivid descriptive powers. Write about the humour of the novel and refer to any episodes that you really enjoyed.

12   Merle Hodge uses Standard English and different dialects of Trinidadian English to make a rich and varied language pattern in the novel. Pick out some examples and use them to comment on Merle Hodge's use of language to reflect what Kenneth Ramchand has called 'orality' (representing the spoken language of the Caribbean people on the printed page).

13   Merle Hodge was one of the first Caribbean women to publish a novel. How does her perception of life as a Caribbean woman influence the novel?

14   Tee says in Chapter 5 (pp. 20 and 23): 'I looked forward to school. ... I had come to this place to read and write and all the other mysteries one performed at school.' The three schools she attended all failed her in different ways. Discuss Tee's experience of schooling.

15   Colour and class prejudice underpin much of what happens in this novel. How does it show itself? Choose three examples and analyse them.

16   Why do you think Merle Hodge called the novel *Crick Crack, Monkey*? Is it a good title in your opinion?

17   Compare *Crick Crack, Monkey* with any other novels of childhood you have read. (You may find the list of Caribbean novels of childhood given in 'Reading links' Section F, p. 84, helpful.)

18   The novel seems to end without any sense of Tee's being able to resolve her dilemma. Do you find this a satisfactory ending?

19   Discuss the ironies in the following remark of Auntie Beatrice's about Tantie and Toddan: "What can that woman teach him, a woman with no culture, no breeding, no sense of right and wrong herself, what can she teach the child, I will live to see him spurn that woman and blush at her name, mark my words" (p. 95).

20   Discuss the symbolic use of (a) names and (b) food in the novel.

(iv) Creative approaches/curriculum links

1   Draw up a chart showing the direct contrasts between Tee's way of life with Tantie and with Auntie Beatrice. You might use headings like holidays, food, clothes, Carnival, names, family relationships, friends.

2   Tee feels torn between two different ways of life. What effect does this have on her? Have you ever felt like this? Write a story or poem about someone who feels torn between two different ways of life.

3   If you had been Tee, how would you have coped with living at Auntie Beatrice's house, given that you wanted to go to St Ann's School? Write or act out a short scene that shows what you would have done in one of the situations Tee found herself in.

4   Some of Tee's ideas change because she is growing up. Have your ideas changed as you have grown up? Discuss this with your group.

5   Auntie Beatrice says she spends her life 'teaching my children to be decent, teaching them what is important'. What do you think Auntie Beatrice was trying to teach them? Did she succeed? What do you think 'being decent' is, and what do you think it is important to teach children? Discuss this in a group and then make a list together of ten rules for bringing up children.

6   Choose any incident in which Auntie Beatrice is involved and write a diary entry as if you were her. Try to use the evidence in the novel to show her thoughts and feelings.

7   At the end of the novel, Tantie has lost Ma, Mikey, Toddan and Tee – all the people who mean most to her. Imagine her five years later, remembering that time and telling a friend all about it. Write or tell it, as a dramatic monologue. You may also want to read Frank Collymore's poem 'Ballad of an Old Woman' (*New Ships*, Oxford University Press, 1975), which fits in very well.

8   At the end of the novel Tantie says: 'Drink one on Rosa, she takin she own chirren an sendin them up in the cold, for what to do?' Write the letter that Tantie must have written to her brother Selwyn in England. If you can, use

Tantie's dialect, but don't worry if you can't, the most important thing is to show her feelings and reasons.

9 Older people have often acquired a lot of wisdom, and sometimes, like Ma, they pass it on to the young. What did Tee learn from her grandmother, Ma? Have you ever learnt something important from an older person? Write about it if you can. You can turn it into a story if you want to.

10 It seems at the end of the novel that Tee has accepted the world of Auntie Beatrice and its values. Imagine that you are Tee, filling in your journal on the plane to England; write about your feelings, hopes, fears and thoughts.

11 What do you think will happen to Tee when she and Toddan go to live with her father? Talk to anyone you know who has come to England from another country and ask them how it felt. You may find it useful to read *Our Lives* (ILEA English Centre, 1979) *Motherland* (Heinemann, 1984) or *So This Is England* (Peckham Publishing Project, 1984). Use your imagination, your own experience and any information you can find to write a really good story about what happens to Tee and Toddan.

12 The early chapters of the novel are based on Tee's memories of important events in her childhood, although she hasn't always understood exactly what was happening. Do you remember any events in your own childhood which seemed very important – although perhaps confusing – at the time? Try to write about them, showing what you understood at the time and what you later realized about the event(s). You could do this in two parts, using childish language for the first and the more grown-up language that you use now for the second part.

13 Find some examples of Trinidadian words and ways of saying things that are different from Standard English. Try to find out where the words come from; you will notice that some are French, some Indian and some African in origin. You could make a chart with the Trinidadian word or expression in one column and the Standard English translation in another. If you want you could make a third column for your own dialect words and expressions.

14 Make a list of Trinidadian proverbs or rhymes and find out what they mean.

15 Try to write either a story in which the narrative is in Standard English and the dialogue is in another dialect or a play using dialect. Discuss with your friends whether it sounds right and what is the best way of writing down a particular word or sound, before you write the final draft. You might like to read your stories and plays aloud or record them into a tape-recorder.

16 Make a list of the foods mentioned in the novel. See if you can find out what they are and how they are cooked. Illustrate your work with photographs or drawings.

17 Find and read (or make a tape of) some of the stories that Ma might have told; they would have been Anancy stories, folk stories and ghost stories. There should be some Caribbean stories in your school library to help you.

18 Make a family tree for Tee.

Section F: Teaching Aids

(i) *Audio-visual material*

Interviews

Some Caribbean Writers, BBC Schools Radio, 3 April 1987. Merle Hodge reads and talks about the novel.

National Identity in our Literature, NCC Radio, 1973. Published, ed. Anson Gonzalez, as *Trinidad and Tobago Literature on Air*, National Cultural Council of Trinidad and Tobago, 1974. Largely readings from the novel.

Films

La Rue Cases-Nègres (106 mins.), Director: Euzhan Palcy, 1983. Excellent film about a boy growing up on plantation in Martinique in 1930s with his grandmother and going to *lycée*; shows schooling and village life in colonial times. Based on the book of same name by Joseph Zobel, translated into English as *Black Shack Alley*, Heinemann Educational Books (Caribbean Writers Series), 1980. Film available from Artificial Eye, 211 Camden High Street, NW1 7BT (16 mm or 35 mm; £50).

(ii) Background reading

Bridget Brereton, *A History of Modern Trinidad, 1783–1962*, Heinemann Educational Books, 1981: pp. 96–116, the newcomers (1838–1917); pp. 117–35, the development of Creole society (1838–1938); pp. 177–98, the emergence of modern Trinidad (1936–50); pp. 205–14, traditional estate agriculture in the twentieth century; pp.223–7, finding a cultural identity.

Steve Garner, *The Caribbean: Trinidad and Tobago, Jamaica, Barbados, Guyana*, Hansib Publications, 1987/8. Specially written for secondary schools.

Lennox Honeychurch, *The Caribbean People*, Nelson Caribbean, 1981, pp. 99–108.

George Lamming, *The Pleasures of Exile*, Michael Joseph, 1960, pp. 38–46.

John Mendes (comp.), *Cote-ce Cote-là: Trinidad and Tobago Dictionary*, Trinidad and Tobago: Syncreators, 1985.

Kenneth Ramchand, *The West Indian Novel and its Background*, 2nd edn, Heinemann Educational Books, 1983.

Keith Warner, *The Trinidad Calypso*, Heinemann Educational Books, 1982, pp. 59–89.

The role of women in the Caribbean

Edith Clarke, *My Mother Who Fathered Me*, Allen & Unwin, 1966.

Lucille Mathurin Mair, 'Reluctant Matriarchs', *Savacou*, no. 13, 1977.

Lucille Mathurin Mair, *The Rebel Woman in the British West Indies*, Institute of Jamaica, 1975.

'Scholarships for Girls', editorial, *The Beacon*, 8 November 1931. Refers to the beginning of scholarships at St Joseph's Convent (St Ann's in the novel).

(iii) Critical bibliography

There is very little published on Merle Hodge's *Crick Crack, Monkey*. One of the most useful analyses is the introduction by Roy Narinesingh to the Heinemann Caribbean Writers Series edition of the novel. Other helpful articles are:

Wayne Brown, 'Growing up in Colonial Trinidad' (review), *Trinidad Sunday Guardian*, 28 June 1970, pp. 6 and 17.

D. Dabydeen and N. Wilson-Tagoe, 'Women Writers', in *A Reader's Guide to West Indian and Black British Literature*, Hansib Publications, 1988.

Leota S. Lawrence, 'Three West Indian Hercines', *College Language Association Journal* (Atlanta), no. 21, 1977.

Marjorie Thorpe, 'The Problem of Cultural Identification in *Crick Crack, Monkey*', *Savacou*, no. 13, 1977.

(iv) Reading links

Other writings by Merle Hodge (not a comprehensive list)

'The Shadow of the Whip', in Orde Coombs (ed.), *Is Massa Day Dead?: Black Moods in the Caribbean*, Anchor/Doubleday, 1974. A comment on male–female relationships in the Caribbean.

'Male Attitudes in Caribbean Family Life', *New Vision* (Trinidad) vol. 1, no. 1, January/March 1974.

'The Peoples of Trinidad and Tobago', in Michael Anthony and Andrew Carr (eds), *David Frost introduces Trinidad and Tobago*, Deutsch, 1975. On the relationship between different ethnic groups.

'Young Women and the Development of Stable Family Life in the Caribbean', *Savacou*, no. 13, 1977.

Is Freedom We Makin': The New Democracy in Grenada (with Chris Searle), Government Information Service, Grenada, 1981.

Other novels of Caribbean childhood

Michael Anthony, *The Year in San Fernando*, Deutsch, 1965; Heinemann Educational Books (Caribbean Writers Series), 1970.

Michael Anthony, *Green Days by the River*, Deutsch, 1967; Heinemann Educational Books (Caribbean Writers Series), 1973.

Austin Clarke, *Among Thistles and Thorns*, Heinemann, 1965.

Geoffrey Drayton, *Christopher*, 1959; Heinemann Educational Books (Caribbean Writers Series), 1972.

Zee Edgell, *Beka Lamb*, Heinemann Educational Books (Caribbean Writers Series), 1982. About girls' experience.

George Lamming, *In the Castle of My Skin*, Michael Joseph, 1953; Longman (Drumbeat), 1979.

Ian McDonald, *The Humming-Bird Tree*, Heinemann, 1969; Heinemann Educational Books (Caribbean Writers Series), 1974.

Grace Nichols, *Whole of a Morning Sky*, Virago, 1986. About girls' experience.

Sam Selvon, *A Brighter Sun*, Alan Wingate, 1952; Longman (Caribbean Writers), 1985.

Joseph Zobel, trans. Keith Warner, *Black Shack Alley (La Rue Cases-Nègres)* Heinemann Educational Books (Caribbean Writers Series), 1980.

Other related writing

Michael Anthony, *King of the Masquerade*, Nelson/Tamarind, 1974. Middle-class boy, helped by maid, takes part in Carnival.

Lorna Goodison, *I Am Becoming my Mother*, New Beacon, 1986. Excellent collection of poetry; encapsulates black women's experience.

V. S. Naipaul, *Miguel Street*, Deutsch, 1959; Penguin, 1971; Heinemann Educational Books (Caribbean Writers Series), 1974.

V. S. Naipaul, *A House for Mr Biswas*, Deutsch, 1961; Penguin, 1969.

Michael Thelwell, *The Harder They Come*, Pluto, 1980.

On the experience of coming to Britain from the Caribbean

Elyse Dodgson, *Motherland: West Indian Woman to Britain in the 1950s*, Heinemann, 1984.

Errol O'Connor, 'Jamaica Child', in *Our Lives: Young People's Autobiographies*, ILEA English Centre, 1979.

Peckham Publishing Project, *So This Is England*, 1984.

Joan Riley, *The Unbelonging*, Women's Press, 1985.

Samuel Selvon, *The Lonely Londoners*, Alan Wingate, 1956; Longman (Drumbeat), 1979.

Two of the magnificent buildings lining the Savannah, Port of Spain (Vicky Unwin).

Unit 10
Derek Walcott: *Ti-Jean and his Brothers* and *Dream on Monkey Mountain*

JOHN THIEME

Section A: Critical Approaches

Ti-Jean and his Brothers (1958) and *Dream on Monkey Mountain* (1967) are plays which explore the nature of West Indian identity and at the same time fuse a broad range of cultural influences to produce a distinctively West Indian drama. So the identity quest which lies at the heart of the plays' thematic concerns is complemented by a parallel quest for a local dramatic aesthetic. The plays are an attempt to emancipate Caribbean theatre from the stultifying influence of the European tradition and to create a drama rooted in the landscape and society of the region, while also drawing on a wide variety of outside forms. These include the Japanese Noh and Kabuki theatres, Shakespearean tragedy, North American expressionism (particularly O'Neill), Brechtian epic theatre, European absurdism (particularly Genet) and the new African drama of playwrights such as Soyinka. Linking these diverse influences is an overriding concern with the ritual and mimetic aspects of drama, and the West Indian folk tradition looms largest of all. Walcott's treatment of the identity quest is similar; he explores the various ancestral strains which have shaped the West Indian psyche and concludes that it is a product of the heterogeneous forces which have gone into its

Derek Walcott, *Dream on Monkey Mountain and Other Plays* (includes both plays); page references in this unit are to the Jonathan Cape edition, 1972.

making. However, within the plays those elements which are most clearly identifiable as African or European are forced to yield pride of place to elements which emanate more directly from the Caribbean landscape and its folk traditions.

Thus form and content work together to suggest that the true strength of West Indian culture and society can emerge only from cultural cross-pollination within the local landscape. In 'What the Twilight Says: An Overture', his introductory essay to the volume of plays in which *Ti-Jean* and *Dream on Monkey Mountain* first appeared, Walcott refers to 'the writer making creative use of his schizophrenia', and this admirably sums up his own practice in the two plays. Like Makak, the protagonist of *Dream on Monkey Mountain*, he transcends the potentially divisive qualities of a mixed racial and cultural heritage by fusing them together.

Both plays readily lend themselves to interpretation as allegories of the West Indian situation. However, they do far more than simply attempt to transfer an observed social reality on to the stage. They employ non-naturalistic techniques – a folk form in *Ti-Jean* and an expressionist dream structure in *Dream on Monkey Mountain* – from which a vision of West Indian creativity and potential gradually emerges.

Ti-Jean and his Brothers is on the surface a fairly straightforward dramatization of a St Lucian folk tale, which has its counterpart in other areas of the world. It is a tale of three brothers, each of whom must in turn do combat with the Devil. A comment in 'What the Twilight Says' makes it clear that Walcott was fascinated by the myth at an early age, not only because of its content, but also because of its structure:

> They sang of children lost in the middle of a forest, where the leaves' ears pricked at the rustling of devils, and one did not know if to weep for the first two brothers of every legend, one strong, the other foolish. All these sank like a stain. And taught us symmetry. The true folk tale concealed a structure as universal as the skeleton, the one armature from Br'er Anancy to King Lear. It kept the same digital rhythm of three movements, three acts, three moral revelations, whether it was the tale of three sons or of three bears, whether it ended in tragedy or happily ever after. (pp. 23–4)

Ti-Jean is the legend of three sons dramatized in a form which initially seems to have more affinity with the tale of Goldilocks and the Three Bears or an Anancy story than with *King Lear*. Each of the three brothers has to answer the Devil's challenge to try to make him feel anger. Success will bring a bowlful of sovereigns and a wish granted; failure will result in being eaten by the Devil. Gros Jean, the eldest, who relies on brute force, and Mi-Jean, the middle brother, who is foolishly enraptured with rhetoric and philosophy, both fail. Ti-Jean (Petit, or Little Jean), the youngest, succeeds because he relies on instinct and common sense.

The play preserves the mythic quality of the legend, but invests it with layers of allegory. The Devil is identified with a colonial Planter and also with Papa Bois (or Father Forest), a traditional figure representative of folk wisdom. The play is clearly not only about the dispossessed West Indian peasantry's fight for survival. It also charts the movement towards a post-colonial consciousness and the West Indian artist's quest for a tradition. This third level of allegory helps to explain why the Devil is equated with Papa Bois as well as with the Planter; both are seen as exercising a stultifying influence on the West Indian imagination. In the final speech of the play, the Frog, who has a choric role, says:

> And so it was that Ti-Jean, a fool like all heroes, passed through the tangled opinions of this life, loosening the rotting faggots of knowledge from old men to bear them safely on his shoulder. (p. 166)

So folk wisdom is rejected as a body of ossifying information, which can inhibit personal growth; but myth is accepted as a legacy to be taken over and metamorphosed. The emphasis is on transformation rather than statically conceived bodies of mythology.

Gros Jean represents the view that direct confrontation is the way to overcome the iniquities of Caribbean society. His belief that 'might is right' makes him seem like a military rebel, but at one point the Devil refers to him as 'a sort of politician' (p. 128). Mi-Jean represents the semi-educated West Indian, brainwashed by the colonial educational curriculum, and also perhaps stands for those Caribbean artists who have totally adopted the metropolitan standard. Ti-Jean, in contrast, is the ordinary West Indian who relies on instinct and common sense, values familial and religious bonds and maintains a reverential attitude to his natural surroundings. Unlike his brothers he is sympathetic to the creatures of the forest, and they consequently aid him as he goes to meet the Devil. He is not, however, simply a flat exemplar of virtue. If the play has the structure of an Anancy story, Ti-Jean himself has many of the attributes of Anancy, the spiderman-trickster of Akan folklore whom the slaves of the Middle Passage brought to the New World with them and who may be seen as a symbol of the ordinary West Indian's descent to subterfuge to ensure survival. Ti-Jean realizes the danger of playing the Devil at his own game and consequently employs trickery to give himself a fair chance.

Other aspects of the play which deserve careful consideration include the figure of the Bolom, whose emergence into life at the end would also seem to represent the transformation of old folk superstitions and the birth of a new West Indian consciousness, which has hitherto been stifled, and the employment of the chorus, Caribbean story-telling conventions, music and dance, and a variety of theatrical traditions (see the analysis of Prologue, in Section C, p. 89).

Dream on Monkey Mountain is written in a much more complex dramatic mode than *Ti-Jean*. Walcott's 'production note' says that 'The play is a dream, one that exists as much in the given minds of its principal characters as in that of its writer' (p. 208). Initially the psychodrama seems to be that of the central figure, Makak, but ultimately it is a product of the collective unconsciousness of all the characters. Together, as the epigraphs to the two parts (taken from Sartre's prologue to Fanon's *Wretched of the Earth*) indicate, they represent the disassociated West Indian psyche, pulled two ways by the schizophrenia which lies at the heart of colonialism.

Once again the form leans heavily on ritual and symbolic elements. The play opens with an elaborate mime in which setting, lighting, movement, dance and song are combined to outline the main themes. This mime gives way to a call-and-response lament sung by a Conteur (tale-teller) and chorus, which introduces the audience to the situation of the black charcoal-burner Makak, arrested and in jail for having been drunk and disorderly. So before the narrative begins, the action has been located in first a non-verbal and then an oral folk context. This opening scene is, along with the Epilogue, the most naturalistic in the play, but even here there are strong symbolic elements; Makak's situation in jail is a metaphor for the mental situation induced by the colonial psychology, and a mock-trial conducted by the Corporal who is his jailer and two fellow-prisoners (suggestive of the two thieves crucified with Christ) parodies Jesus's appearance before Pilate and thus establishes Makak as some kind of messianic figure.

The long central section of the play deserts any semblance of naturalism for the expressionist structure of the dream. Initially the dream seems to be Makak's vision of a White Goddess figure, a European Muse who, paradoxically, instils in him a belief that he must act as the redeemer of his race by leading them back to Africa. He descends from his home on Monkey Mountain, performs acts of healing and acquires a reputation as a messianic deliverer. He is imprisoned, escapes from jail after wounding the Corporal and returns to the mountain in the company of his two fellow-prisoners. Back on Monkey Mountain, Makak appears deranged. With the two felons humouring his madness in different ways, and Makak realizing he has been a 'king among shadows' (p. 304), this episode seems strongly redolent of *King Lear*. It ends with the 'Apotheosis' scene (Part II, scene 3; see the analysis in Section C), which culminates

with Makak's beheading of the apparition of the White Goddess and apparently achieving psychological liberation as a result.

In the Epilogue, Makak awakes from the dream to find himself still in prison. Hitherto he has been called only Makak (or Monkey), but now he moves beyond being a mimic man, aping European or African modes of behaviour, and is given an individual name, Felix Hobain. The play ends with his realizing:

> Lord, I have been washed from shore to shore, as a tree in the ocean. The branches of my fingers, the roots of my feet, could grip nothing, but now, God, they have found ground. . . . Now this old hermit is going back home, back to the beginning, to the green beginning of this world. (p. 326)

The image of the uprooted tree strongly suggests the legacy of the Atlantic slave trade, but the conclusion argues against a return to Africa. 'Home' for Makak is the Caribbean landscape from which he has come and it is now viewed as a place of Edenic promise which offers a new beginning. This notion is in keeping with Walcott's belief that historical determinism must be rejected in favour of an aesthetic in which the New World artist creates the Americas anew through an Adamic vision. As in *Ti-Jean*, the quest for a Caribbean identity is enacted on the level of form as well as theme. With the beheading of the European Muse who has stirred up African atavism, the two levels combine to plead for a distinctively Caribbean tradition.

Though Makak is the central figure of *Dream on Monkey Mountain*, the identity quest is also played out in the minds of other characters. Makak's partner Moustique acts as a Sancho Panza to his Don Quixote, since he is as much a pragmatist as Makak is an idealist. When in the central scenes he exploits Makak's messianic appeal by pretending to be him, he may be regarded either as an opportunist who sells the dream or as an Anancy, who justifiably seizes the material opportunities it offers.

Corporal Lestrade, a vivid study in the negative aspects of cultural schizophrenia, provides another interesting foil to Makak. Named after the bumbling Scotland Yard inspector of the Sherlock Holmes stories, the racially mixed Lestrade initially appears as a staunch defender of the colonial order. He separates himself off from the island's Blacks, regarding them as existing on a lower evolutionary level than himself, and thus repudiates half of himself. However, during the course of the dream, he does a complete about-face and replaces his Eurocentric perspective with an Afrocentric one. Finally it is he who persuades Makak to behead the White Goddess. In the Epilogue he re-emerges as the colonial administrator he was at the outset. This may incline one to the view that the dream has been Makak's after all; but in the latter half of Part II, Lestrade occupies the centre of the stage, and the action seems to issue primarily from his mind, as he provides as powerful a study of the split consciousness as Makak does.

Section B: The Setting

Both *Ti-Jean* and *Dream on Monkey Mountain* are set in an unnamed West Indian island. Language, folklore and topography are all, however, suggestive of Walcott's native St Lucia.

St Lucia is a small mountainous island (233 square miles in area) situated to the south of Martinique and to the north-east of St Vincent in the Windward Islands. It is primarily rural, and the capital Castries is the only city of any size. The split between capital city and countryside is one of the most extreme in the Caribbean. A 1963 commentator wrote in the island's newspaper: 'The poor, barefoot, uneducated, unsophisticated, shy people in the out-districts looked up with awe and fawning respect to the well-dressed, well-spoken and better-read city folk. . . . Castries was St Lucia in every way. . . . The out-districts were a Never-Never land' (quoted by Gordon Lewis, *The Making of the Modern West Indies*, MacGibbon & Kee, 1968, pp. 151–2).

Dream on Monkey Mountain reflects this division, in the distance between the peasant Makak and the colonial administrator Lestrade. *Ti-Jean* is set exclusively in the countryside, but here too there is a conflict between two worlds, those of peasantry and 'plantocracy'.

In the past, possession of St Lucia was hotly disputed by France and Britain. The island changed hands more than a dozen times between 1660 and 1802, after which it remained British. Nevertheless outside Castries it is primarily a Francophone, Catholic island. As in the other formerly British Windward Islands, where English is the 'official' language but a French patois is the main means of communication, language has been an especially significant factor in the alienation of the local culture from the colonial. This is reflected in Lestrade's infuriation at Makak's answering his formally phrased questions in patois (pp. 218–20).

St Lucia became independent in 1979. Both plays are set in the colonial period. The generalized nature of the allegory in *Ti-Jean* can be related to various periods of West Indian history; the moment of *Dream on Monkey Mountain* is more specifically identified as the 'Twilight of Empire' (p. 297).

Section C: A Closer Look

(1) Prologue to *Ti-Jean and his Brothers*

The curtain rises on four forest creatures and an impoverished mother. The Frog and the Cricket begin a dialogue, which quickly makes it clear that the creatures function as a chorus, which will comment on the action:

> FROG: Greek-croak, Greek-croak.
> CRICKET: Greek-croak, Greek-croak.
> [The others join.]
> FROG: [sneezing]: Aeschylus me!
> All that rain and no moon tonight.
> CRICKET: The moon always there even fighting the rain
> Creek-crak, it is cold, but the moon always there
> And Ti-Jean in the moon just like the story.
> (p. 85)

This opening also establishes a cross-cultural frame of reference from the outset. 'Greek-croak' suggests that the creatures have the same role as the chorus in an ancient Greek play (and perhaps contains a specific allusion to Aristophanes' comedy *The Frogs*). There is also a punning reference to Greek drama, when the sound of the Frog's sneeze is rendered by the name of one of the three great masters of Athenian tragedy, Aeschylus. However, by the Cricket's second speech 'Greek-croak' has given way to 'Creek-crak', a phrase much used by speaker and listener – in a call-and-response manner – in Caribbean story-telling (cf. the title of Merle Hodge's *Crick Crack, Monkey*).

So the Prologue begins by locating the narrative within the conventions of West Indian oral tale-telling; audience and reader are made aware that a traditional story is being reworked and that it comes from the folk tradition. At the same time the punning references to Greek drama extend the framework beyond the Caribbean.

Immediately after this the Frog outlines the tale which is to be told. He says that Ti-Jean can be seen in the moon:

> He got the heap of sticks
> From the old man of the forest
> They calling Papa Bois
> Because he beat the devil,
> God put him in that height
> To be the sun's right hand
> And light the evil dark. (p. 86)

He then goes on to tell the story of the three brothers' encounters with the Devil in the manner of a simple folk tale. So the main story is known before the action commences. The effect of this is to leave the author free to develop variations on the story-line and the audience free to ponder the significance of the tale and the way it is being treated. It also implies that Ti-Jean has achieved a kind of immortality. He has become a guide for travellers, as well as a mythic figure who is brought alive each time his tale is told. This passage has the further effect of arousing curiosity about the significance of Papa Bois and the bundle of sticks.

By the end of the Prologue the strange figure of the Bolom has appeared and issued the challenge of his master, the Devil. The Bolom represents life strangled before birth, while the Devil longs to be made to feel emotion. So neither character has fully become human. Ti-Jean's achievement in the play lies not only in finding a way to defeat the Devil and

what he represents, the iniquities of the colonial order; he is also responsible for bringing a new Caribbean consciousness into being when he asks for the Bolom to be born at the end, and for humanizing the Devil or 'plantocracy'. As in his later play *Pantomime* (1977), Walcott is concerned with the plight of the white ruling class in a time of social change, even though his main emphasis is on the predicament of the ordinary black West Indian.

Throughout the Prologue, Walcott uses a simple but moving lyrical poetry, which seems ideal for the folk theme. Elsewhere (in a prefatory note to his play *The Joker of Seville*, 1974) he has said: 'The verse play is not a literary exercise in the West Indies [of today]', because the folk tradition is vibrant and alive in the Caribbean.

The Prologue to *Ti-Jean* also uses music very effectively: a roll of drums and a 'comic quatro' when Mi-Jean enters; sad flute music to evoke the situation of the mother; and clashes of cymbals to herald the appearance of the Devil and his followers.

(2) *Dream on Monkey Mountain*, Part II, scene 3

This scene portrays the comic apotheosis (or deification) of Makak as an African chieftain. Like the mock-trial of the play's Prologue, it is a highly stylized scene which employs elements of parody. It functions as a kind of dream-within-the-dream, and since it has been initiated by Lestrade (at the end of the previous scene), it may seem to be primarily a product of his mind. It is, however, introduced by the Chorus and so, like the whole of the central section, is best viewed as a collective fantasy.

The Chorus is not to be identified with the Conteur of the Prologue, nor, as in *Ti-Jean*, with a Greek chorus. It is later called 'the tribes' and represents a communal African identity. It sings a 'chant of a tribal triumph' (p. 308) and functions like the praise-singers of West African society. Some of the scene's detail is drawn from specific African traditions – thus the reference to the 'golden stool' (p. 309) alludes to the central symbol of the Ashanti nation (cf. Edward Brathwaite's *Masks*, part of *The Arrivants*, 1973, see Unit 12, p. 104) – but much of it is generalized parody. Earlier Walcott has ridiculed West Indian mimicry of European standards; here he mocks Caribbean 'back to Africa' movements. This is particularly apparent in the portrayal of Lestrade, who, from being a staunch defender of 'Roman law', has now become an advocate of 'tribal law' (p. 311).

At Lestrade's instigation, prisoners are brought before Makak in a fantasy of black revenge. They include such disparate figures as Sir Francis Drake, Mandrake the Magician, Sir Cecil Rhodes and Al Jolson. Their crime is said to be whiteness, but in some cases it is clearly more specific. Drake and Rhodes were archetypal imperialists; the comic-strip hero Mandrake has a black servant, Lothar; Al Jolson performed in black-face. In fact, all the prisoners seem to be people who have in some way contributed to the repression of Blacks, by either exploiting them economically, appropriating their culture or excluding them from official versions of history. 'Tribal law' quickly condemns them to be hanged.

Next a comic catalogue of tributes is brought before Makak. These include:

> An offer to revise the origins of slavery. A floral tribute of lilies from the Klu Klux Klan. Congratulations from several Golf and Country Clubs. . . . A silver of bone from the thigh of Lumumba. An offer from Hollywood. (pp. 313–14)

The tribes quickly reject all these offers of restitution from the white world. While the comic way the tributes are presented makes them far from convincing, their summary rejection suggests black intransigence.

At this point Moustique is brought before Makak, accused of having betrayed his dream. He tells Makak he is in danger of replacing his love for the white moon with a deep hatred which will want it destroyed. Makak orders Moustique to be taken away, but the warning proves to be prophetic. In the remainder of the scene Lestrade urges Makak to behead the apparition of the White Goddess, telling him:

> She is lime, snow, marble, moonlight, lilies, cloud, foam and bleaching cream, the mother of civilization, and the confounder of blackness. I too have longed for her. She is the colour of the law, religion, paper, art, and if you want peace, if

you want to discover the beautiful depth of your blackness, nigger, chip off her head! When you do this, you will kill Venus, the Virgin, the Sleeping Beauty. She is the white light that paralysed your mind, that led you into this confusion. It is you who created her, so kill her! kill her! (p. 319)

Makak is finally persuaded, and the scene ends with his beheading the apparition. This is the play's climax, but its exact meaning is complex. Lestrade, not completely committed to a black standpoint, had advocated the killing of the European Muse. However, since the apparition has been responsible for initiating Makak's African dream, the beheading has a significance of which Lestrade is unaware. It represents a repudiation of the African heritage as well as the European. The Epilogue ends with Makak returning to his Caribbean home, free from the stultifying influence of both legacies.

Section D: The Author

Derek Walcott was born in Castries, St Lucia, in 1930. Both his grandfathers were white, both his grandmothers black. Though St Lucia is predominantly Catholic, his family were Protestants; his mother was headteacher of a Methodist infant school. He was brought up in an atmosphere conducive to culture. His father, who died a year after his birth, had been an amateur painter, and during his formative years Walcott was instructed in art and literature by his father's friend, Harold Simmons. Simmons was later to commit suicide. In Walcott's poetic autobiography of his early years, *Another Life* (1972), this suicide symbolizes the difficulty of the artistic life in the Caribbean.

Another Life dramatizes the conflict which Walcott felt existed between the local world and the world of art. The latter seemed to offer him the heightened awareness of 'another life', but one which was inextricably entangled with foreign cultural values. Along with his friend Dunstan St Omer, who went on to become St Lucia's foremost painter, Walcott vowed he would not leave the island until he had chronicled it in art.

In fact Walcott left with this task only partly completed when he went to the Jamaican campus of the University of the West Indies in 1950. Since then he has continued to live away from St Lucia, mainly in Trinidad and more recently in the United States. However, his work as both poet and dramatist has made St Lucia the subject of internationally acclaimed art.

Walcott is generally regarded, along with Edward Brathwaite, as one of the Caribbean's two finest poets. Where Brathwaite's poetry embodies the values of community, the oral tradition and the African heritage, Walcott's speaks with the voice of the New World exile, trying to create its own tradition where none had existed before. The dominant figure of his early work is the castaway, who emerges as a type of the West Indian artist, a Robinson Crusoe marooned thousands of miles away from the metropolis, trying to fashion art from the sparse raw materials at his disposal.

While Walcott's poetry reflects the isolation of the individual colonial artist, his plays dramatize a quest not only for tradition, but also for community. After settling in Trinidad, he played a very active role in promoting local culture, particularly the theatre. As arts reviewer for the *Trinidad Guardian* in the 1960s he wrote numerous articles on theatre which, taken together, come to constitute a manifesto arguing specifically for the establishment of a national theatre and more generally for a West Indian drama rooted in the local experience. As founding director of the Trinidad Theatre Workshop, Walcott was actively involved in trying to create such a theatre in practice, by staging his own plays and those of other dramatists. Walcott's journalism represents the most probing exploration of West Indian theatre aesthetics yet to have appeared, while the Workshop's productions over two decades have come close to fulfilling his ideal of a national repertory company. Most significantly of all, his own plays stand unrivalled as the finest achievement of West Indian drama to date. *Ti-Jean* and *Dream on Monkey Mountain* are foremost among them, his masterpieces of the 1950s and 1960s respectively. More recent plays include his brilliant Creolized version of the Don Juan legend, *The Joker of Seville* (1974), *Pantomime* (1977) and *Remembrance* (1978).

Section E: Classroom Use

(i) Level of use

Ti-Jean can be taught with virtually all age groups. The simple folk-story at the heart of the play is accessible even to infants, who could act out a shortened version excluding the Prologue. Older groups may be expected to appreciate the allegory on various levels. First or second years in secondary schools (ages 11–13) might be asked to discuss the strengths and weaknesses of the three brothers' approaches to the Devil on a fairly straightforward level. Sixth-formers might be introduced to the notion of allegory and asked to discuss how it functions in the play.

The complexities of *Dream on Monkey Mountain* make it suitable only for older, A-level groups.

(ii) Points of focus and emphasis

Ti-Jean

1 Departure and encounter with the creatures:
   - Gros Jean, scene 1, pp. 102–4;
   - Mi-Jean, scene 2, pp. 115–17;
   - Ti-Jean, scene 3, pp. 132–8.
2 Working for the Planter:
   - Gros Jean, scene 1, pp. 107–10;
   - Mi-Jean, scene 2, pp. 123–7;
   - Ti-Jean, scene 3, pp. 143–54.
3 Downfall and triumph:
   - Gros Jean's downfall, scene 1, pp. 110–14;
   - Mi-Jean's downfall, scene 2, pp. 128–30;
   - Ti-Jean's triumph, scene 3, pp. 155–66.

Dream on Monkey Mountain

1 Makak's dream:
   - production note, p. 208;
   - poetic vision on the mountain, Prologue, pp. 226–7;
   - prose vision on the mountain, Part I, scene 1, pp. 234–5;

- destruction of the apparition, II, 3, pp. 317–20;
- awakening, Epilogue, pp. 321–6.

2 Moustique's role:
- his practicality, Part I, scene 1, pp. 231–2; and Epilogue, pp. 325–6;
- his superstition, I, 1, p. 238;
- his attitude to the return to Africa, I, 1, p. 241;
- trickster figure, I, 2, pp. 244, 251–4;
- impersonating Makak, I, 3, pp. 265–70;
- his 'death', I, 3, pp. 271–5.

3 Music and mime:
- opening mime, Prologue, p. 212;
- Conteur and Chorus's lament, Prologue, pp. 212–13;
- mock-trial and monkey mime, Prologue, pp. 220-5;
- *burroquite* or donkey-dance, Part I, scene 1, p. 242;
- religious sisterhood's dancing and singing, I, 2, pp. 243, 251;
- impromptu market dance, bongo and healing mime, I, 3, pp. 262–4;
- 'monkey' song and mime, I, 3, p. 266;
- Basil's spider movements around Moustique, I, 3, pp. 269–70;
- demons carry off Moustique's body, I, 3, pp. 274–5;
- final song, 'I going home', Epilogue, p. 326.

(iii) Questions for essay writing or classroom discussion

1 What does each of the three brothers in *Ti-Jean* represent? Do you agree that Ti-Jean's attitude is the best?
2 What is the importance of the creatures in *Ti-Jean*?
3 What is a chorus? How is it generally used in drama? How does Derek Walcott use it?
4 Why is the Devil portrayed as a Planter?
5 What does Papa Bois represent? Why is the Devil portrayed as Papa Bois as well as the Planter?
6 What do you think the figure of the Bolom represents? Why has he not been born? Why *is* he born at the end of the play?

7 Derek Walcott draws on various cultures in *Ti-Jean* and *Dream on Monkey Mountain*. Can you give examples of this? (See the discussion of the opening of *Ti-Jean* in Section C, p. 89.)
8 Dance, mime and song figure prominently in both plays. Give examples. Why do you think they are used so much?
9 Why is Makak so influenced by the apparition of the White Goddess?
10 What details suggest that Makak is a Christ figure? How seriously do you think this suggestion is to be taken?
11 Mimicry is important in *Dream on Monkey Mountain*. In what parts of the play can this be seen most clearly?
12 What attitude does *Dream on Monkey Mountain* suggest towards the influence on the West Indies of (a) Europe, and (b) Africa?
13 The opening Stage Direction of *Dream on Monkey Mountain* outlines many of the play's concerns. How many can you spot?
14 Who was Frantz Fanon? What is the significance of the quotations from Sartre's Prologue to his work, *The Wretched of the Earth*, which serve as epigraphs to the two parts of the play?
15 What is an expressionist play? What expressionist elements can you find in *Dream on Monkey Mountain*?

(iv) Creative approaches/curriculum links

1 Compare the relationships the three brothers in *Ti-Jean* have with their mother with those you and your friends have with your mothers.
2 Gros Jean tells his mother, 'The world not the same it was in your time,/ Tell my brothers I gone. A man have to go' (scene 1, p. 104). Do you think it is true that there comes a time when children have to break with the values of their parents? If so how complete should this break be?
3 The way Mi-Jean is presented suggests that book-knowledge is not enough to help him win through in his situation. How helpful do you find book-knowledge in your own life?
4 In the Prologue to *Dream on Monkey Mountain*, Corporal Lestrade mockingly

refers to Makak as the 'King of Africa' (p. 214) and 'the Lion of Judah' (p. 217). Rastafarians call the late Emperor Haile Selassie of Ethiopia, whom they greatly admired, 'Lion of Judah'. What attitude does the play suggest to the Rastafarian stress on African roots? Do you think Makak should be mocked for his desire to return to Africa? Do you think this is a realistic goal for black people living in Britain? [Answers will clearly vary, but students may be encouraged to think in terms of the need to foster African elements in black culture rather than an actual return to Africa.]

5   In *Dream on Monkey Mountain* there seems to be a fairly sharp division between life in the country and life in the town. Do you think there is much difference between life in rural and in urban areas in your own country? If so, what would you say are the main differences?

6   Improvise a situation where three brothers or sisters are faced with a challenge (or bet), and each one tackles it.

7   At one point in *Dream on Monkey Mountain*, Moustique tells Makak, 'you will have to sell your dream, your soul, your power, just for bread and shelter' (Part I, scene 2, p. 254). What do you think of this view? Would you be prepared to sell a dream of your own for this reason?

8   Investigate other versions of the legend of the three brothers and see how they compare with *Ti-Jean*. Possibilities include the Three Little Pigs and the Three Billy-Goats Gruff.

9   Stage a simple production of *Ti-Jean*. Particular tasks will involve the making of masks for the Devil/Planter/Papa Bois character and the Bolom, finding or making costumes (especially for the animals), designing a simple set, arranging the performance of the songs and dances and, of course, acting and directing.

10   Find out as much as you can about West Indian speech and the language of St Lucia in particular. What differences do you notice between the way in which particular characters in the plays speak? How does the language of the plays differ from the way you speak?

Section F: Teaching Aids

(i) *Audio-visual material*

Videotapes

Ti-Jean and his Brothers, U-matic (1 hour; colour), Stage One Productions, Barbados. Obtainable from Dr Michael Gilkes, Department of English, University of the West Indies, Cave Hill, Bridgetown, Barbados. Videotape made for use primarily in Barbadian schools; regrettably available only on the US line monitor system, but can be used in the UK with the appropriate equipment, though colour is lost.

This tape is an invaluable aid which raises questions about enactment. Pupils watching it could be asked what they think of:
(a) the way particular aspects have been presented, e.g. the Devil, the Bolom;
(b) the standard of the various acting performances;
(c) the use of settings, e.g. outdoor locations, a scene in which the Devil appears in a Barbados disco;
(d) the use of music;
(e) departures from the printed text.

The Art of Derek Walcott, U-matic (30 mins; colour). Obtainable from Dr Michael Gilkes (address as above). Also produced for use in Barbadian schools and on US format. Walcott's own work as a pictorial artist. Again very useful. Slides include St Lucian scenes and Walcott's own drawings for his plays (set designs, etc.), including *Ti-Jean* and *Dream on Monkey Mountain*. Study of these would again raise questions about drama in performance.

St Lucia: People and Celebrations (25 mins.; colour), Open University Unit 204/15v. Obtainable from Open University Enterprises Ltd, 12 Stony Stratford, Milton Keynes, MK11 1BY. Useful background on the setting of the two plays. Illustrates the fusion of various cultural and religious influences in St Lucia.

Record

The Joker of Seville (LP, 12 tracks). Semp Productions, Port of Spain, unnumbered. Music from the Trinidad Theatre Workshop production of this Walcott play. Lyrics by Walcott; music by Galt MacDermot, composer of the rock musical *Hair*. Gives an excellent idea of the way Caribbean music is used in Walcott's plays – in this case to Creolize a European story, the Don Juan legend.

(ii) Background reading

Ken Corsbie, *Theatre in the Caribbean*, Hodder & Stoughton, 1984.

Gordon Lewis, *The Making of the Modern West Indies*, MacGibbon & Kee, 1968; particularly Chapter VI on the Windward Islands.

(iii) Critical bibliography

Albert Olu Ashaolu, 'Allegory in *Ti-Jean and His Brothers*', *World Literature Written in English*, 16, 1977, pp. 203–11. Finds no less than six levels of allegory in *Ti-Jean*.

Robert Hamner, *Derek Walcott*, Twayne, 1981. The only book on Walcott to consider his plays in any detail.

Diana Lyn, 'The Concept of the Mulatto in Some Works by Derek Walcott', *Caribbean Quarterly*, vol. 26, nos. 1–2, 1980, pp. 49–69. On Walcott's poetry and plays. Included in a Walcott/ Brathwaite special issue of *Caribbean Quarterly*.

John Thieme, 'A Caribbean Don Juan: Derek Walcott's *Joker of Seville*', *World Literature Written in English*, 23, 1984, pp. 62–75. Shows how this later Walcott play uses Trinidadian music to Creolize a Spanish original. Could be used with the Trinidad Theatre Workshop record to illustrate the folk element in Walcott's plays.

(iv) Reading links

Other works by Derek Walcott

Selected Poetry, Heinemann Educational Books (Caribbean Writers Series), 1981; particularly 'The Castaway' (p. 16), 'The Almond Trees' (p. 21), *Another Life*, Extract A (pp. 42–4).

Another Life, Cape, 1972.

The Joker of Seville and *O Babylon!*, Cape, 1979.

Pantomime and *Remembrance*, Farrar, Straus & Giroux, 1980.

Other plays

Shakespeare, *King Lear*. Compare the scenes on the heath with *Dream on Monkey Mountain*, Part II, scene 2.

August Strindberg, *The Dream Play* (1902). A pioneer expressionist play and a major influence on *Dream on Monkey Mountain*.

Eugene O'Neill, *The Emperor Jones* (1920). The expressionist night-journey of a black dictator in flight.

Wole Soyinka, *A Dance of the Forests* (1960). Written for Nigerian independence celebrations and concerned with the reconstruction of a Nigerian identity. Compare the figure of the half-child with the Bolom in *Ti-Jean*.

Other West Indian treatments of Africa

Edward Brathwaite, *The Arrivants*, Oxford University Press, 1973. Particularly compare the apotheosis scene in *Dream on Monkey Mountain* (II, 3) with Brathwaite's much more detailed and sympathetic portrayal of the African heritage in *Masks* (1968), the second part of *The Arrivants* trilogy.

Another Devil

Milton, *Paradise Lost*, particularly Books I and II. Milton's Satan would make an interesting comparison with the Devil in *Ti-Jean* for any A-level students reading *Paradise Lost*. For others the teacher might introduce one or two of Satan's speeches from the first two books.

Fiction on mimicry in colonial cultures

V. S. Naipaul, *Miguel Street*, 1959; Penguin, 1971; particularly the stories 'Bogart' and 'B. Wordsworth'.

V. S. Naipaul, *The Mimic Men*, 1967; Penguin, 1969.

Albert Wendt, *Leaves of the Banyan Tree*, 1979; Penguin, 1981; particularly Part III. An unexpectedly close parallel in this novel from Western Samoa.

Unit 11
Derek Walcott: *Poems*

STEWART BROWN

Section A: Critical Approaches

'Ruins of a Great House' (*Selected Poems*, p. 4)

The poem is set among the ruins of a plantation 'great house', the symbol of European authority and status in the Caribbean through the slavery period. The poet is struck by the irony of such a grand and pretentious building being reduced to 'stones only' and is reminded of the frailty of all human endeavour. He acknowledges the beauty of the 'great houses' (they were architecturally striking and represented the positive aspects of European culture that came with colonialism: the language, the poetry, the art) and of the 'moth-like girls' who graced them in the days of candle-lit ballrooms. Though it carries an ironic charge, the quotation from Blake recognizes that the 'plantocracy' was itself a community in exile, separated from the green fields of its homeland and heartland. But 'deciduous beauty prospered and is gone', and despite the pretensions of its imperious masters and their ladies, that whole 'great house' world has 'paid the worm's rent'.

Images of death and decay pervade the scene, the black crows, the haunting echo of bone struck beneath dead leaves and the stench of rotting limes.

Limes were the major crop of the plantation, it seems, illustrating how dependent the whole economy was on slavery; for the limes were used to prevent scurvy among the sailors plying the Middle Passage. This brings into focus the theme of slavery which counterbalances the beauty of the 'great house' and infects like a moral leprosy any pretension to gentility or culture its inhabitants may have had. The corruption of values that could institutionalize slavery ensured, the poet implies, that the empire of which the 'great house' was an expression would be eaten away to 'stones only', just as the other great empires built on the practice of slavery had been; hence the reference to Greece and to Faulkner's American South.

The brutality enacted in the name of that empire is not necessarily forgiven by the levelling of time, even though 'the river flows, obliterating hurt'. The poem swings between outrage and compassion as the poet considers the implications of the 'great house' site: rage against the injustice and barbarism of slavery – 'some slave is rotting in this manorial lake' – counterbalanced by an understanding of the ambition and weakness of men that could pervert even the 'green' promise of human growth that the Renaissance heralded into nothing but a 'charnal galleon's text' by their greed. The figure of Raleigh, both 'ancestral murderer *and* poet', embodies the contradiction for Walcott, who is himself struggling to reconcile a patriot's natural outrage with a sensibility nurtured by the very culture against which that rage must be directed.

Finally the poem asserts a humanistic compassion, eschewing the close focus of a racial reading of Caribbean history, which 'limits the memory to the suffering of the victim', for a longer perspective that understands cruelty and greed to be a weakness of humanity rather than the burden

Page references in this unit are to Derek Walcott, *Selected Poems*, Heinemann Educational Books (Caribbean Writers Series), 1981.

of a particular race. Britain, too, had been just a colony of another passing empire in its turn. So, Walcott asserts, with Donne, 'no man is an island'; we must share or forget the guilt which is history. For, as he puts it in his essay 'The Muse of History', the urge to revenge is in fact a 'filial impulse', the response of one who is still enslaved by the past he or she would avenge.

The difficulties that students have with 'Ruins of a Great House' are often to do with the welter of literary references that threaten to choke the poem but are in some ways crucial to its meaning. Obviously, unless one knows the context of the final quotation from Donne, the end of the poem is meaningless. Once the 'reference barrier', as it were, is breached, the issues the poem raises can be approached. Besides the general historical and moral questions, the poem raises all the issues of audience, relevance, cultural commitment and context that dogged Walcott's early work. Who was he writing for? Who was he writing *as*? Is the persona in any sense a 'representative' West Indian? How far can a sensibility so obviously steeped in European culture understand the view of history that people who regard themselves still as 'African' might have? These are questions generated by the poem itself and are as fundamental to a full response to the poem as more traditional 'lit. crit.' type forays into imagery and style.

'The Almond Trees' (*Selected Poems*, p. 21)

In a lecture he gave at the University of the West Indies in Trinidad in 1965,[1] Derek Walcott explained that in the opening stanzas of 'The Almond Trees' he was 'trying to describe the absence of history, tradition, ruins' in the Caribbean. Instead of such ruins he saw 'the figure of ancient almond trees in a grove past Rampanalgas on the north coast [of Trinidad] as a grove of dead, transplanted uprooted ancestors' (p. 10). He also

explained that the opening two lines of the poem – 'There's nothing here/this early' - embrace the idea of both an empty beach at dawn and the beginnings of 'historic time'.

Within that 'set' the poem can be understood as a reaction against the negativism of commentators like V. S. Naipaul who have dismissed the region as being without any meaningful history because nothing significant ever occurred or was created there. That 'nothing' condition is symbolized by the 'absence of ruins': the fact that there are few historic monuments or heroic characters in the Caribbean's 'official' chronicle (except those that relate to the colonial powers' in-fighting) and that there can *be* none that relate to the pre-colonial past of the great majority of the islands' peoples. The poem offers a different view of history, opposing the obsession with ruins, with 'visible history', by an understanding of the historic and the heroic as 'the endurance of the tribe, the race of all the nameless people'.[2]

It is significant that the poem is set at Rampanalgas, a tiny and unexceptional fishing village on the Atlantic Coast of Trinidad, 'the further shore of Africa'. By its very ordinariness the place both serves to embody the 'nothing' that the ruin-hunters complain of and yet speaks of the people's achievement in creating a distinct, viable culture *despite* the brutalization of generations of slavery. The achievement is embodied in the figure of the 'one/foam haired, salt grizzled fisherman', a figure emblematic throughout Walcott's work of the stoic, culturally assured self-reliance of the 'folk'. The poem marks the beginning of a radical, 'Adamic' view of history in Walcott's work, which sees in the lone figure on the beach not a hopeless castaway but a representative man with the potential to create the New World, a new civilization from the rich 'nothing' that is Rampanalgas.

Somewhat paradoxically it seems, the poem makes that assertion via classical mythology, using the story of Daphne and the idea of the sacred grove to locate the brown girls 'toasting their flesh' as descendants of the ancestral spirits represented by the 'frieze of twisted coppery sea-almond trees'. What the poet is offering is a view of history that acknowledges the European 'classical' inheritance of the islands that came with colonialism but sees it

---

[1] 'The Figure of Crusoe', unpublished text on file at the University of the West Indies, St Augustine, Trinidad.

[2] Edward Baugh, 'The West Indian Writer and his Quarrel with History', Part 2, *Tapia* (Trinidad), 27 February 1977, p. 7.

assimilated and transformed by an African tradition tempered in the furnace that was slavery. The twisted, scorched ancestral grove bears witness to the experience of the race:

> Welded in one flame,
> huddling naked, stripped of their name,
> for Greek or Roman tags, they were lashed
> raw by wind, washed
> out with salt and fire-dried . . .

From this perspective the girl carefully kneeling to spread her towel within the shade of the almond trees in the final stanza is, unconsciously, expressing and acknowledging 'that past and [her] own metamorphosis' from African, from slave, to West Indian, with all the resonances of history that identity implies.

'The Bright Field' (*Selected Poems*, p. 75)

'The Bright Field' is set in London but it recalls the concerns and attitudes of 'Ruins of a Great House' and can usefully be compared with that poem. London, as 'the heart of our history', focuses the contrasting emotions of collective rage and individual compassion that are the keys to the earlier poem but now turn on the present state of England and that country's own traumatic re-evaluation of its history.

Caught in a self-protective rage against the herd mentality of the crowd jostling him towards the Underground at rush hour, the poet is struck by the experience as a metaphor for the individual lost in that surge of antagonisms between races, classes or nations that is the traditional notion of history. Developing the metaphor, he acknowledges the helplessness of any member of the crowd wishing to stand aside or to assert their individual humanity against the tide of events or ideas that dominate their time. Tied in with this sense of helplessness is the image of the crowd-that-is-all-humanity surging towards the underground destination of the grave.

Such visions of a common experience and destiny for all humankind, regardless of race or creed, neutralize the rage of one whose racial history gives him cause to move 'against a bitter sea', to contrast the guilty affluence of London with the poverty of Balandra (a fishing village on Trinidad's east coast) and take refuge in historic animosities. His compassion, his 'mercy', is in its way a kind of standing against the tide – of racial hostility and the urge for revenge – that characterizes black–white relations in *his* time. The image, a recurring one in Walcott's poetry (borrowed most directly from Traherne), of humanity as 'sheaves of harvest' waiting for the 'one end', which they may reach by tube train or by bullock cart, is the key to the poet's 'mercy'.

In *Another Life* the decline of Britain's influence in its former empire is often suggested by images of sunset and twilight. In 'The Bright Field' the harsh, artificial twilight of the city, illuminating the 'flushed faces' sinking down the steps, ironically recalls the 'sun that would not set' and the jingoistic slogan (that the 'sun would never set on the British Empire') which camouflaged the self-delusion of generations of Britons sent out to service the colonies. The kind of society Britain has become, suggested by the anonymous, driven, automaton image of the city emptying its factories and offices on to 'the loud belt of the street', is the price paid for the amoral obsession with power and profit which was the real motivation of the empire. That soulless society is the fulfilment of Blake's nightmare vision of a future dominated by the ethos of the dark Satanic mills, and is the antithesis of Samuel Palmer's pastoral vision. Such a personal, human and humane society as Palmer celebrated still exists, the poem suggests, in the very corners of the old empire that the British were so keen to leave: in places like Balandra. So history pays its debts; humanity – slaver or slave, stockbroker or stock minder – is subject to the same natural justice and will answer the same bell (Donne's bell), which tolls for 'everything'.

'Forest of Europe' (*Selected Poems*, p. 87)

Although 'Forest of Europe' is essentially an assertion of the fundamental importance of poetry to human civilization, not least because of its power to defy and redress the corruption of political systems over time, it relates in several ways to the historical themes that run through the three poems discussed above. Poetry, 'Forest of Europe' argues, never loses sight of 'the single human through the cause', and this is the key to the compassion that characterizes Walcott's much discussed humanism. Dedicated to the exiled Russian poet Joseph Brodsky and invoking, through that poet's association with Mandelstam, the unmuzzled voice of Russian poetry in the twentieth century, the poem avoids the trap of becoming a one-sided critique of political repression by considering a wider definition of the political abuse of the human spirit. It makes repeated references to the injustices done to the American Indians, for example, and to the inheritance of slavery that must jar the conscience of any in 'the land of the free' who would rest too smugly on political slogans. Walcott's insistence on looking beyond the immediate horror, resisting easy condemnations in an attempt to see events and issues in a wider context – as he also does in 'Ruins of a Great House', for example – is one source of the considerable moral authority his 'public' poems command.

'Forest of Europe' is also a poem about exile, a theme that runs through Walcott's poetry. Brodsky is a poet forced by political oppression into exile:

> far from Russia's canals quivered with sunstroke
> a man living with English in one room . . .

Walcott has himself chosen exile as a means of escape from the philistine indifference to art that he feels characterizes the post-independence Caribbean ('the tourist archipelago'); in a deeper sense, his very status as a West Indian makes him an exile from the 'heartland' traditions of Africa or Europe. These two exiled poets are sharing a cabin through a winter in Oklahoma. The life and work of Osip Mandelstam, a poet cruelly persecuted and censored by Stalin, is an inspiration to both and is the measure of their suffering and of their achievement. His example brings these two poets, from such different backgrounds, to understand a shared allegiance to a concept of the poet as 'the conscience of the tribe'; in some way the truth of their art is vouchsafed by the hostile reaction it evokes from their respective governments. Though such rejection hurts, and exile is a kind of prison, Walcott can assert that 'there is no harder prison than writing verse'. Such an assertion might seem melodramatic. But the ambition to make a poetry that 'men can pass from hand to mouth' –

> From hand to mouth, across the centuries,
> the bread that lasts when systems have decayed,

> when, in his forest of barbed-wire branches,
> a prisoner circles, chewing the one phrase
> whose music will last longer than the leaves

– validates the anguish which both poets endure as a consequence of their commitment, above all else, to their art.

Section B: The Author

(For more about Derek Walcott life and background, see Unit 10, Section D, p. 91.)

Derek Walcott was born in St Lucia in 1930. In various autobiographical accounts of his upbringing he has described himself as a 'divided child'. He has always been torn between conflicting loyalties and consequently felt himself something of an outsider. That sense of being 'divided' stems from several factors in his own background and experience. First and foremost he is a mulatto – that is, he has both black and white ancestors, in his case as recently as his grandparents. In the Caribbean of the 1930s such a background had both positive and negative connotations; it was difficult, to put it crudely, for the mulatto to 'side' with either of the racial groups who have been historically antagonistic in the region. Walcott has always been as 'proud' of the one ancestry as of the other. As he has put it: 'mongrel as I am, something prickles in me when I see the word Ashanti as with the word Warwickshire, both separately intimating my grandfathers' roots, both baptizing this neither proud nor ashamed bastard, this hybrid, this West Indian' ('What the Twilight Says', in *Dream on Monkey Mountain and Other Plays*, 1972, p. 10).

Walcott was an outsider in other ways, too. His father died when he was just a baby, and his mother, a schoolteacher, had to bring up Walcott, his twin brother and elder sister, alone. The family was culturally part of the island's middle class but was not at all well off. Walcott's mother had to supplement her teaching salary by doing dressmaking on the side. However, in the hierarchical social structure of colonial St Lucia, Walcott was separated from the mass of his peers by class and colour. The family were also Methodists, while St Lucia is a profoundly Roman Catholic country; although there was no open hostility between the two denominations, the Methodists were regarded with some suspicion. Perhaps most crucially of all, Walcott's family were among the educated élite who used English as their everyday language. Because for long periods in its history St Lucia had been a French colony, the common language of the society was a version of French Creole – a mixture of French and African languages. Walcott knows this language, but it was not the language of his identity.

The sense of his own 'outsiderness' which these various factors encouraged in Walcott is important to an understanding of his attitude to both history and the role of the poet, the two obsessions which dominate his poetry as a whole and the four poems discussed here particularly. However, in much of his writing about poetry Walcott has been concerned to refute the idea that the Caribbean poet has some kind of *duty* to delve into history, to 'repair foundations' (as the Nigerian writer Chinua Achebe has put it), to make sense of the region's complex and disturbing past. He has rejected the idea of the human being as 'a creature chained to his past'. He has labelled the confrontation with history which has so obsessed the region's writers – and has arguably dominated its people's collective psychology – as the 'Medusa of the New World'.[3]

This paradox, between the apparent concerns of his poetry and his declared mistrust of the whole concept of linear history, is a matter of definitions. Walcott regards linear history – as told by the professional historians – as a sham, a 'fiction' subject to 'the fitful muse, memory'. He argues that, if 'everything depends on whether we write this fiction through the memory of the hero or the victim', then the replacement of one distorted chronicle by another is hardly going to repair

foundations in any meaningful sense. Walcott, rather, has perceived the role of the poet to be to attack the very foundation of linear history, of the memory of degradation and abuse, victory and conquest, by inhabiting 'the timeless habitable moment' which acknowledges history but 'neither explains nor forgives it'. So his humanism, his even-handed consideration of even the most emotionally searing issues – slavery, racialism, the poverty of the Third World – is not the classical or Eurocentric conservatisim that many critics have accused him of, but rather a refusal to simplify. We might say that for someone of Walcott's background the traditional racial, social and religious divisions of linear history are evidently untrue. In Walcott's poetry, especially the more recent work, history is drama not polemic. His attitude is summed up in the line from 'Forest of Europe': he has always refused to 'lose sight of the single human through the cause'.

If the New World poet's task is to take a position 'beyond history', then the language he uses must, itself, be somehow beyond the contamination of its own history. Walcott has been accused of speaking *away* from a Caribbean audience because of the formality of his language, the English the colonizer forced on his slaves. Walcott opposes the idea of English as the residue and detritus of a demeaning past, however, with the image of it as one of the 'spoils of history'. He would refute the notion that to have a *mastery* of the English language (to the extent that the user can improvise, modulate, abuse and re-create it to his or her own ends) is yet to be still a victim of the history which the language, as received, bears and signifies.

Walcott has striven for an English which echoes the essential and characteristic tones of West Indian speech, which is 'fertilized by dialect', as he puts it. The poet's function, he maintains, is to be 'filter and purifier, never losing the tone and strength of the common speech as he uses the hieroglyphs, symbols or alphabet of the official one'. He has striven, then, to make English speak *his* language. In some poems this 'fertilization' is overt – the poet employing a version of Creole speech – but even the four poems discussed here, which appear to be written in conventional 'Standard English', assume and move to a distinctly West Indian voice.

[3] This and all following quotations from Walcott's essay, 'The Muse of History', in Orde Coombs (ed.), *Is Massa Day Dead?*, Anchor/Doubleday, 1974.

Section C: Classroom Use

(i) Level of use
Fourth- to sixth-form students; GCSE and A-level.

(ii) Questions for essay writing or classroom discussion

'Ruins of a Great House'

1 'Deciduous beauty prospered and is gone'. One critic has written that this line is 'a rather unexpected tribute to the lives once lived in the big house'. Why 'unexpected', do you think? Why might the critic have expected anything other than a 'tribute' to those lives?

2 Find and read John Donne's essay that contains the lines 'No man is an island, entire of itself; every man is a part of the continent, a part of the main. If a clod be washed away, Europe is the less, as well as if a manor of thy friend's or thine own were.' How do Donne's sentiments in that essay bear on the situation the poet in 'Ruins of Great House' finds himself in?

3 When was 'Albion too . . . once/a colony like ours'? Why is that a relevant observation?

4 This poem is often criticized as being obscure and relying too much on references to European literature for a work concerned with the issues of Caribbean history. Other people feel that the range of allusions and echoes enriches the poem, giving the issues it raises a more universal context. What do you feel? List four allusions or echoes of such European literature.

'The Almond Trees'

1 The beach at dawn is empty, with 'no visible history'. How *could* history be 'visible'?

2 What do you understand by the description of the Caribbean underlying a whole strand of Walcott's work as 'the New World Mediterranean'? What comparisons is the poet making — just geographical, or are there cultural and historic similarities, too? Do you think it is a useful comparison?

3 '. . . their leaves' broad dialect a coarse/enduring sound/they shared together'. The poet is making a point here about the importance of language as a factor in a people's sense of identity. How important is your language to your sense of who *you* are? What would you feel if you were suddenly banned from using it and forced to adopt another? Why is this an important consideration for anyone thinking about Caribbean history or literature?

4 'One sunburnt body now acknowledges/that past'. In what ways does the past bear on *your* behaviour? How much, if at all, are you a product of events that happened years, perhaps centuries, before you were born?

'The Bright Field'

1 The poet in 'The Bright Field' is struck by his own helplessness in the surge of the crowd towards an Underground station. Have you ever felt a similar sense of being swept along, out of control? When? Try to describe your feelings.

2 Discuss the resonances of the phrase 'London/heart of our history, original sin'. Are you conscious of London being a city with a 'guilty' history? Why might it seem so to a West Indian or an African from one of the former colonies?

3 Consider the image of the crowd 'like walking sheaves of harvest'. Do you know any other poems – traditional or modern – that make a similar comparison? How does the traditional idea of death as 'the grim reaper' bear on the image?

4 John Donne's remark 'ask not for whom the bell tolls, it tolls for thee' is an important echo in this poem; in what way is it relevant?

'Forest of Europe'

1 What has the treatment of the American Indians by the European settlers in the USA got to do with the Gulag Archipelago? How valid is the comparison?

2 Consider the image of true poetry as 'the bread that lasts'. How might one phrase from such a 'loaf' sustain a prisoner trapped inside a 'forest of barbed wire'?

3   Why do politicians, governments, sociologists, statisticians, historians and journalists 'lose/sight of the single human through the cause'? What does Walcott mean by the phrase? Can you give a recent example of where, in your opinion, this has happened?

4   In the final stanza, with its comparison of the poets to grunting 'primates' in their cave and the forces of civilization to 'mastodons', the poet is directing us to something prehistoric, to do with the origins of human society. What do you think he is suggesting?

Background to the poems

1   The plantation economy of the West Indies depended on slavery. Find out all you can about the slave trade. When did it begin, where did the slaves come from, how did the slaves live on the plantations, what was a slave's daily routine like? When you have found these things out, read 'Ruins of a Great House' again and see if you feel that the 'rage' the poet speaks of is justified.

2   Find out all you can about the classical origins of the following: Pompeii, Daphne, the laurel, hamadryads, the Sacred Grove.

3   Look up the work of the painter Samuel Palmer. What 'vision' brought him 'peace'?

4   Find out all you can about the Russian poet Osip Mandelstam. Why was he persecuted? How did his work survive?

(iii) Creative approaches/curriculum links

1   Can you imagine a Jewish poet wandering through the remains of, say, Auschwitz, being able to write a poem like 'Ruins of a Great House'? If you think this is an unreasonable comparison, discuss your reasons why? Remembering that 'Albion, too, was once/a colony', might a contemporary English person have similar feelings when walking round the remains of a Roman fort? What are the differences between the three situations?

2   Imagine that you are either one of the 'moth-like girls' or one of the 'imperious rakes' who lived in the 'great house' in the days of slavery. Write a paragraph about the kind of life you lead, the people you come into contact with and your feelings about the West Indies and about Britain.

3   What 'visible history' is there in your district? How does your knowledge of it affect your sense of identity? Do you take your own heritage, your national, racial or family history for granted, or are you conscious of it as a shaping force in your life and in the life of your society?

4   The 'twisted coppery sea-almond trees' stand as a kind of emblem for the West Indian experience in history in 'The Almond Trees'. What might stand as an emblem for your region's history in a similar way, and why?

5   'The Bright Field' opposes two worlds: the hustle of London at rush-hour against the pastoral, bullock-cart-paced life of Balandra. Write two paragraphs – one imagining yourself a Balandra peasant suddenly in the centre of London, the other as a Londoner in Balandra. These two paragraphs will inevitably concentrate on what is different about the lives people lead in those two worlds; write a third paragraph about things they share in common.

6   Imagine yourself suddenly exiled by the government of your country, to a land where you had no relatives, whose language you didn't speak and which you had no particular wish to go to. How would you feel? What would your priorities be in your new situation?

7   Imagine that you have been sentenced to solitary confinement in a Siberian prison camp. What line or passage of poetry that you know might serve as the 'bread that lasts' in your despair and isolation? Try to say what it is about the line(s) that particularly moves or inspires you.

Section D: Teaching Aids

(i) Audio-visual material

Video
St Lucia: People and Celebrations (25 mins.), Open University, U204/15V. A useful general survey of St Lucia and the environment Walcott grew up in. Available for purchase from the Guild Organization Ltd, Guild House, Oundle Road, Peterborough PE2 9PZ.

Record
Poets of the West Indies, Caedmon, 1971, TC1379. Walcott reads four poems (not any of the poems discussed here).

(ii) Background reading

Historical background
Eric Williams, *Capitalism and Slavery*, Deutsch, 1944, new edn 1964.

Eric Williams, *From Columbus to Castro,* Deutsch, 1970.

Walcott's place in Caribbean poetry
Stewart Brown (ed.), *Caribbean Poetry Now,* Hodder & Stoughton, 1984.

John Figueroa (ed.) *Caribbean Voices*, Evans, 1971.

Andrew Salkey (ed.), *Breaklight*, Hamish Hamilton, 1971.

Anne Walmsley and Nick Caistor (eds), *Facing the Sea*, Heinemann Educational Books, 1986.

Background to 'Forest of Europe'
Nadezhda Mandelstam, *Hope against Hope*, Oxford University Press, 1970.

Nadezhda Mandelstam, *Hope Abandoned*, Oxford University Press, 1970.

Walcott's writing on his childhood and his 'world-view'
'Leaving School', *London Magazine*, vol. 5, no. 6, September 1965, pp. 4–14.

'Meanings', *Savacou*, no. 2, 1970, pp. 45–51.

'What the Twilight Says: An Overture', Introduction to *Dream on Monkey Mountain and Other Plays*, Cape, 1972.

Another Life, Deutsch, 1973.

'The Muse of History', in Orde Coombs (ed.) *Is Massa Day Dead?*, Anchor/Doubleday, 1974, pp. 1–27.

(iii) Critical bibliography

Edward Baugh, *Memory as Vision: Derek Walcott — Another Life*, Longman, 1978.

Edward Baugh, 'The West Indian Writer and his Quarrel with History', *Tapia* (Trinidad), 20 February 1977, pp. 6–7; 27 February 1977, pp. 7 and 11.

Joseph Brodsky, 'On Derek Walcott', *New York Review of Books*, 10 November 1983, pp. 39–42.

Lloyd Brown, *West Indian Poetry*, Heinemann Educational Books, 1984.

Robert D. Hamner, *Derek Walcott*, Boston: Twayne, 1981.

D. S. Izevbaye, 'The Exile and the Prodigal: Derek Walcott as West Indian Poet', *Caribbean Quarterly*, vol. 26, nos. 1/2, 1980, pp. 70–82.

Bruce King (ed.), *West Indian Literature*, Macmillan, 1979.

Mervyn Morris, 'Walcott and the Audience for Poetry', *Caribbean Quarterly*, vol. 14, nos 1/2, 1968, pp. 7–24.

Kenneth Ramchand, *An Introduction to the Study of West Indian Literature*, Nelson, 1976.

J. A. Ramsaran, 'Derek Walcott: New World Mediterranean Poet', *World Literature Written in English*, 21, 1982, pp. 133–47.

Ned Thomas, *Derek Walcott: Poet of the Islands*, Welsh Arts Council, 1980.

(iv) Reading links

Edward Brathwaite, *The Arrivants*, Oxford University Press, 1973. Another perspective on Caribbean history.

Wole Soyinka, *The Man Died*, Penguin, 1975. An account of an imprisonment in which 'the bread that lasts' sustains a hard-pressed spirit.

Derek Walcott, 'Dream on Monkey Mountain', from *Dream on Monkey Mountain and Other Plays*, Cape, 1972. Brilliantly explores the issues of race, history and identity.

Denis Williams, *Other Leopards*, Heinemann Educational Books, 1983. On the complexity of the relationship between history and identity for the West Indian.

Unit 12
Edward Brathwaite: *Poems*

NANA WILSON-TAGOE

Section A:
Critical Approaches

'New World a-Comin'' (*The Arrivants*, pp. 9–11)

The poem is the second section of 'Work Song and Blues', the opening sequence of Brathwaite's long poem *Rights of Passage*. It evokes the experience of the Middle Passage, exploring both the shock of the slaves' encounter with the white slaver and the devastation and possibilities of their traumatic movement from Africa to the New World. This dual view of the Middle Passage is a characteristic both of Brathwaite's poetry and of contemporary West Indian poetry as a whole. The experience of the Atlantic crossing generally functions as a symbol of displacement and loss, but in the best of West Indian poetry it is also explored in a search for meaning and vision. Thus in 'New World a-Comin'' the fact of dispossession, of being wrenched from landscape, community and tradition, becomes both the 'silence' of defeat and a journey of possibilities, precisely because Brathwaite gives the experience a historical significance and a meaning. By locating it in the wider historical context of the earlier migration of Africans from the North African desert to the forest regions of West Africa, he is able to enlarge the black West Indian's perception of space, sense of origin and consequently conception of self.

The dominant impressions, especially in the first section of the poem, are the shock of capture and the helplessness of the uprooted. These are made immediate not just by the poet's skilful exploitation of action, sound and scene, but also by his suggestive use of the gospel song, dramatized as the creative offshoot of an essentially negative experience.

Of central relevance to Brathwaite's purpose is the way the Middle Passage itself is presented as the traumatic sequel to the process of defeat, disintegration and renewal, dramatized in 'Prelude' as part of Africa's history. Thus, in this poem, captivity and enslavement are projected as partly the consequence of internal tribal disintegration. Like defeat and destruction in the desert they are symbolized by dumbness:

> Soft foot
> to soft soil
> of silence:
> We met in the soiled
> tunnel of leaves . . .

In a similar linking of detail and experience, the passage across the seas become part of the pattern of African migrations recalled in song by the slaves as they journey across the seas into a new world. This dramatic linking of experiences becomes an act of memory. The poet's imagination travels backwards and forwards, discovering associations between events of the past, linking the past with the present and in the process heightening our awareness of the relationship between them.

The drama of the Middle Passage is concluded in the second section of the poem. Brathwaite dramatizes the transition from Africa to the New World, capturing the gradually receding consciousness of the slaves and their persistent

Page references in this unit are to Edward Brathwaite, *The Arrivants*, Oxford University Press, 1973.

efforts to remember the past. The progression from tribal to New World consciousness is suggested in the extension and juxtaposition of images portraying the interplay between the two worlds and suggesting at the same time that Africans of the New World appraised their new condition in relation to their old experiences and with reference to a particularly African mode of apprehension. The paradox of the 'chained' and 'welcoming' port, with which Brathwaite concludes the drama, projects a sense of the future and reflects the slaves' hopes of a new inheritance, of new and interesting combinations of past, present and future experience:

> . . . new soils, new souls, new
> ancestors . . .
> . . . the pride of our ancestors mixed
> with the wind and the water
> the flesh and the flies . . .

This is a reasonably accessible poem and a good introduction to the themes, methods and perspectives of Brathwaite's poetry. The only difficulty it may raise is a problem of context and association, a peculiar difficulty caused by our having to isolate a single poem in a closely related sequence of poems. The best way to counteract this problem is to be generally aware of the closely knit structure of *Rights of Passage* and of the interrelationships within its sequence of poems. For a good understanding and appreciation of Brathwaite's purpose, this poem should be related to the 'Prelude' of 'Work Song and Blues' and thus to the poet's declared intention of evoking aspects of African history in the variety of moods suggested by 'sing', 'shout', 'groan' and 'dream',

On a thematic level, a combined reading of this poem and 'Prelude' will throw more light on the association and extension of images through which Brathwaite enlarges the context of the Middle Passage. In the first section of 'New World a-Comin'' such manipulations of image occur in almost every stanza, and we have to move backwards in time to build up relationships between past and present, between forest and desert, between the flames of slave-traders and the flames of tribes, between 'fire-locked captive slaves' and 'fly-bitten warriors', between the journeys of migrating tribes and the new wrenching and traumatic journey across the seas. Only from making such connections can we fully appreciate Brathwaite's relationship to his material: his visual projection of the Passage, the rhythms in which he enacts it and his earnest attempts at creating a poetic language to carry the meaning of the experience.

'Folkways' (*The Arrivants*, p. 30)

'Folkways' is the second section of the sequence entitled 'The Spades', and it relates to 'New World a-Comin'' in several senses. In one sense, it dramatizes the failure of the first slaves' hope of a continuity and of a creative mixing of past, present and future experiences. In substance, structure and rhythm it appears also to subvert the very mood and pattern of associations which Brathwaite establishes in 'Work Song and Blues'. Its background is the United States city, and the voices are the voices of urban Blacks, a generation removed from the first slaves and already distanced from them in experience, vision and speech patterns. Brathwaite explores the pressures of confronting a white ex-slave society from the narrow perspective of the urban black world, and in the process reveals the dangers of discontinuity and of the 'limbo' from which urban Blacks choose now to survive and define themselves. The ironically presented portrait of urban Blacks examines both this world and their particular mode of existence and definition.

The method is simple but effective; a series of ironic juxtapositions separate the stereotypes behind the Blacks' façade from the reality of what they feel. The juxtapositions set up contrasts between the carefree brashness which is the pose of people without illusions and the frightening self-rejection and despondency of people unable to transcend frustration and pain. To understand the significance of these contrasts we should be able to unravel the characteristics which these stereotypes denote and to determine the extent to which urban Blacks accept, exploit or reject them. In the third stanza especially, we should be able to identify the dissonance of tone which enacts the clash between carefree pose, easy cynicism and the reality of pain and suffering:

> steel
> hits the rock

and the broad blade
shivers, eye
sockets bulge

Such a clash of tones fulfils a particular purpose in Brathwaite's dramatization of discontinuity. We should explore it by noting the significance of the different sounds, rhythms, moods and images in the rest of the stanza. The carefree urban Black when unmasked reverts to a kind of urban blues; it would be interesting, for instance, to compare the substance, tone and effect of this type of blues with the blues of the first slaves. Are these urban Blacks able like the first slaves to sublimate anguish? Are they able, like 'Tom' in *Rights of Passage*, to make creative use of suffering? Or is their blues merely an escape from pain? Does the comparison suggest any statement about the relationship between humanity's present and its past, between humanity and history?

Besides these contrasts there are parallel movements in the poem built up as a series of paradoxes and constantly coming between the clashes and contrasts. There is, for instance, on one hand, the sickening cynicism that rejects the sense of continuity implied in accepting the work-song:

keep them
for Alan Lomax, man, for them

swell

folkways records, man
that does sell for two pounds ten. But get
me out 'a this place you hear, where my dreams
are wet

as hell.

and, on the other, the quiet intrusion of 'dreams' in the last line of the stanza, gently mocking the persona's cynicism and stressing the need for a more meaningful dream. Again, the persona's rejection of the culture and ties of the blues, on the one hand, relates paradoxically to his incisive insight into its exploitation by the white world and its tendency therefore to falsify and pervert the pain of black experience, on the other. There is, above all, the more pertinent paradox in the second section, where the shortened lines and the quick rhythms of 'come'/'come'/'bugle'/'train' imitate the

hurried journey out of the 'hell' of the South yet manage at the same time to suggest the anguish of parting, the pain of separation from the South and a fear of the unknown. Brathwaite plays on such paradoxes and tensions to suggest ambivalences in the West Indian's history of loss. In this poem the ambivalences seem to confirm what he sees as the lingering 'memory', the lingering 'dream' and the possibility, however slight, of a reaffirmation of that sensibility which the urban Black appears to have lost.

'South' (*The Arrivants*, p. 57)

This poem appears to be the climax of the second movement of *Rights of Passage*. Written in 1956 when Brathwaite was living and working in Africa, it is deeply autobiographical and is in part a self-assessment and a scrutiny of that New World restlessness which finds its expression in journeys and exile. 'South' was written years before the publication of the collection and yet (in its revised form) fits in amazingly well with it. The poem should be regarded as the turning-point in Brathwaite's exploration, the point at which the poet's voice begins gradually to extricate itself from the other voices and becomes more assertive. The alternation between 'I' and 'We' is the familiar device with which Brathwaite both roots himself in his society's ills and rises above them; but the maintained reflective tone marks the voice out as principally the poet's own.

From the rootlessness of exile the poet summons a positive response to the New World and for the first time recognizes the area's violent history as a possible source of strength. The ocean becomes now a symbol of turbulence and largeness, suggesting the widening of perspective that could come out of a response to the historical upheavals of the New World. The African river comes to symbolize time and continuity; its continuous, purposeful movement to its destination in the sea is seen by the poet as a contrast to the purposelessness, the denial of history and the discontinuity which exile must signify for the West Indian. The poet's identification with the river's movement is an attempt to inhabit those ancestral qualities of patience and sureness which keep the travelling river going in spite of historical disruptions. Symbolically it marks the poet's decision to accept his island, to confront the turbulence, the disorder and the pain of its history and to see these as the background from which any movement forward can be made. The decision enlarges his consciousness, for in the next stanza his vision of his island is a remarkably positive one. The island's landscape has not changed. His own exile and the exile of his compatriots have not signified a break. Continuity is possible after all, and the returning exile can look forward to infinite possibilities:

> A starfish lies in its pool.
> And gulls, white sails slanted seaward,
> fly into the limitless morning before us.

In terms of theme, image and tone, the poem appears to be a dream, a psychic wish through which the poet counteracts the purposelessness of exile and convinces himself of the possibility of continuity. Indeed, the original version of the poem, published in *BIM* (vol. 7, no. 28, p. 191) in 1959, has an extra stanza (omitted from the version in *Rights of Passage*) which brings the poet back to the reality of the African forest and to the possibilities of further exile:

> Night falls and the vision is ended
> Frogs croak and fireflies shimmer like stars
> I turn down the slope from the murmuring river
> Old dreamer remembering summer.

At the time it was written way back in 1956, the poem must have been principally an auto-suggestive response with which the poet fought his fear of the African forest. The sounds and images of the forest in this stanza suggest a return to the 'shadows', to the poet's old fears, and the reference to summer hints at further exile. This last stanza is rightly omitted from *Rights of Passage*, because by the time of the latter's compilation the 'dream' has come to mean so much more than a reaction to the poet's personal fears and now represents the

awakening of a whole new perspective on the New World. Significantly, the positive insights grasped in 'South' dominate the next section of *Rights*, entitled 'The Return'; and the poet's dream of awakening becomes a superior contrast to the delusions of grandeur exhibited by the new breed of New World leaders.

'Bosompra' (*The Arrivants*, p. 136)

The title of this poem is a reference to the river Pra in Ghana, which marks the boundary between the Fante and the Asante peoples. The poem is the first section of 'Crossing the River', the fifth chapter of Brathwaite's *Masks*. In spite of its brevity it marks an important transition in Brathwaite's relationship to his ancestral world and to history. In *Rights of Passage* this relationship is suggested mostly through the poet's skilful use of memory and dream as symbols of connection between the New World and the Old. In *Masks* memory and dream culminate in the poet's actual encounter with Africa and its past; and in his poignant exploration of his relationship to this world. 'Bosompra' marks a transition because it reveals the difference between memory and history, between dream and reality. The poem is the point at which the poet becomes aware of the wounds of history and of the historical scars that separate the New World from Africa.

'Bosompra' is structured in such a way that its explorations shift between the present experience of the returning New World Negro and the poet's examination further back in time, of cultural failure in Africa. The explorations begin with the poet's journey in space and time, a journey which unlike the journey of his slave ancestors begins from the sea and progresses inland into the forest regions around Kumasi, the heart of 'Akan' land,[1] the central city of the Asante Empire[2] and in the poet's consciousness the very symbol of that achievement and decadence which culminated in the aberration of the slave trade and in the poet's agony of homelessness and exile. The drama begins with the poet's attempt at establishing contact with the Old World. His desperate questions wonder if a link still exists between the returning 'exile' and his kinsman in Africa. The fact of there being no real contact and no answers to his questions reflects the ambiguity of the exile's situation in Africa and reveals at the same time the frightening reality of

---

[1] A reference to the Asante, the Akwapim, the Fante and the Akyem, the Twi-speaking people of Ghana.

[2] A confederacy of six major states of the forest regions of the Gold Coast led by the then Osei Tutu, these states came together as a nation and remained for two centuries (1697–1900) a powerful military and economic force.

the wounds of history. Although this discovery momentarily shatters the exile, it nevertheless helps to clarify his own position in relation to the Old World, for the persona now identifies himself as

I who have pointed my face
to the ships, the winds' anger . . .

– defining a new sense of separateness which marks a growth in his consciousness of himself.

In the light of this discovery, the persona's questions and entreaties become extremely important. As we would remember from the poem 'South', the African river has appeared in the poet's dream as a symbol of purposefulness and continuity, a contrast to the discontinuity and purposelessness which exile had signified for the poet. Now, in the face of the real threat of history, of scars that really separate the New World from the Old, the river is also a protective, healing and purifying symbol. The poet asks of it:

can you soothe
the wind's salt
scorching my eye,

blue finger of water,
heat's solace?

And what he hopes for is solace, protection, deliverance from and reconciliation to the failures and aberrations of the past. Yet what becomes paramount, instead, is the pervading sense of the river's invulnerability, of its continual flow through centuries of building and disintegration. This serves to remind the poet of the movement of time, of cycles of death and rebirth, of the unalterable fact that time moves on in spite of breaks and discontinuities. This lesson is enacted in the very words which the stories give to the river in the poem:

asuo meresen
asuo meresen

asuo meresen . . . [3]

As can be seen, the poem marks a transition from a fluid attitude to history in *Rights* to a new, tougher

and more realistic approach in *Masks*. Appropriately called 'Crossing the River', this entire section of *Masks* enacts the poet's transition from one set of consciousness to another. 'Bosompra', the first poem in this section, thus questions earlier positions and attempts to clarify certain issues raised in *Rights*.

First, the poet's discovery of the wounds of history and of the scars that separate New World and Old World experiences is made against the background of Tom's memories in *Rights*:

Atumpam talking and the harvest branch-
es, all the tribes of Ashanti dreaming the dream
of Tutu, Anokye and the Golden Stool, built
in Heaven for our nation . . .

Throughout the poem, memory of this 'dream' seems to lie behind the poet's discovery of its perversion and of the resulting aberration that led to discontinuity and to his own exile.

Secondly, memory of the past and the idea of return and reconnection are given a new, realistic qualification. Against the symbolic background of the African river and its perennial lessons the poet clarifies his view of the exile's relationship to the past and to history. The wounds of history are not necessarily diminished by the fact of return; nor does reconciliation to the pains of history necessarily re-establish the continuity lost through the Middle Passage. From now on and throughout *Islands* this qualification is to inform the poet's search for a relationship to the past and to Africa.

'Homecoming' (*The Arrivants*, p. 177)

'Homecoming' bears a thematic relationship to 'South' (*Rights*) and to sections on 'The Return' in *Rights* and *Masks*. In contrast to 'South' it marks a return not to possibilities in the Caribbean but to the reality of new doubts and pains. In another sense it registers the lonely cry of the poet persona – 'unmasked', no longer distanced from reality and from the past as in *Masks*, and unable to find solace or consolation in the reality of the present-day Caribbean. The poem also portrays a new persona, stripped of illusion and expectation, armed with a new grit and ruthlessness and prepared to start again, to re-explore the essence of home in the Caribbean. The poem's bleak picture of the

---

[3] Translated as 'River, I am passing'.

Caribbean and its possibilities makes an interesting contrast to the 'dream' of possibilities in 'South'; the significance of the contrast can be worked out by exploring the implications of metaphor, tone and rhythm in the two poems.

There is a sense in which a superior intelligence in the poem distances itself both from the persona and from Caribbean society in order to measure the real impact of the poet's return. We should explore the nuances of such distancing in order to get as much from the poem as possible. The absence of rapport between poet and people, the distance between the consciousness and sensibility of the poet and his society, are suggested in the third stanza of the poem:

> No clan or kinsman turns
> my self-respect
>
> into a claw, a tooth
> a dagger.

The reasons for this absence can be traced in the poet's devastating portrait of society and sensibility in the Caribbean. This portrait eventually colours and defines the poet's negative view of Caribbean possibilities. For the image of the Caribbean poor – denuded, incarcerated and trapped by the exploiting 'bulldogs' (their fellow countrymen) in a crassly materialistic colonial society – not only limits the horizons of the Caribbean people but also diminishes their potential for creative development. The real nature of the human condition in the Caribbean, the degree of spiritual impoverishment, is finally related to people's lack of a sense of self and home and to the absence of that revolutionary consciousness needed to create this feeling of home and identity:

> we have no name
> to call us home, no turbulence
>
> to bring us soft –
> ly past these bars to miracle, to god,
> to unexpected lover.

The pessimism and despondency that engulf 'Homecoming' should not be seen as ends in themselves but in the overall context of Brathwaite's purposes in *Islands* as the ruthless re-examination which forms the basis of the poet's search for vision. The poem should present no difficulties except perhaps in relation to the working out of the various images. But with good guidance the exercises in explication and association should reveal dimensions to enhance students' understanding and enjoyment.

Section B: The Author

Edward Kamau Brathwaite was born in Barbados in May 1930. He was educated there until 1950, when he won an Island Scholarship to the University of Cambridge, UK. He read history in Cambridge from 1950 to 1953 and in 1954 took a Certificate in Education at the same university. From 1955 to 1962 Brathwaite worked as an education officer in Ghana, living and interacting with various communities in the country. He returned to the West Indies in 1962 and worked first at the extramural department of the University of the West Indies, St Lucia, and later as a lecturer in history at the Mona campus of that university. In 1965 he took up a research award at the University of Sussex, UK, working on the development of Creole society in Jamaica for a doctoral degree which he obtained in 1968.

Brathwaite began writing poetry as far back as 1950. Whether written in England, the West Indies or Africa, his poetry has been informed both by his experience of life in these areas and by his researches into the development of Creole society in the West Indies. His early poetry and critical essays were concerned with examining those sources from which the West Indian artist could draw inspiration and perspective. This early work lamented the alienation and spiritual poverty of the growing middle class but saw the alternatives of despair and exile as negative and soul-destroying. In the early essays and poems Brathwaite tended rather to identify himself with a new generation of artists willing to rise above despair and feelings of 'historylessness'. He saw the real barrier to freedom and achievement in the West Indies not in the facts of slavery and dispossession *per se* but in the dichotomy between West Indians' real background and the direction of their education.

In an early poem entitled 'Journeys', Brathwaite sees a young poet's attempt to 'leap the saddle', to 'reach the moon', as a series of juxtapositions in which images of his background clash with and are blotted out by images of his superficial education:

> the black night longs for the moon
> an old cracked face looks up from the well
> And the dish runs away with the spoon.
> (*Other Exiles*, Oxford University Press, 1975)

Even as early as 'Journeys', Brathwaite saw the reintegration of personality – a confrontation with history – as the necessary condition for creativity. The poet's cracked face, impaired but not quite fractured by history, cries out to be confronted, but the reflection is blotted out by the meaningless line from an English nursery rhyme. Unable thus to reconcile his experience and his learning, the poet cannot, as his vocation is, save his people:

> he watched the seas of non-dragged aunts and
>   mothers:
> but all his thoughts were chained
> which should have sparked and hammered in his
>   brain.

In another early poem the poet seems on the verge of perception as he discovers his islands:

> Stuffed away in his pockets
> the fingers tightly clenched
> around a nervousness . . .

But the process of unclenching, of exploration and discovery, is hampered by his deficient and uncertain methods. Already a product of a colonial system, his raped brain can manage only their little tricks and trade:

> he unpacked the wired apparatus of his eyes
> so that he could assess not only surfaces but
> doubts and coils.

This kind of perception, however, achieved through an inorganic world of steel, is not true creation. True creation, as Brathwaite demonstrates in a later poem, 'Cat', demands a submission both to the intellect and to the senses. Not only must the poet assess; he must also uncurl, create with the sensitivity of a cat. His eyes should not be wired apparatus but 'green doors that dilate greenest pouncers'. He must plumb the depths of the world and create pouncing:

> be a cat eeling through alleys
> slipping through windows of odours
> to feel swiftness slowly.

Brathwaite saw the prospects for the emergence of this kind of sensibility blunted by the fact of cultural discontinuity. He saw the Western Black's history of rootlessness and exile as a barrier against true creativity and he searched relentlessly for a way of confronting this barrier. In the process he recognized creative possibilities in the folk values that had survived precariously in the Caribbean, and his essays debated these possibilities continually. An early essay written in 1957, for instance, hinted at the creative prospects which the folk background could hold for the artist able to exploit it with imagination and insight:

> Can our society produce enough writers with
> the talent and insight to use folk material
> creatively, not as reporters, but with sufficient
> maturity to establish a tradition, or will the
> unique circumstances of our society be too
> much for them?
> ('Sir Galahad and the Islands', *BIM*, vol. 7, no. 25,
> 1957, p. 9)

By folk values Brathwaite meant the attitudes, beliefs and values that had crystallized from centuries of Creole adaptations to historical and social conditions in the Caribbean. Three centuries of such adaptations, he felt, should unfold a way of life that could provide a mythology and an aesthetic basis for a West Indian definition and for a tradition of poetry.

Brathwaite's own major work, *The Arrivants*, comprising *Rights of Passage*, *Masks* and *Islands*, began such an exploration on a monumental scale. The trilogy is an epic evocation of the black West Indian's history and culture. Its very broad framework allows Brathwaite to provide West Indians with a historical context, just as its various moods, tones, rhythms and points of view reflect the variety of historical experiences which he draws upon. Relating to this material Brathwaite squeezes out various historical, spiritual and linguistic lessons, thus making his poetry an act of recollection that heightens his awareness of the past, links it with the conditions of the present and creates a sense of an evolving West Indian consciousness. Interestingly, the very rationale of this kind of poetry is demonstrated in the archetypes of experience and the creative models that emerge especially in *Rights of Passage*. It was invariably the vision of themselves and of their historical conditions that propelled most slaves and New World Blacks to create. Brathwaite implies that the very capacity to survive and create is inextricably bound up with the ability to remember the conditions of the present as they have evolved from the past and as they affect individual and community. This is the context and the role which Brathwaite claims for the black poet in the New World.

Section C: Classroom use

(i) Level of use

Fourth- to sixth-form students; GCSE and A-level.

(ii) Questions for essay writing or classroom discussion

'New World a-Comin'' (to be studied with reference to the 'Prelude' of 'Work Song and Blues')

1 Soft foot
   to soft soil
   of silence:
   We met in the soiled
   tunnel of leaves . . .

   Describe the atmosphere and mood surrounding the meeting of slave-trader and slave. How does the poet create this atmosphere and why does he see the meeting in these terms?

2 Why does the poet describe the encounter as a meeting in the 'soiled' tunnel of leaves?

3 Consider the following lines from the poem 'Bosompra' in relation to 'New World a-Comin'':

Can you hide me now

from the path's hope —
less dazzles, halts,
meetings, leaves' sudden

betrayal of silence . . .

Distinguish between the two contexts and examine the connection between 'leaves' sudden/betrayal of silence' and the 'soiled/tunnel of leaves'.

4 Examine the poet's presentation of action in the second stanza. What makes it dramatic?

5 Consider the following lines:

   Our firm
fleshed, flame
warm, fly
bitten warriors
fell . . .

Why does the poet describe the captured slaves in these images? How do the images relate to the experience of migrating Africans in the 'Prelude'? What does the poet achieve by linking experiences in the desert with those in the forest?

6 The pride of our ancestors mixed

   with the *wind* and the *water*
   the flesh and *the flies*, the *whips* and *the fixed fear of pain* in this chained and welcoming
      port.

What does each of italicized words symbolize? Why does the poet link them in this way?

7 Would you agree that the poem ends on a paradoxical note? Give reasons.

'Folkways'

1 From your reading of the poem distinguish between the setting of this poem and that of 'New World A-Comin''.

2 Compare the mood, tone and rhythm of the speaking voice in 'Folkways' with the voices in 'New World a-Comin''.

3 In this poem the poet sets up contrasts between: (a) the speaking voice of the persona in the first and second sections; (b) the picture he paints of himself in the two sections. Can you identify and explain these

contrasts? What judgement of the persona does the poet reveal through these contrasts?

4   Just Watch
me fall in the mud
O' my dreams
With my face in the cow-
pen, down
at heart, down
at hope, down
at heel.

What is the effect of the repetition of the word 'down'?

5   But bes'leh weget to rass o' this place, out o' this ass hole, out o' the stink o' this hell.

Can you identify the particular speaking voice? What type of folk Negro is being described here?

6   keep them
for Alan Lomax, man, for them
swell
folkways records, man,
that does sell for two pounds ten.

Who was Alan Lomax? Why does the poet isolate the word 'swell'? What aspect of the blues do you think the persona rejects? Why? What does his rejection imply?

7   Do you find any irony in the persona's reference to his 'dreams' in view of the general tone of despondency in the poem? What is the point of the irony in terms of the poet's theme?

8   Come
come bugle
train

What impression does this stanza create? Can you identify the particular blues on which this section is based? Are the contexts the same in the poem and the blues?

9   Consider section (3) of the poem. Whose voice is recorded here? Write down two or three adjectives to describe the tone of the speaker's voice. What is the particular effect of the word-breaks in 'land-/less' and 'harbour-/less'?

'South'

1   From what special situation does the poet recapture this vision of his island?

2   '. . . life heaved and breathed in me then/with the strength of that turbulent soil'. In what light does the poet view his island now?

3   'We who are born of the Ocean can never seek solace/in rivers: their flowing runs on like our longing.' What difference does the poet draw between the symbolic meaning of 'Ocean' and 'rivers' in these lines? What comment is he making through this differentiation?

4   What does the travelling river symbolize and what is its relationship to the poem's theme?

5   Consider the last two stanzas of the poem. Examine all the images that celebrate the poet's return and explain their implications.

6   Sum up in one sentence what you consider to be the poem's resolution.

'Bosompra'

1   What is the general *mood* of the persona in this poem. How does it come across to you?

2   Consider stanzas 4, 5, 6 and 7 and identify the implications of the following references:

the wind's salt
scorching my eye
     the path's hope
less dazzles, halts
meetings, leaves' sudden
betrayal of silence, the sun's
long slant sloping
to danger?

3   I who have pointed my face to the ships, the wind's anger today have returned.

How does the poet define himself here? How important is this definition in the circum-stances of his return?

4   Why does the poet describe himself in stanza 9 as a 'mudfish' eating time?

5   [I] have returned
where the stones

give lips to the water:
asuo meresen
asuo meresen

asuo meresen . . . [translated as: 'River, I am passing')

Study the structure and the punctuation of these lines. What does the river enact? What special significance does the enactment hold for the poet?

'Homecoming'

1 Compare the context of the poet's return in this poem with the context of his return in 'South'.

2 In the first four stanzas identify all the images that describe the 'character' of the poet's return.

3 Whips do not flinch
from what they will destroy:
strips, strips of flesh, flash
of the black forked tongue

licking these scars.

What kind of images are these? What pictures do they conjure up? Who are being described in these images?

4 In stanza 8 who or what is being referred to as: (a) the 'clanking bulldog'; (b) the 'starved ankles'?

5 Explain the connotations of these images:

Walking bone
Without flesh
Cannot travel too far.

What do they suggest about Caribbean possibilities?

6 In stanza 9 what are the 'stars' symbolic of? Who is the persona's 'master'?

7 clinks
of dew in the grass
is the nearest we will get to god.

Work out and explain the implications of the images in this stanza. What statements do they make about possibilities in the Caribbean?

8 Discuss the significance of the poem's animal imagery, relating it to the human condition in the Caribbean as seen by the poet.

9 What saves this poem from total pessimism and despair?

(iii) Creative approaches/curriculum links

'New World a-Comin' '

1 Find out all you can about the following groups of people mentioned in the poem. Suggest reasons why 'helpless', 'horse-/less', 'leader-/less' slaves should call on them on their lonely journey to the New World: (a) Hawkins and Cortez; (b) Tawiah, Prempeh and Asantewa; (c) Geronimo, Jackie and Montezuma. What links the characters in each of these groups?

2 Read about the Middle Passage in any history book and work out if the account you read is the same (in terms of the shock of capture and dislocation) as what the poet has evoked in 'New World a-Comin' '.

3 Read about the background to the creation of the gospel song. Consider how the poem's fourth stanza fits into this musical type.

4 The title 'New World a-Comin' ' is an allusion to Duke Ellington's concert of sacred music RCA SF7811. (See Gordon Rohlehr, 'Black Ground Music to *Rights of Passage*', in *Pathfinder: Black Awakening in 'The Arrivants' of Edward Kamau Brathwaite*, Trinidad: self-published, 1981, p. 333.) Play the record and compare its subject and theme to Brathwaite's poem.

5 If you had to present this poem as a dance, how would you choreograph it?

'Folkways'

1 Increase your knowledge of the background of the poem by reading about the various migrations that created the situation of the urban Black: (a) migrations from the US South to North; (b) migrations from the Caribbean to the northern cities of the USA.

2 Get an idea of the character of urban city areas like Harlem and note their special contribution to music, art and thought during the 'Negro' Renaissance of the 1920s and 1930s.

3 Read Leroi Jones, *Blues People* (1963) and J. and M. W. Stearns, *Jazz Dance* (1968) for information about urban blues. How does this type of blues differ from the gospel song in

'New World a-Comin' ' and from the spiritual in 'Tom' (*Rights*)? Moving from gospel song to urban blues, do you see any sense of progression in black feeling and sensibility?

'South'

1 Two scenes are evoked in this poem: the scene in the forest by the river in Ghana and the scene by the ocean on a West Indian island. Read about the landscape, vegetation and particular associations of the two regions.

2 Have you ever been away from your own familiar surroundings? Have you ever felt a similar nostalgia? Imagine that like Brathwaite you had a similar feeling about being away from home. Express this feeling in a poem, a song or a story.

'Bosompra'

1 In this poem the poet returns to his ancestral land. Can you think of similar instances of 'return' in fiction or travel writing? Read V. S. Naipaul's *An Area of Darkness* (1964).

2 Look up the meaning of the term 'diaspora'. How many instances of 'diaspora' can you recall from history? Consider the following: 'And they took their journey from Elim, and all the congregation of the children of Israel came unto the wilderness of Sin, which is between Elim and Sinai, on the fifteenth day of the second month after their departing out of the land of Egypt' (Exodus 16: 1). What particular diaspora is Brathwaite referring to? Why do you think he uses this passage as an epigraph to *Rights of Passage*?

'Homecoming'

1 Read: (a) Derek Walcott, 'Return to Denerry Rain', (*In a Green Night*, Cape, 1962) and 'Homecoming Anse La Raye' (*The Gulf*, Cape, 1969); (b) Aimé Césaire, *Return to My Native Land* (Penguin, 1969), p. 82; (c) Edward Brathwaite, 'South' (*Rights of Passage, The Arrivants*, 1973) and 'Homecoming' (*Islands, The Arrivants*, 1973).

  Then write an essay or prepare a project, drawing on the writers you have read, based on this quotation from Walcott: 'there are homecomings without home' ('Homecoming Anse La Raye').

Section D: Teaching Aids

(i) Audio-visual material

Rights of Passage (double LP), London: Argo, 1969, PLP 1110/1. Poems read by Edward Brathwaite.
Masks (LP), London: Argo, 1972, PLP 1183. Poems read by Edward Brathwaite.
Islands (double LP), London: Argo, 1973, PLP 1184/5. Poems read by Edward Brathwaite.
Mother Poem (2 cassettes), London: ATCAL. Brathwaite reading and discussing his work. The cassettes are held by the British Institute of Recorded Sound.

(ii) Background reading

Edward Brathwaite, *The Development of Creole Society in Jamaica, 1770–1820*, Clarendon Press, 1971.
J. K. Fynn, *Asante and its Neighbours, 1700–1807*, Longman, 1971.
R. Hart, *Slaves Who Abolished Slavery*, 2 vols, Institute of Social and Economic Research, University of West Indies, Mona, Jamaica, 1980.
Leroi Jones, *Blues People*, Morrow, 1963.
J. H. Parry and P. M. Sherlock, *A Short History of the West Indies*, Macmillan, 1971.
M. W. Stearns, *The Story of Jazz*, Oxford University Press, 1956.

(iii) Critical bibliography

E. Baugh, *West Indian Poetry, 1900–1970: A Study in Cultural Decolonization*, Kingston, Jamaica: Savacou Publications, 1970.
J. D'Costa, 'The Poetry of Edward Brathwaite', *Jamaica Journal*, vol. 11, no. 3, 1968.
D. Grant, 'Emerging Image: The Poetry of Edward Brathwaite', *Critical Quarterly*, vol. 12, no. 2, 1970.
M. W. Lewis, 'Odomankoma Kyerema Se', *Caribbean Quarterly*, vol. 19, no. 2, 1973.

M. Morris, 'This Broken Ground: Edward Brathwaite's Trilogy of Poems', *New World Quarterly*, vol. 23, nos. 2–3, 1977.

W. Risden, 'Masks', *Caribbean Quarterly*, vol. 23, no. 243, 1977.

G. Rohlehr, *Pathfinder: Black Awakening in 'The Arrivants' of Edward Kamau Brathwaite*, Trinidad: self-published, 1981.

(iv) Reading links

The theme of journeying is common in Caribbean writing, and the reader is encouraged to make comparisons between Derek Walcott's poetry (*The Castaway*, Cape, 1965; *The Gulf*, Cape, 1969) and novels like George Lamming's *In the Castle of my Skin*, (Michael Joseph, 1953; Longman (Drumbeat), 1979) and Denis William's *Other Leopards* (Heinemann Educational Books, Caribbean Writers Series, 1983). V. S. Naipaul's *The Middle Passage* (Deutsch, 1964), which deals with the processes of uprooting and resettlement, is valuable journalistic reading to complement the poetry and fiction.

Captured Africans being shipped to the Caribbean in the slave trade.

SELECT BIBLIOGRAPHY

E. Baugh, *West Indian Poetry, 1900–1970: A Study in Cultural Decolonization*, Savacou, Jamaica, 1970.

E. Baugh (ed.), *Critics on Caribbean Literature*, St Martin's Press, New York, 1978.

L. Brown, *West Indian Poetry*, Heinemann Educational Books, London, 1984.

K. Corsbie, *Theatre in the Caribbean*, Hodder & Stoughton, London, 1984.

D. Dabydeen and N. Wilson-Tagoe, *A Reader's Guide to West Indian and Black British Literature*, University of Warwick Centre for Caribbean Studies, in conjunction with Hansib Publications, London, 1988.

J. D'Costa, *Roger Mais: 'The Hills Were Joyful Together' and 'Brother Man'*, Longman, London, 1978.

M. Gilkes, *The West Indian Novel*, Twayne, Boston, 1981.

J. Grant, *Samuel Selvon: Ways of Sunlight*, Longman, London, 1979.

R. D. Hamner, *Critical Perspectives on V. S. Naipaul*, Heinemann Educational Books, London, 1979.

R. D. Hamner, *Derek Walcott*, Twayne, Boston, 1981.

M. Hughes, *A Companion to West Indian Literature*, Collins, London, 1979.

Louis James, *Jean Rhys*, Longman, London, 1980.

B. King (ed.), *West Indian Literature*, Macmillan, London, 1979.

H. Maes-Jelenik, *The Naked Design: A Reading of 'Palace of the Peacock'*, Dangaroo Press, Denmark and UK, 1976. Distributed in UK by PO Box 186, Coventry CV4 7HG.

S. P. Paquet, *The Novels of George Lamming*, Heinemann Educational Books, London, 1982.

K. Ramchand, *An Introduction to the Study of West Indian Literature*, Thomas Nelson, Walton-on-Thames, 1976.

K. Ramchand, *The West Indian Novel and its Background*, revised edn., Heinemann Educational Books, London, 1983.

T. A. Staley, *Jean Rhys*, University of Texas Press, Texas, 1979.

INDEX